Palgrave Studies in Oral History

Series Editors
David P. Cline
SDSU Center for Public and Oral History
San Diego State University
San Diego, CA, USA

Natalie Fousekis
California State University
Fullerton, USA

'A premier publisher of oral history.' - CHOICE

The world's leading English-language oral history book series, *Palgrave Studies in Oral History* brings together engaging work from scholars, activists, and other practitioners. Books in the series are aimed at a broad community of readers; they employ edited oral history interviews to explore a wide variety of topics and themes in all areas of history, placing first-person accounts in broad historical context and engaging issues of historical memory and narrative construction. Fresh approaches to the use and analysis of oral history, as well as to the organization of text, are a particular strength of the series, as are projects that use oral accounts to illuminate human rights issues. Submissions are welcomed for projects from any geographical region, as well as cross-cultural and comparative work.

Ricardo Santhiago • Miriam Hermeto
Editors

The Unexpected in Oral History

Case Studies of Surprising Interviews

Editors
Ricardo Santhiago
Federal University of São Paulo (Unifesp)
São Paulo, Brazil

Miriam Hermeto
Federal University of Minas Gerais (UFMG)
Belo Horizonte, Brazil

ISSN 2731-5673 ISSN 2731-5681 (electronic)
Palgrave Studies in Oral History
ISBN 978-3-031-17748-4 ISBN 978-3-031-17749-1 (eBook)
https://doi.org/10.1007/978-3-031-17749-1

© The Editor(s) (if applicable) and The Author(s), under exclusive licence to Springer Nature Switzerland AG 2023
0th edition: © Letra e Voz 2022
This work is subject to copyright. All rights are solely and exclusively licensed by the Publisher, whether the whole or part of the material is concerned, specifically the rights of reprinting, reuse of illustrations, recitation, broadcasting, reproduction on microfilms or in any other physical way, and transmission or information storage and retrieval, electronic adaptation, computer software, or by similar or dissimilar methodology now known or hereafter developed.
The use of general descriptive names, registered names, trademarks, service marks, etc. in this publication does not imply, even in the absence of a specific statement, that such names are exempt from the relevant protective laws and regulations and therefore free for general use.
The publisher, the authors, and the editors are safe to assume that the advice and information in this book are believed to be true and accurate at the date of publication. Neither the publisher nor the authors or the editors give a warranty, expressed or implied, with respect to the material contained herein or for any errors or omissions that may have been made. The publisher remains neutral with regard to jurisdictional claims in published maps and institutional affiliations.

This Palgrave Macmillan imprint is published by the registered company Springer Nature Switzerland AG.
The registered company address is: Gewerbestrasse 11, 6330 Cham, Switzerland

Acknowledgments

This book would not have been born were it not for Juniele Rabêlo de Almeida, who brought us together and whom we thank for her unstinting partnership, friendship, and encouragement. It took shape within discussions in the working group "Oral History and Memory of Arts, Culture, and Creativity," which we two have coordinated since 2009 at national and regional conferences of the Brazilian Oral History Association (ABHO). We are grateful to the ABHO and to all the working group participants who, over the years, have provided invaluable inputs to this project. We could not have completed this work without the diligence, competence, and generosity of the contributors. We thank Daphne Patai for her contributions and suggestions throughout all stages of the work involved in this book. We also thank the Graduate History Program at the Federal University of Minas Gerais, which allocated resources from the Coordination for the Improvement of Higher Education Personnel (CAPES) to partially fund the translation of the chapters. Finally, we thank the Palgrave Macmillan Oral History Series team and the careful and generous reviewers of the proposal, who believed in this project and helped us formulate this international dialogue on the unexpected in oral history—a practice in which we deeply believe—with a strong Brazilian flavor.

Contents

1   Foreword   1
    Mercedes Vilanova

2   Introduction   7
    Miriam Hermeto and Ricardo Santhiago

Part I   Scratching the Silence: The Unexpected as an Outbreak   15

3   Introduction to Part I   17
    Miriam Hermeto and Ricardo Santhiago

4   My Grandfather's Unknown History   21
    Luiza Porto

5   Florence Richard, Childhood Sexual Violence, and the
    Unsettling of Local History   29
    Steven High

6   An Unexpected Gift: Oral History and the Documentation
    of Michfest   37
    Ann Cvetkovich

7   *Commentary*: The Elaboration of What Has Been Lived   45
    Ana Maria Mauad

Part II Between Lies and Half-Truths:
         The Unexpected as Falsification   53

8   Introduction to Part II   55
    Miriam Hermeto and Ricardo Santhiago

9   The Must-See Play that so Many People Staged:
    A Mosaic of (False) Memories   59
    Miriam Hermeto

10 New Looks at Old Interviews:
    Racism and Privilege Around Black Folk Festivities   69
    Lívia Nascimento Monteiro

11 "Sincere Lies Interest Me": The Power of Falsehood
    in Oral History   79
    Heliana de Barros Conde Rodrigues

12 A Love Story That Never Happened   89
    Ricardo Santhiago

13 *Commentary*: Leftovers, Their Unexpected Forms,
    and the Act of Gleaning: Re-encounters with Interviews   97
    Luciana Kind

Part III Deviating Routes: The Unexpected
          as a Mnemonic Device   107

14 Introduction to Part III   109
    Miriam Hermeto and Ricardo Santhiago

15 "Who rode in my car? Who do you think? Jesus!":
    Subversion and Displacement in the Rereading of an Interview   113
    Luciana Heymann and Verena Alberti

16 Metabolizing the Leftovers of Memory   121
    Daisy Perelmutter

17 The Unexpected in an Archive:
    Interferences in a Soccer Memory Collection   127
    Bernardo Borges Buarque de Hollanda and
    Raphael Rajão Ribeiro

18	*Commentary*: Revisiting Oral Sources: The Unexpected and the Anticipated in Oral History Praxis Jorge Eduardo Aceves Lozano	135
Part IV	The Answer Is Another Subject: The Unexpected as a Generative Device	141
19	Introduction to Part IV Miriam Hermeto and Ricardo Santhiago	143
20	Looking for Heroes, I Found Conventional Workers: A Labor Community in the Argentine Dictatorship Camillo Robertini	147
21	The Devious Paths of Memory: Reflections on the Experience of Interviews with Residents of the Caparaó Sierra Plínio Ferreira Guimarães	155
22	"Everything Has Been Said": Surprising Encounters from Oral Histories in Ireland Dieter Reinisch	161
23	*Commentary*: The Answer Is Not Only Another Subject: It Is Also Another Set of Questions Linda Shopes	169
Part V	Nothing but Surprises: The Unexpected as a Given	175
24	Introduction to Part V Miriam Hermeto and Ricardo Santhiago	177
25	The Case of the Baffling Bandit Indira Chowdhury	181
26	Tragedy, Trauma, and the Transformations of Local Memory Regina Helena Alves da Silva and Leylianne Alves Vieira	189
27	Uncomfortable Stories and Tensions in the Official Memory of an Institution Iara Souto Ribeiro Silva	197
28	*Commentary*: Oral History as a Culture of Research Gabriel Amato	207

Part VI Avenues and Openings: The Unexpected as a Method — 213

29 Introduction to Part VI — 215
Miriam Hermeto and Ricardo Santhiago

30 Listening to Young Geeks in a Different City's Cosplay Scene — 219
Monica Rebecca Ferrari Nunes

31 "Ain't You Afraid to Be around a Drifter Like Me?": Beyond the Nothingness and the Fragments of the Life on the Streets — 227
Joana Barros

32 Struggling Through Speech in the Midst of Grief: A Non-interview and the Indigenous Xakriabá Cosmopolitics — 235
Juliana Ventura de Souza Fernandes

33 Ethnic Classification and Trauma During the Rwandan Genocide — 241
Philippe Denis

34 *Commentary*: How Do We Face the Unexpected? Constitutive Practices of Oral History — 249
María Laura Ortiz

35 Afterword: Expecting the Unexpected — 257
Alessandro Portelli

Index — 265

Notes on Contributors

Jorge Eduardo Aceves Lozano is a professor at the Center for Research and Higher Studies in Social Anthropology, in Guadalajara, Mexico. He is the author of works on oral history, local history, urban cultures, and social movements.

Verena Alberti is a professor at the School of Education at the State University of Rio de Janeiro and at the Professional Master's Degree in History Teaching and a history teacher at the Corcovado German School, Brazil. She has published works on history teaching, Brazilian contemporary history, oral history, and the history of laughter.

Gabriel Amato is a teacher at the Federal Institute of the South of Minas Gerais, Campus Três Corações, Brazil. He has published works on Brazilian contemporary history, military dictatorship, youth, oral history, and memory.

Joana Barros is a professor at the Federal University of São Paulo, Brazil. She has published works on the formation of Brazilian Society and Brazilian thinking, social movements and popular participation, public policies, and social rights.

Indira Chowdhury is the founder-director of the Centre for Public History at the Srishti-Manipal Institute of Art, Design, and Technology, Bengaluru, and a founding member of the Oral History Association of India. She was President of the Oral History Association of India (2013–2016) and President of the International Oral History Association (2014–2016).

Ann Cvetkovich is a professor in the Feminist Institute of Social Transformation at Carleton University in Ottawa, Ontario, Canada. She is the author of *An Archive of Feelings: Trauma, Sexuality, and Lesbian Public Cultures* and *Depression: A Public Feeling*. She is working on a book about the current state of LGBTQ archives and the creative use of them by artists to create counterarchives and interventions in public history.

Philippe Denis is Senior Professor of the History of Christianity at the University of KwaZulu-Natal, South Africa. He is the founder and presently a Board member of the Sinomlando Centre for Oral History and Memory Work in Africa and an associate member of the Royal Academy of Belgium. His most recent book is *The Genocide Against the Tutsi, and the Rwandan Churches: Between Grief and Denial* (2022).

Juliana Ventura de Souza Fernandes is a teacher at the Federal Institute of Minas Gerais, Campus Ribeirão das Neves, Brazil. She has published works on indigenous history, racism, race relations in education, and human rights.

Plínio Ferreira Guimarães is a teacher at the Federal Institute for Education, Science, and Technology of Espírito Santo, Campus Ibatiba, Brazil. He has published works on oral history and memory, military dictatorship, and history teaching.

Miriam Hermeto is a professor at the School of Philosophy and Human Sciences at the Federal University of Minas Gerais (UFMG), Brazil. Her research is on the teaching of history and the memory of the Brazilian military dictatorship. Also a singer, she creates and performs historical-themed concerts that combine music and documentation.

Luciana Heymann is a researcher at the Oswaldo Cruz House at the Oswaldo Cruz Foundation and a professor at the Graduate Program in the Preservation and Management of Cultural Heritage in the Sciences and Health, Brazil. She has published works on personal archival collections, memory, and cultural heritage.

Steven High is Professor of History and co-founder of Concordia University's Centre for Oral History and Digital Storytelling in Montreal, Canada. He is the author of many books and articles on oral history.

Bernardo Borges Buarque de Hollanda is a professor at the Social Sciences School at the Getúlio Vargas Foundation, Brazil. He is the author of works on the social history of soccer and the social history of literature in Brazil. He is a National Council for Scientific and Technological Development (CNPq) Productivity Fellow.

Luciana Kind is a professor in the Psychology Graduate Program at the Catholic University of Minas Gerais, Brazil. She coordinates the research group "Narratives, Gender, and Health." She has authored works on narrative methods, political subjectivation, participatory processes in health, and violence against women. She is a National Council for Scientific and Technological Development (CNPq) Productivity Fellow.

Ana Maria Mauad is a full professor at the Institute of History and the History Graduate Program of the Fluminense Federal University, Brazil, as well as a researcher at its Laboratory for Oral History and Image. She is the author of works on visual history, oral history, history of memory, and public history. She is a National Council for Scientific and Technological Development (CNPq) Productivity Fellow and a Faperj's "Our State" fellow.

Lívia Nascimento Monteiro is a professor at the Alfenas Federal University, Brazil. She has written on folk culture, the teaching of Afro-Brazilian history and culture, oral history, and public history.

Monica Rebecca Ferrari Nunes is a professor at the Graduate Program in Communication and Consumption Practices at the Superior School of Advertising and Marketing, in São Paulo, Brazil. She is the author of several works on communication, memory, and consumption. She is a National Council for Scientific and Technological Development (CNPq) Productivity Fellow.

María Laura Ortiz is a professor at the Philosophy and Humanities School at the National University of Córdoba, Argentina. She directs and is involved in research projects on Córdoba's recent history and oral history, with an emphasis on labor, activism, labor culture, political violence, and terrorism. She is the author of the book *Con los vientos del Cordobazo* (2019) and a member of Argentina's Oral History Association.

Daisy Perelmutter is a postdoctoral fellow at the University of São Paulo, Brazil, and an adjunct coordinator of the Center for Studies and Research on Oral History and Memory. She has published works on oral history, local history, family history, and the social history of education institutions.

Alessandro Portelli is an Italian scholar of American literature and culture, oral historian, writer for the daily newspaper *il manifesto*, and musicologist. He is Professor Emeritus of American literature at the University of Rome and was for many years a faculty member of the Columbia Oral History Summer Institute. He is the author of *They Say in Harlan County: An Oral History* (2011), among several other books.

Luiza Porto is a graduate student in the Graduate History Program at the State University of Santa Catarina, Brazil. She is involved with the Marginal Archives Project.

Dieter Reinisch is a postdoctoral researcher in the School of Political Science and Sociology at the National University of Ireland in Galway and teaches international relations and history at Webster Vienna Private University. He is the author of *Learning Behind Bars: How IRA Prisoners Shaped the Peace Process in Ireland* (2022).

Raphael Rajão Ribeiro is a historian at the Abílio Barreto Historical Museum. He has published works on cultural heritage, memory, sports history, and urban history.

Camillo Robertini is a researcher at the International Studies Institute at the University of Chile. He has authored essays on oral history, the use of social networks in historical research, and the labor memory of the dictatorships in Argentina, Chile, and Brazil.

Heliana de Barros Conde Rodrigues is a professor at the Psychology Institute at the State University of Rio de Janeiro. She has authored books and articles about French institutional analysis, oral history, and Foucault's concept of genealogy.

Ricardo Santhiago is a professor at the Institute of Cities at the Federal University of São Paulo (Unifesp), Brazil. An oral and public historian with a focus on Brazilian culture, he is the author of articles and books on Brazilian popular music, oral history methodology, and memory studies. He is a National Council for Scientific and Technological Development (CNPq) Productivity Fellow.

Linda Shopes has been involved with oral history for more than four decades. She has written widely in the fields of oral and public history, was the founding co-editor of Palgrave's Studies in Oral History series, has taught oral history in venues ranging from community workshops to graduate seminars, and is a past president of the US Oral History Association. She works as a freelance consultant and editor.

Iara Souto Ribeiro Silva is a staff member at the Federal University of Minas Gerais, Brazil, and a coordination of archives at the Center for the Memory of Physical Education, Sports, and Leisure. Her research focuses on oral history and the Brazilian military dictatorship.

Regina Helena Alves da Silva is an adjunct coordinator of the National Institute of Science and Technology in Public Policies and Territorial Development, as well as a professor at the History Graduate Program at the Federal University of Minas Gerais, Brazil.

Leylianne Alves Vieira is a researcher of the National Institute of Science and Technology in Public Policies and Territorial Development.

Mercedes Vilanova is the author of numerous articles and books on oral history, illiteracy, women's history, and Spanish history. In 1996, in Gothenburg, she contributed to the foundation of the International Oral History Association (IOHA) and served as its first president. She is the founder and editor of the journal *Historia, Antropologia y Fuentes Orales*.

CHAPTER 1

Foreword

Mercedes Vilanova

The Unexpected in Oral History is a joyful and vital book, one that collects experiences without bargaining, without attempting to disguise failures. It is a brave book, about that which is tough to accept and costly to say. At times, it conveys these things silently; at others, it cries out to our hearts. In either case, its purpose is to transform how we see things. It opens gaps, gathers scraps, and discovers mistakes—that may or may not be or ever have been noticed—and, for that very reason, may be read in any number of ways. Its pages insist that we should be "more" than what we are.

This was, for me, the challenge in reading it: to force myself to learn. The book's subtitle, *Case Studies of Surprising Interviews*, reveals the progress of a still unknown journey into our classic bibliography. The essays that follow successfully bring us close to dialogues with historical content and teach us to live in a plenitude that is absent from colder and more exacting methods. The creation of oral sources not only allows the written history to be better, but also transforms both those who question and those who answer, since, otherwise, it would have no meaning. Furthermore, revisiting the interview—a process known at least since Herodotus—brings us closer to other disciplines and, thanks to the ability to record, opens up a new dimension to archiving and helps us rethink what has been said: the Gordian knot in our craft.

The creators and organizers of this collection, Miriam Hermeto and Ricardo Santhiago, hit the target by suggesting themes that are as solid as cliffs: the *silence* we didn't wish for as we go in search of words; the *deception* that alerts us to the untrue, to those half-lies that are the spice of life; the *unexpected* that

---

M. Vilanova (✉)
Barcelona, Spain

baffles and disrupts; the fruitful path to gather *data* as a key to interpretation; and the *sine qua non* in oral history, recording and active listening, time and again, to the spoken, the unspoken, or the unasked.

To re-ask what is the meaning today of what was told to us yesterday transforms the recorded oral word into a memory of the past and also converts it into another source to study, consult, and squeeze. To reuse the interviews created by us or created by others and made available to us, in public or private archives, guides us into new interpretations and diverse times: how many experiences were gathered, in a few pages, by Hermeto and Santhiago! We owe so much to Willa Baum's feat, which, since the mid-twentieth century, at the Regional Oral History Office (ROHO) at the Bancroft Library at the University of California, Berkeley, has taught us the importance of not only transcribing the interviews, but also storing the original tapes.[1]

In this book, I was amazed to read the goals of the people who converse, as well as how that which is never or rarely told emerges: the Hansen bacillus, sexual abuse, lesbian love, theater, the imposture, or fantasy of what one wishes to believe oneself to be or have been; the transversality in situations of armed conflict, clandestine struggles, and dictatorships; or in the creation of new personalities, which can transform us from outlaws into "respectable" beings and, sometimes, may convert us into specialists who, upon discovering the "center of gravity" that moves the interviewee, feel compelled to dedicate years to analyzing this center—for example, reflecting on what soccer practice meant to a prisoner reluctant to dialogue.

Many texts present us with targets we didn't even know existed and discover unexpected paths that alter and deepen written history. All while facing the dilemma of knowing if our questions and hypotheses are more important than the objectives of the interviewees who, deliberately or not, do whatever they choose. What is most decisive: to discover that a grandfather remained secluded for years for being a "leper" or to have him share this experience and leave it as a legacy before passing away? Is it more decisive to recognize that there was sexual abuse, for the sake of having a record in an archive, or is it equally decisive to reveal that the interviewer also suffered abuse in childhood, although this was never before publicly acknowledged until the offer to participate in this book had been presented? *Noblesse oblige*—this is the *leitmotif* of *The Unexpected in Oral History*: the desire to share, extend a hand, and value failures, errors, and experiences.

Reading the initial chapters, about leprosy and sexual abuse, left me trembling—perhaps because my father, in 1937, in Colombia, was the director at the Agua de Dios leprosarium. A few years later, I, still a child, followed him as he visited people with the Hansen bacillus, living in seclusion near Barcelona; I

---

[1] At Columbia University, still in the 1970s, once the interviews were transcribed, the magnetic tapes were reused in other recordings, destroying the originals; my dismay and anger at this lack of thought were great when I visited them in 1976.

saw them behind the tall, barred windows, noticing their screams of joy, their applause, and smiles as they observed us arriving with gifts because Christmas was approaching. I have never forgotten this image. Now I rework this recollection: joined by Luiza Porto's grandfather, "I go through the mirror," and my recollections grow richer.

If the beginning of the book causes an impact, the last chapter synthesizes the essential in oral sources, as it affirms that the scientific method should not be a limit, but a complement to our work, for the voices we choose are the flesh of experiences in which we, historians, also take part. For María Laura Ortiz, it is time to recognize that the unexpected are not exceptions—they are the rule in our method, the path that allows us to access interpretations that we might not have discovered otherwise. This is the strength residing in the oral source; without it, something dies, ends up buried, is forgotten, and disappears.

Case Studies of Surprising Interviews approaches major themes and questions; I have chosen some, at random, such as seeking heroes and discovering they were hardly that, simply because of something trivial and obvious: they have not written a story that is the usual triumphant report. Ronald Fraser, upon publishing his book on the Spanish Civil War (1979), commented to me: "I will no longer interview activists, because most of them talk like a broken record, repeating what they believe in and not what they have lived; telling what they wish had happened and, therefore, lying when claiming what hasn't been." Not surprisingly, I myself, after analyzing interviews with miners, peasants, or fishermen from Catalonia, converted myself into a "spoken word inspector," because whoever spoke the most, who talked the most, was always the one who wished that the story had been that which they had dreamed of— and that which perhaps I myself also wished would have happened. Ever since, I have sought out people who belong to the invisible majorities, who are considered expendable and hence not worthy of being interviewed.

I have spent so many years in this job that I, unwillingly, relate to many surprises and discoveries collected in *The Unexpected in Oral History*—despite opposing the use of the "oral history" designation, because I find it more adequate to refer to a "history written without adjectives with oral sources."[2] Neither the book nor I believe that we give voice to the oppressed, who have their own voice—but one that we are frequently unable to listen to—and, sometimes, do speak, and out loud.[3] But an example of this activist understanding can be found in a book published in Germany, relatively recently. A group of doctoral students from Friedrich-Schiller University Jena became interested in researching the history of the so-called international oral history movement, which began, in Europe, in the early 1970s. They were able to do it, thanks to

---

[2] In 1989, *Historia y Fuente Oral* magazine was founded, and the first published issue was entitled "¿Historia Oral?", because we intended to defend the creation of oral sources, not oral history in particular.

[3] I have defended this idea since the 1992: "we began to think the majorities had a voice, but we the intellectuals, historians and politicians weren't able to distinguish it" (Vilanova 1996, 38).

an idea set forth by Lutz Niethammer. The title is suggestive: *Giving a Voice to the Oppressed? The International Oral History Association as an Academic Network and Political Movement* (Arp et al. 2013, 2019). In the first chapter, by Agnès Arp, Raphael Samuel's view of the importance of questioning whether researchers give voice to the oppressed is underscored, which, by the way, is what the book title claims. Samuel states: "They are not just described; but have the possibility to speak for themselves." I have always felt more attracted to Alessandro Portelli—who is dear to the concept of this collection—who makes a resounding defense of oral history as an "experiment in equality," based on the recognition (and power) of difference.

Another question that has always struck me, and that is pertinent to the scope of this book, is, "Is it possible to write history solely with oral sources?" I will mention two cases in which I found myself forced to do it, somewhat unexpectedly, in order to search for answers to questions pivotal to my own projects. First: Why did the 1936 social revolution in Spain fail? What people told me is common sense but is also something that historiography is unaware of. Laborers who were illiterate, or poorly literate, gave me blunt answers: they claimed that neither they nor their union leaders had the necessary knowledge to manage the economy and boost the social change they yearned for. Since then, I have learned that, without an elite culture and the capacity of imagining a different system, it is not possible to achieve radical change in our ways of living, personal and collectively—a great lesson given to me by oral sources.

Secondly, in the Mauthausen Survivor Documentation Project (MSDP), coordinated by Gerhard Botz, I could not find written documents but was able to use oral sources thanks to having interviewed Spanish republicans who had been in the Mauthausen concentration camps and managed to survive. The way they describe their lives and what helped them to survive amazed me: "The world of Mauthausen prisoners is like the world outside. I understood this right away, but others didn't ... Even though it's true that the category you belonged to [inside] had nothing to do with what you had been outside, but with what you were in there." And what they were inside could be so brutal, such as having to take care of the camp's daily operations in order not to die—or so extraordinary, such as what Manuel Azaustre managed to do. "I learned to be human and, when I left, I left as a man, carrying a humanity, a thing ...," he said.

In 2005, I asked Jorge Semprún how and why he wrote the book *El largo viaje*, in 1963, which, *ipso facto*, transformed him into a famous writer. Published in Spanish and French, the book received many awards, including the Premio Formentor (in Spain) and the Prix Littéraire de la Résistance (in France). His answer was:

> The possibility to write appeared to me with amazing ease, when I was about to be expelled from the party, at an activist couple's [Manuel Azaustre and his wife, María Gascón, activists of the Communist Party] residence in Concepción

Bahamonde, in Madrid. And there was this amazing casualty. I was very lucky Manolo Azaustre had been deported to Mauthausen … He'd tell me about it and I would think: 'He had such a deep experience, but narrates it so badly'. So, I had the idea to tell it myself. In other words, the book was written thanks to (or by) Manuel Azaustre."[4]

Could it be that, like Janaína Amado, I, too, met with a "great liar"? Rereading Amado, thanks to *The Unexpected in Oral History: Case Studies of Surprising Interviews*, for which her article provides an important grounding, allowed me to recover my recollections about her, the Brazilian partner with whom I shared a year, between 1989 and 1990, at the Smithsonian Institute's Woodrow Wilson International Center for Scholars, in Washington, DC. She researched social movements and land issues, and I dedicated myself to interviewing illiterate people living in the Baltimore area. Another contributor to this book also crossed my path years ago. The first time I referred to the need for a "history without adjectives with oral sources" was a bit later, in Rio de Janeiro, at the invitation of Marieta de Moraes Ferreira. To some extent, this foreword allows me to return to Brazil, one of my dearest places, where this book was generated.

One last comment, before concluding. A key subject for my study of illiteracy in Catalonia was the comparison between oral sources and statistical studies, because statistics, despite its many errors, provide a social framework; it raises questions that we would be unable to formulate otherwise; it helps us to insert our speakers' answers into a broader historical narrative. The importance of statistics is central to understanding the meaning and reach of censorship, as I demonstrated in "Trozos perdidos de la historia. El tapiz de Walter Benjamin" [Requested pieces of history: The Walter Benjamin tapestry] (2016), where I expose the evil face of those who restrict freedom of expression and, consequently, freedom itself. Statistics are of help, especially, when our hypotheses are not confirmed—as happens with many authors in this book—because it pushes us toward other paths. After intense experiences with statistics creation and analysis, I would, in my research, search for real people through the paper trail that would point to them instead of using, for example, the snowball method. I was convinced that the invisible majorities carry answers to the world's most complex problems today. However, we will hardly find the bearers of these answers if we try to reach them only through our friends, or our friends' acquaintances, or acquaintances of other friends' acquaintances.

Interviewing illiterate people is a responsibility we should not avoid, because they are those who leave no other kind of trace or source, except in census or certain companies' archives. Still, if I were younger today, I would approach another pressing challenge: I would seek the excluded people, a term even more atrocious because the excluded aren't even labeled as poor and nobody

---

[4] Jorge Semprún's interview is part of the project by the Foundation Remembrance, Responsibility and Future, coordinated by Alexander von Plato et al. (2010).

cares whether they are literate or not. The excluded don't matter; what defines their lives is to be apart. Undoubtedly, by talking to excluded people after a fine statistical study, we would find mountains of surprises, unexpected, and "truths," as the authors in this collection have, precisely because history-writing is a tale that never ends and to do it we must absolutely rely on life and on the words that take us back to the world.

References

Arp, Agnès, Annette Leo, and Franka Maubach, eds. 2013. *Den Unterdrückten eine Stimme geben? Die Internationale Oral History Association zwischen politischer Bewegung und wissenschaftlichen Netzwerk*. Gottingen: Wallstein Verlag.

———, eds. 2019. *Giving a Voice to the Oppressed: The International Oral History Association between Political Movement and Academic Networks*. Berlin: De Gruyter.

Fraser, Ronald. 1979. *Recuérdalo tú y recuérdalo a otros: historia oral de la guerra civil española*. Barcelona: Crítica.

von Plato, Alexander, Almut Leh, and Christoph Schlesinger, eds. 2010. *Hitler's Slaves: Life Stories of Forced Labourers in Nazi-Occupied Europe*. Oxford, UK: Berghahn Books.

Vilanova, Mercedes. 1996. *Las mayorías invisibles: explotación fabril, revolución y represión*. Barcelona: Icaria.

———. 2016. Trozos perdidos de la historia. El tapiz de Walter Benjamin. In *¿Y ahora qué?: nuevos usos del género biográfico*, ed. Henar Gallego Franco and Mónica Bolufer Peruga, 195–219. Barcelona: Icaria.

CHAPTER 2

Introduction

Miriam Hermeto and Ricardo Santhiago

Running an informal survey with oral history practitioners could easily lead us to an inventory of the essential qualities needed for enthusiasts of this art of listening: tenderness, patience, attention, balance between respect for the narrator and commitment to a reliable construction of knowledge. While other abilities—those at the level of procedure—may be more easily submitted to regulation and reproduction, these contain a touch of the unfathomable or untransferable at the least. The flexibility and dexterity needed to adjust creatively to the unexpected can certainly be included in this second set.

In the mid-1990s, when oral history was spreading across Brazil thanks to the vigor of a new generation of researchers attracted to the force of dialogue, an essay by historian Janaína Amado made an impression on her readers. Not because she brought them good news, definitive solutions to the problems that afflicted them; on the contrary, because she drew attention to the limits of methodological dogmatism and called for them to be suspicious of their own certainties and denials.

Under the title "O grande mentiroso: Tradição, veracidade e imaginação em história oral" [The Great Liar: Tradition, Veracity, and Imagination in Oral History] (1995)—published in a slightly shorter version, in English, as "The Brazilian Quijote: Truth and Fabrication in Oral History" (1998)—the essay

M. Hermeto
Federal University of Minas Gerais (UFMG), Belo Horizonte, Brazil

R. Santhiago (✉)
Federal University of São Paulo (Unifesp), São Paulo, Brazil
e-mail: ricardo.santhiago@unifesp.br

© The Author(s), under exclusive license to Springer Nature Switzerland AG 2023
R. Santhiago, M. Hermeto (eds.), *The Unexpected in Oral History*, Palgrave Studies in Oral History,
https://doi.org/10.1007/978-3-031-17749-1_2

introduced readers to a character named Fernandes. An exuberant narrator from whom Amado had collected a 16-hour-long life story, Fernandes had been contacted for a clear purpose: the historian was investigating the 1950s farmworkers' uprising in the small town of Formoso, in the north region of the state of Goiás. Fernandes had been her first interviewee in this thematically circumscribed project and, perhaps as a sort of beginner's luck, seemed to foretell its success. That narrator, Amado wrote in the original Portuguese-language essay,

> seemed to represent all a researcher could wish for in a first research interview: the informant demonstrated deep knowledge and experience of the subject, as well as a will to collaborate with the work; displayed a prodigious memory, meticulously recollecting even seemingly unimportant events; expressed strong opinions on all the subjects, with no lack of a sense of humor; and expressed affinity with folk culture, reciting proverbs and popular poetry, chanting songs, performing dance moves, and describing in great detail the garments, manners, and traditions of the region. (Amado 1995, 126)

Nonetheless, as she scrutinized written documents and examined the oral histories of other interviewees, Amado could come to no other conclusion than that Fernandes had lied—or, more appropriately, fabricated a story that operated with real episodes, people, and events, but scrambled with his own connections, spatiality, and temporality. Disappointed and angered with the unexpected trap she had fallen into, she shoved the interview into her personal files and only came back to it later, when her research on the Formoso uprising had already been concluded.

And yet, when listening to her "great liar" interview for a second time, outside the investigative framework that led her to him, Amado experienced a different reaction and was able to appreciate the unique creativity in Fernandes's narration. The essay she published, a Brazilian classic on oral history, expressed her dilemmas in coping with Fernandes's story. She made way for other interpretations, exploring the relations between the interviewee's narrative, his personal library, the Western literary tradition, and the modes of transmission of cultural memory. Above all, she pondered how that interview led her to reconsider both her research questions and, more extensively, her view on oral history.

Could it be—Janaína Amado's text compels us to ask—that the best (or only) solution to handling an unusual narrative is to discard it, as the researcher herself did at first, deeming her narrator a liar? Both in this text and in much of what oral history shows us, the answer is a resounding "no": on the contrary, many of our most significant experiences occur precisely due to the incongruity between our research expectations and what we effectively encounter in the field. In a word, the *unexpected*—a foundational and inescapable theme in oral history methodological debates, but as elusive as it is commonplace.

In this book, inspired by Amado's landmark work, we defy the elusive nature of the unexpected and place it at the center of a shared, collective reflection. Joined by some 30 authors, we pursue dialogue situations that produce unexpected research encounters and data that seem apparently unusable. We ponder how some field experiences not only redirect the steps of a given research project, but also often reconfigure the *ethos* of the researchers, destabilizing their hypotheses and certainties about their subjects and work methods.

Beyond the Anecdotal

Perhaps the unexpected does in fact constitute one of the foundations of each and every instance of participatory research—an ever-present reality oral history practitioners try to avoid, relying on exploratory research, carefully prepared interview scripts, recorders and backup tech supplies, and interview release forms. We tend to take care of every possible development, drawing supposedly flawless research plans, only to enter the swampy ground of actual experience, inside which we still bathe in the rich procedures of our method.

Whoever accumulates a handful of interviews is capable of constructing their own anecdotes of situations that generated a rerouting. They may vary from tense negotiations between both parties involved in a dialogue to the simple discourtesy of an interviewee. Many of these episodes end up restricted to hallway conversations, in which we confide to our colleagues the pains and delights of producing oral history (once considered a "simpler" method than, for instance, archival research). And, if some of these shenanigans end up as mere curiosities in these personal anecdotes, others can highlight the inherent complexity of our practice and paving the way to more complex readings, positioning *our* interviews on a spectrum distinguishable from interactions of a different nature. "Would you like to have an instrument that will tell you what, when and how to do an interview?" asks a popular book, one that promises to teach its readers to "dominate the process of a job interview." It is hard to believe its method is flawless in any context, and the mere enunciation of this hypothesis is already exasperating.

Several manuals in our field—works that have played an introductory role of enormous value—state that "interviewers need to be sufficiently prepared to know both what to expect and what not to expect from an interview" (Ritchie 2014, 75), but also warn that "circumstances apparently external to the interview might disrupt its progress" (Alberti 2013, 196). Therefore, these books anticipate conciliations as well as conflicts that are carefully analyzed in the theoretical literature, where silence, hesitation, relief, distortion, and the switch from verbal to gestural expression, have been—starting from its "theoretical turn" in (Thomson 2007; Shopes 2014)—not only recognized but embraced as constitutive memory operations in oral history interviews.

Strictly connected to the concepts of narrative and (most significantly, in our case) intersubjectivity, such a turn has highlighted the conversational and negotiated nature of interviews and their results. Alessandro Portelli's work in this aspect was seminal. His influential text from 1979, "Sulla diversità della storia orale" [On the Diversity of Oral History] paved new roads for work with oral history and memory, at the intersection between the individual and the collective. Arguing in favor of the requalification of aspects considered to be weak in oral history, by seeing them as points of strength, Portelli indicated orality, narrative, subjectivity, credibility, objectivity, and authorship of oral sources as their axes. He also discussed the relational nature of the source and its product, an issue enriched by his resounding defense of history as an "experiment in equality," based on the acknowledgment (and strength) of difference (Portelli 1991).

His essays, collapsing the strict frontiers between theory and empiricism, have become an entry portal to questions that continue to both stimulate and disturb oral historians. The unexpected that emerges in Portelli's fieldwork is treated with skill and rigor while not leading to attempts to regulate the practice of oral history. In addition to the unannounced events that temper encounters and performances in oral history, his interpretations are also replete with appreciations of the unexpected: what should we do, after all, with the errors, inconsistencies, and individual and collective evasions in the oral histories we collect? Along this path, Luigi Trastulli—an iconic character whose death is incorrectly dated in the memory of Portelli's interviewees—became one of his most famous interviewees, shedding light on possible readings of inconsistent, and therefore intimidating, research data.

From another perspective, feminist oral history—definitely concerned with the procedural dimension of research and the balance of power surrounding and influencing the interview—has brought public light to debates on the practical implications of gender, ethnicity, and class differences among research participants, on tensions resulting from failures in meeting the counterparts' expectations, and on the inconvenient discoveries in investigations caused by the expectations on both sides. Valuing the researcher's self-reflexivity resulted in a widespread vigilance over how one can act in face the narrators and their narratives (Gluck and Patai 1991; Srigley et al. 2018).

In short, in many ways, scholarship in our field has dealt with either the traces or the imposing presence of surprise, often under the guise of incompatibility, incoherence, or even failure. From a strictly traditional perspective, most scientific fields are essentially formed by narratives of success and achievement, whereas the knowledge our kind of research creates, dialogically produced—which does not delegitimize the specific inputs of experience and expertise, in Michael Frisch's terms (2011)—is largely formed by narratives of processes, of pathways. In it, things that are not calculated become a stimulus for a sophisticated analysis of how people depict both themselves and their circumstances.

Learning from the Unexpected

On many, and mostly fortuitous, occasions, we have eventually shared tales about our field experiences. We have enjoyed each other's surprises and adventures, yet quickly perceived the possible formative power of these behind-the-scenes stories about the practice of oral history—as Anna Sheftel and Stacey Zembrzycki stress in the introduction of *Oral History Off the Record: Toward an Ethnography of Practice* (2013), with which this book forges a connection. We have agreed that case studies of unexpected interviews may stress, and assist in revising and incrementing, the *corpus* of established knowledge—in theoretical, methodological, and documental terms—in our field. And we have sought to expand these informal and private conversations into a larger web of dialogues, woven not only by mere descriptions of unusual situations but by theoretical-methodological problematizations about dialogue, production of oral sources, and personal narratives within the framework of oral history.

We believe the encounter with the unexpected raises questions that otherwise might not have occurred or would hardly occur if we were to engage in a merely formal reflection. This new focalization (to borrow Gerard Genette's term) seems to generate a virtuous cycle within the methodological debates in our field, attentive to the scrutiny both of sources and of its conditions of production. Oral history, after all, is a reflexive practice dependent not only on the experiences of our storytellers, in Walter Benjamin's sense—the "experience which is passed on from mouth to mouth" (1968)—but also the researchers' experiences. These put to the test the body of theoretical, methodological, and content-related assumptions that are intertwined in our projects.

Incited by Janaína Amado's Brazilian "classic," we invited colleagues from various disciplinary fields, in distinct moments in their professional careers, and also from other national contexts, to focus on experiences with narrators who did not speak about the subjects proposed to them; who guided their accounts in a thematic way when invited to elaborate a life story, or vice versa; who built their narrative identities differently from those socially attributed to them; who denied and produced intentional silences; who narrated partially or completely invented memories, based on recollections from other individuals, reference groups, and/or on whatever reached them through popular media or reading habits. We presented them with a broad invitation to place the mobilizing nature of the "unexpected" into the center of a first-person methodological reflection, capable of extracting lessons from practice but without incurring the over-theorization that often plagues our field, imposing a gap between the aesthetic, foundational experience of dialogue, and the texts that are disseminated.

We had broad-spectrum consultations with possible contributors, creating an open environment so our colleagues—researchers we admire and who we knew would respond creatively to our invitation—could draw on the different circumstances relating to their oral history training, conceptualization, or research. We embraced occasions where the unexpected emerged in the field, face-to-face with narrators, in the heat of the dialogue; the contexts where it forced researchers to reconsider their goals and review their research design; as well as the situations where the unexpected was confronted *a posteriori*, away from the urgency of field research, or of personal, professional, and institutional commitments. We looked to the unexpected showing up in terms of method, theory, politics, psychology, and identity. We included even those research contexts so prone to the eruption of the unexpected that we would actually be amazed if they had not implied some surprise. By doing so, we—as the curators of case studies of surprising interviews—consequently opened this volume to a kind of unpredictability that we deliberately choose to keep, and that is expressed by the heterogeneity of themes, origins, assumptions, methodological practices, and theoretical framings found in the chapters that follow.

We later had extensive discussions about the contributions, identifying affinities and recurrences that could be translated into thematic sections and the suggestion of possible paths for reading. In the organization of these sections, we opted for stressing methodological (and not thematic) axes, thus preserving the primary nature of the book. The unexpected as an outbreak, as falsification, as a mnemonic device, as a generative device, as a given, as a method: these are half a dozen of the many faces the unexpected can assume. Axes we defined while still acknowledging that they are arbitrary, a result of our readings, and do not always match the very nature of the unexpected as imagined or insinuated by the authors. Then, when we received the remarks by the invited commentators—remarks that close each of these sections, duplicating the conversational genesis of this book—a new surprise: not even they match the authors' nor our emphases. In a revealing way, these many seams interweave into one of the pillars of our practice: recognizing that every interview is polysemic and not limited to a single interpretation.

It would be daunting to extract generalizations from the full set of chapters; and in fact, when reading these reports and the ways in which unexpected events were faced, the readers will be tempted to offer alternative paths, different from those of the authors, that do not claim to be univocal. Nevertheless, given the mission of this volume—to highlight a phenomenon that lies at the very heart of oral history, both in its fieldwork and scholarship—it is inevitable to point to some nodal points that are less lessons in avoiding the unexpected than windows for it to be accepted as an unavoidable presence.

Also collaborating with this book, Luciana Heymann and Verena Alberti (2018) have previously written about the "silent heritage" that oral history collections embody: the interviews stored in archives that could tell us much more than what they were asked in previous readings. No doubt our field is strongly powered by the harvesting of new sources—and there is no denying that the thrill in meeting our narrators and getting involved in their often-fascinating contexts plays a role in a tacit inclination to record new interviews instead of more actively exploring those produced by others. Additionally, oral history in Brazil has always been more associated with the logic of producing sources for immediate employment in academic research than with the creation of collections for future use. The richness implied by the recovery of past interviews performed in many chapters of this volume leads us to agree with Heymann and Alberti's call for the reuse of previously done oral histories, and to add that, beyond enriching our knowledge of the topics raised in the dialogue, these materials also have a lot to teach about the methodology itself.

A second element we find in these texts is the extensive use of researchers' observations, consubstantiated in field notes, personal and research diaries, as well as other resources that may be linked with the interviews *a posteriori*, such as the correspondence between researchers and interviewees. The benefits brought to the scholarship by this ethnographic dimension fortify the understanding of oral history as an endeavor that holds the recording of a human voice at its center—but that also amplifies the reach and depth of its hypotheses and speculations when it is combined with other sources and registers which allow us to grasp whatever remained unspoken and amenable to the intuition (a priceless predicate) of the researcher.

As a final remark, the texts collected here confirm the significance of distinguishing thematically oriented interviews and biographical interviews or life stories. Under the oral history framework, both hold similarities: they demand quality preliminary research, give rise to open questions, and require full attention and attentive listening from the researcher. However, they also present differences extending to the distinct interpretative flexibility offered by them in the core of the projects that originated them; these differences, in addition, impact the scope of possible research for generations of new hypotheses and conclusions upon reuse.

As we have said and wish to repeat, this book emphasizes a tension that is immanent in our practice: that between expectations and the reality of oral history fieldwork and interpretation; it highlights how shared is the authority created by oral history interviews and their condition as an experience of intellectual and personal discovery. We suspect that the unexpected dimensions reported by the authors who accepted to engage in this collective reflection are parallel to what they have encountered and pursued in their own intellectual projects, to their views on knowledge in the humanities, and on the ways to produce and share it.

These chapters, thus, point to the permanent and inescapable incompleteness of methodological discourses, which also accounts for their beauty. Theoretical dogma and institutional restrictions may threaten the embrace of surprise but do not mitigate it: any researchers who throw themselves into the practice of oral history quickly discover that it is not a path that will always lead to the same ends. Each interview is unique, no matter how many we may have conducted, how overarching our prior research may have been, how eloquent our narrators prove to be, how resilient we may be as researchers. And, if so, to what extent can we claim a pedagogical nature for reflections built on unexpected dialogues, on surprising oral history interviews? What the following chapters teach us is that such experiences must indeed be documented, scrutinized, criticized, shared, and salvaged from mere casual behind-the-scenes talks, not so that the unexpected stays within our line of sight—which will remain beyond our control—but only so we may better deal with it in the (many) future times it crosses our paths again.

References

Alberti, Verena. 2013. *Manual de história oral*. 3rd ed. Rio de Janeiro: Editora FGV.
Amado, Janaína. 1995. O grande mentiroso: Tradição, veracidade e imaginação em história oral. *História* 14: 125–136.
———. 1998. The Brazilian Quijote: Truth And Fabrication In Oral History. *Luso-Brazilian Review* 35 (1): 1–9.
Benjamin, Walter. 1968. The Storyteller: Reflections on the Works of Nikolai Leskov. In *Illuminations*, ed. Hannah Arendt, 83–109. New York: Harcourt Brace Jovanovich.
Frisch, Michael. 2011. From A Shared Authority to the Digital Kitchen, and Back. In *Letting Go?: Sharing Historical Authority in a User-Generated World*, ed. Bill Adair, Benjamin Filene, and Laura Koloski. Philadelphia: Pew Center for Arts & Heritage.
Gluck, Sherna Berger, and Daphne Patai, eds. 1991. *Women's Words: The Feminist Practice of Oral History*. New York: Routledge.
Heymann, Luciana, and Verena Alberti. 2018. Acervos de história oral: um patrimônio silencioso? In *História oral e patrimônio cultural: potencialidades e transformações*, ed. Leticia Bauer and Viviane Trindade Borges, 11–29. São Paulo: Letra e Voz.
Portelli, Alessandro. 1979. Sulla diversità dela storia orale. *Primo Maggio* 13: 54–60.
———. 1991. Research as an Experiment in Equality. In *The Death of Luigi Trastulli and Other Stories: Form and Meaning in Oral History*, 29–44. Albany: State University of New York Press.
Ritchie, Donald A. 2014. *Doing Oral History*. 3rd ed. New York: Oxford University Press.
Sheftel, Anna, and Stacey Zembrzycki, eds. 2013. *Oral History Off the Record: Toward an Ethnography of Practice*. New York: Palgrave.
Shopes, Linda. 2014. 'Insights and Oversights': Reflections on the Documentary Tradition and the Theoretical Turn in Oral History. *Oral History Review* 41 (2): 257–268.
Srigley, Katrina, Stacey Zembrzycki, and Franca Iacovetta, eds. 2018. *Beyond Women's Words: Feminisms and the Practices of Oral History in the Twenty-First Century*. New York: Routledge.
Thomson, Alistair. 2007. Four Paradigm Transformations in Oral History. *Oral History Review* 34 (1): 49–70.

PART I

Scratching the Silence:
The Unexpected as an Outbreak

Introduction to Part I

Miriam Hermeto and Ricardo Santhiago

We oral historians often nurture the desire—sometimes secret—that an interview should surprise us, that it should invariably unveil new aspects of events, details never before exposed, experiences hitherto unconfessed, perceptions never formulated until we appeared with our equipment in pursuit of an interview. This appetite for novelty is an equivalent of the "scoop" in the world of professional journalists. In our field, however, it is a sort of scooping within the apparently limitless terrain of established social memory. And, while oral history is now usually understood as a method prone to creating a space for the narrators' self-expression and for the interpretation of the meanings of their recollections (including the reiteration of stories crystallized by past repetition), its conceptualization as a resource to register "original information" remains alive.

So established is the wish to mine for novelties that we may often find ourselves dismissing as "minor" those interviews that mainly collect episodes and impressions already of public knowledge. Alessandro Portelli, author of the afterword to this book and a leading exponent of an interpretive approach to oral sources—sometimes conceptualized as the heart of its "theoretical turn"—taught quite a long time ago that "what is spoken in a typical oral history interview has usually never been told *in that form* before." This shift of

---

M. Hermeto
Universidade Federal de Minas Gerais (UFMG), Belo Horizonte, Brazil

R. Santhiago (✉)
Universidade Federal de São Paulo (Unifesp), São Paulo, Brazil
e-mail: ricardo.santhiago@unifesp.br

© The Author(s), under exclusive license to Springer Nature Switzerland AG 2023
R. Santhiago, M. Hermeto (eds.), *The Unexpected in Oral History*, Palgrave Studies in Oral History,
https://doi.org/10.1007/978-3-031-17749-1_3

perspective led him to shrewdly qualify as a "literary fiction" the image of a "grandparent who takes a grandchild on his or her knee and tells the story of his or her life" (1997, 4). Portelli perceived the dialogue that unfolds in oral history as a narrative space in which even the stories already told in former situations are newly shaped as "untold stories," starting from, and producing, unprecedented meanings in the light of their new circumstances.

As oral history practitioners, we heard him, but we could not deny that the imperative of novelty persists. It stays alive today, in our expectations, and it is frequently expressed in carefully constructed questions. Even when not trying to induce memory work, these questions betray our hopes for the emergence of the unspoken.

If the desire for "breaking the silence"—one of the clichés of current vocabulary—is still latent in our imagination, it derives from the field's own tendency, particularly in the 1960s and 1970s, to define and justify itself in those very terms. Gathering testimonies of those who had never been heard was once a must-do, not infrequently accompanied by the supposed urge to "give voice to" the marginalized, the forgotten, the ignored. This further cliché is largely viewed today as a mistake on epistemological, methodological, political, and ethical grounds. Nonetheless, challenging structural silences was one aim of numerous committed researchers from whom we learned much. In fact, these silences are still the target of many research agendas—which, if no longer labeling their subjects as "voiceless" or "marginal," continue to privilege minorities relegated to public invisibility.

One unexpected surprise for our field was to realize that creating spaces for expression would not, as a natural consequence, amount to eradicating all that is silent, ignored, or unspoken. Why, when invited to speak out, would our interviewees take the floor but not always break social and individual silences? Biographical and autobiographical studies, literary criticism, *testimonio* studies—sometimes brought together by interdisciplinary memory studies—have offered eloquent answers to this question. Robyn Fivush (2010) emphasized a key difference between *being silenced* and *being silent*; she considers the latter a form of agency, an active way of constructing oneself through narrative (or the lack of narrative). Well before her work, however, oral history scholarship (from the late 1970s onwards) began to consider the identification and understanding of silences within oral narratives, produced in the context of interviews, as being of fundamental importance. As she did with humor, Luisa Passerini (1984) reinterpreted the city of Turin's working-class silences about fascism: from being dismissed as "irrelevant," they became central to her influential analysis. Alistair Thomson (1999), in his well-known analysis of oral history and migration studies, stated that "the need to combat the silences" would be one of the motivations for undertaking migrant and ethnic oral history; he, too, simultaneously stressed that "emphases and silences" are themselves forms of revealing the migrant experience. Marco Aurélio Santana (2000), interviewing workers who fought against the Brazilian military dictatorship, noticed that the silences in the narratives he gathered mirrored the very experiences of fear and consternation they sought to communicate.

A number of other cases could be raised, given that interpreting silences as much as verbalized evocations has become an inescapable task of oral historians. From the "memory framing" and "underground memories" suggested by the sociologist Michael Pollak (1989) to the official/state production of forgetfulness in times of an apparent "memory boom," as alerted by the literary critic Andreas Huyssen (2014), conceptual categories for interpreting the unsaid that remains in the narratives of those who agree to speak (but who cannot or do not wish to "break the silence") abound. Under the inspiration of Paul Ricoeur (2007), no memory research today can do without the effort of understanding the maintenance and role of silences as an inescapable part of memory work.

This is the framework for the question posed by the first section of this book: what happens when, at the moment when the silence seems to have been "broken," something emerges that is not only new, but in one way or another unexpected? What does an oral historian do when the novelty, so ardently desired, goes too far or moves in a different direction from the one the interviewer had in mind? How to behave when "breaking the silence" raises personal, political, and ethical dilemmas? On these occasions, one can feel that the oral narrative seems to stutter, scratching the silences. By doing this, our narrators may be promoting disconcerting irruptions of meanings, themes, and objects, inciting unusual interpretations for the initial constructions of memory about the narrated events. If the silence itself was uncomfortable, what now breaks through causes still greater unease—like a sudden invasion, an unexpected overflow.

The chapters that make up this section deal with these types of occasions. We encounter three researchers overwhelmed by the unexpected: Luiza Porto, Steven High, and Ann Cvetkovitch. Or four, considering what Ana Maria Mauad narrates in her commentary following the three essays. Invasions are not, in themselves, a surprise for these scholars, who fully embrace the intersubjective, cooperatively managed dialogue that defines oral history. What is unique are the forms the invasions assume.

Porto recounts the hidden story of her grandfather, *Seu* João Batista, who, in his old age, gathered his family together and narrated a truth that abruptly burst over his children and grandchildren: he and his wife had met in an isolation facility for patients suffering from leprosy (Hansen's disease). His silence about that experience, which he had hidden to avoid stigmatizing his family members, invaded his granddaughter. Still a historian in training, she became an oral history researcher constructing *Seu* João's life story and, in the process, discovering many other family secrets.

In High's case, what broke out unpredictably was Florence Richard's account of sexual violence, narrated in the midst of High's calm summer of research, in his early days as an oral historian, from which he imagined that he would emerge unscathed—after all, it was supposed to be merely an internship intended to record bland interviews about local history! That was definitely not the case. The forthright essay written by High, now a seasoned oral historian, represents a brave confrontation with the silence in his own life experience.

In the third chapter of this section, Ann Cvetkovich recounts how the Covid-19 pandemic broke into her idea of documenting the legendary Michigan Womyn's Music Festival (Michfest), which included a plan to conduct a life story interview with Lisa Vogel, one of the festival's founders. The problem was that Vogel was not eager to narrate. The solution was that, during the pandemic, her stories flowed out via Facebook through her performative livestreams: silences being scratched. The richness of these digitally constructed memories allowed Cvetkovich to create an astute analysis of the internal tensions of the festival.

Finally, Mauad—who touches on the concepts of the "unspeakable," "hidden memories," and "memory framing" when commenting on the three preceding authors—also narrates her own unexpected experiences. She mentions a secret truth about her grandmother that was unveiled during her research involving family photographs—a secret that still remains under lock and key. Before commenting on the three chapters that preceded her, Mauad also reveals the hidden trajectory of an award-winning newspaper photo, only made possible by the work of oral history.

These, as we will see, are reports on irruptions and novelties that changed not only the research projects but the researchers as well.

References

Fivush, Robyn. 2010. Speaking Silence: The Social Construction of Silence in Autobiographical and Cultural Narratives. *Memory* 18 (2): 88–98.
Huyssen, Andreas. 2014. *Culturas do passado-presente: modernismos, artes visuais, políticas da memória*. Rio de Janeiro: Contraponto.
Passerini, Luisa. 1984. *Torino Operaia e Fascismo: Una Storia Orale*. Bari: Laterza.
Pollak, Michael. 1989. Memória, esquecimento, silêncio. *Estudos Históricos* 2 (3): 3–15.
Portelli, Alessandro. 1997. Oral History as Genre. In *The Battle of Valle Giulia: Oral History and the Art of Dialogue*, 3–23. Madison: University of Wisconsin Press.
Ricoeur, Paul. 2007. *A memória, a história, o esquecimento*. Campinas: Editora da Unicamp.
Santana, Marco Aurélio. 2000. Militância, repressão e silêncio: relato de uma experiência com a memória operária. *História Oral* 3: 35–47.
Thomson, Alistair. 1999. Moving Stories: Oral History and Migration Studies. *Oral History* 27 (1): 24–37.

CHAPTER 4

My Grandfather's Unknown History

Luiza Porto

João Batista Pereira is my maternal grandfather. He was born on January 5, 1930, in the small town of Andrelândia, in the countryside of the Brazilian state of Minas Gerais, son of Maria da Glória Pereira and Rufino Pereira Junior—a man who played a key role in his life narrative. João spent his childhood with his parents and sisters at "Granja Tiradentes," a corral near the city's downtown area. In 1944, he was attending the high school preparatory course in the city of Lavras, larger than that where he was born, when he received a letter from his colleague Francisco Manuel Pereira, a.k.a. "Chico Padeiro," talking about Rufino's death. João returned to Andrelândia immediately and took over his father's role as responsible for his mother and sisters. For the next four years, João remained in the city and sought to provide for his family any way he could.

In 1948, due to an open ankle wound, he went through clinical tests on his feet and ears. His physician, Dr. Alípio, also collected a blood sample for a leprosy prophylaxis test. The diagnosis confirmation came shortly thereafter, transforming João Batista's life, and he was admitted to the Roça Grande Leprosarium a few days later.

About this part of my grandfather's story, we, his descendants, only came to learn a few years ago.

L. Porto (✉)
Universidade Estadual de Santa Catarina (UDESC), Florianópolis, Brazil

The First Unexpected Event

Provisional measure 373, dating from 2007, authorizes the concession of a special pension to people affected by Hansen's disease who were compulsorily admitted to leper colonies across the country, a procedure officially adopted in Brazil from 1924 to 1962, and continued until the mid-1980s. João Batista only came to learn about the law in 2009, reading the morning news. This was the trigger to uncover a past that had been subjected to many layers of oblivion. It was, as well, the first unexpected event, which enabled my research to exist: a life history interview which I conducted with him and analyzed for the completion of my bachelor's degree in Historical Studies at the Federal University of Minas Gerais.

Upon reading the news, João called his youngest son, his only male offspring, to talk. It was the first time he had told his story, 61 years after the appointment with Dr. Alípio. Together, João and his son guaranteed the reparation and planned the moment in which João would tell his other kids about his past.

Until then, João had never spoken about his complete path. In family talks, his life had been narrated in a segmented way: his childhood in Andrelândia and his adult life. The first stage, marked by the father's strong influence, and the other, by the duties implicit in masculinity. The realities were separated by the confinement period and were projected as a discontinuous narrative, and, I only then understood, characterized by deliberate silence. A silence that broke, indeed, during the life history interview—from which I extracted the narratives about the period of his confinement that I now deliver.

Between 1948 and 1953, João Batista was a patient at the Roça Grande Leprosarium. During the first two years, he was admitted as a pensioner, a condition guaranteed by the institution's director, Dr. Valério de Resende, in response to Dr. Alípio's request: "Valério called me in. He came and said: 'Alípio is my friend, my relative, private. You will remain here until you are cured.' So, I stayed. In there."

In 1950, João became an employee at the leprosarium and began to share a room with other workers. The management assigned him a variety of daily tasks, for which, he proudly told us, he stood out for his organization and discipline. The estimated wage, 150 *réis*, was accumulated and paid sporadically.

His greatest wish was to be cured and be able to leave, but the release process was not simple. It happened in two stages, as he told us. First, the patient should test negative for skin, earlobe, and mucus for 12 consecutive months. If all tests for the leprosy bacillus came back negative, the biopsy was then evaluated by a medical board from São Paulo, which visited sporadically.

In 1953, with fifteen negative tests, João Batista was discharged. But he could not return to Andrelândia: "There was no such thing as an ex-leper."

During the following months, he would go to the capital of Minas Gerais—the city of Belo Horizonte—daily seeking a job, returning to the leprosarium to sleep, since he lacked the financial conditions to afford a stay at the capital. He responded to a listing by Brahma brewery for a "city driver" and was shortly ruled out. His driver's license, issued in Andrelândia, was not legally valid in the capital. After a few other unfortunate events, he could finally make a living by fixing showers and irons, a skill he had learned at the leprosarium.

João then started to work for a man, Mr. Alfredo, who trained him to be an electrician. He resided at various addresses as his financial condition improved. He maintained his relationship with Guiomar Porto, whom he had started to date inside the leprosarium—she was also an inmate—and they married in 1962. The couple moved that very same year to the shack where they had their three children, to whom, in 2009, they told this story.

This narrative, from 2009, had, as a starting point, the social stigma silenced for six decades, as well as the narrator's solitude. The only person who could join him in telling the story no longer remembered the script: Guiomar, his companion for over 60 years, suffered from advanced Alzheimer's and could not add to the story. She merely sat by his side, carrying the indelible marks from a shared past: the feet marked by burns resulting from the treatment for Hansen's disease. Traces from which the source none of us, in the family, knew of.

And why did they choose to remain silent about this past, both within the family and to society? According to João, as he told us about the reparations, because they did not want their children and grandchildren to live under the social stigma hovering over the (ex)lepers and their descendants.

Faced with the narrative, different reactions in the family followed. Some of us embraced the past: we transformed the experience of past pain in collective meetings. Some of us wanted to learn what João and Guiomar had gone through; we wanted to understand their story, which was also ours. Nevertheless, diverse family reactions soon emerged—for example, against sharing any past experience concerning Hansen's disease. Not only public sharing, with other social groups, but also talking about it within the nuclear family.

As a major in historical studies, I started to think about how interesting it would be to transform what my grandfather had narrated to us into an oral history research project. I approached one of my professors, Miriam Hermeto, seeking a supervisor, and, upon the first readings, began to conduct informal conversations with my grandfather João, in order to elaborate a biographical summary within which I could locate the experiences that were, until then, unknown to us. When did he learn he was sick? When and where was he first sent to a hospital? When did he meet my grandmother? What kind of treatment did he go through?

From Family History to the Research Project

As I began this dialogue, however, I would hear displeased whispers through the hallways of the house, where the other children and grandchildren of the couple frequently gathered. Some values nurtured within that family—health, success, work—began to be questioned. I started to see my relatives acting like cornered animals, reacting, by instinct, to the loss of a feeling of comfort thanks to the breaking of the silence about an inconvenient past. This was the second unexpected event in the research, which I had to deal with for quite some time—and it only ceased, actually, when I concluded my monograph, about a year-and-a-half later.

It is possible to say that the pre-interview stage with João was a period of considerable vulnerability. As a researcher, I was seeking my theoretical-methodological footing, and the research, like a child, grew at its own rhythm. Sometimes right under my wings, sometimes slowly widening my hand. Certain relatives reacted badly to my initial steps in the research. In the meantime, my grandmother, *Dona* Guiomar, passed away, and *Seu* João lived through period of intense mourning, which, in fact, related directly to my investigation: he had not only lost his life partner, but the only person with whom he could, throughout six decades, break the silence about the experience at the leprosarium.

With that in mind, I organized the interview schedule to take place weekly and away from João's home. I assumed this would allow for a physical distance from the memories of daily life in that house, which was also a place of silence over those experiences I wanted to learn about. A distance, as well, from the relatives who disapproved of these memories coming to light.... It was necessary to guarantee a welcoming environment that did not add up to an inquisitorial tone. We arranged to meet at the university, in the oral history research center's room. João was accustomed to the routine and I was attentive to the methodological guidelines from oral history manuals and articles: we decided the interviews would take place on Mondays at 9 a.m. Feeling rather insecure with the situation—that is, of conducting my first research interview, with my grandfather, and about such a sensitive subject—I was pleased when my supervisor, Professor Hermeto, came forward to join the interview encounter.

He, doubtful; I, anxious. After all, what were we doing? As a granddaughter, could I be the researcher who was going to write the history of his life? João, suspicious, as someone who might have lived for many more years than he wished, seemed apprehensive and protective: "What do you mean, you have the key to a university room?" was his first question. I was still only his granddaughter.

Taking the Floor

As the first interview began, as he sat between myself and Hermeto, João turned the chair towards me—his body posture made it clear he was there responding to my invitation. Professor Miriam understood the situation and adopted a posture of full interest, dedicating herself to listen, exclusively, until invited to participate.

Rather succinctly, he responded to the questions, presenting, in few words, the memories he carried. As a person who had to reconstruct his identity built on the model of masculinity—a man dedicated to his work and family—he would never arrive unprepared. His recollections arrived organized in notes and finely sorted, possibly as a reflex of the eagerness to understand, group, and, thus, bring sense to the entanglement of memories which, individually captured in themselves, might lack meaning. A third unexpected issue appeared: he had done his research, his "homework," and did not want to be caught off guard.

In the second meeting, a new unexpected twist. From that point, up to the fourth and last interview, the person who conducted the thread of the conversations was, indeed, and unassumingly, the narrator himself. He arrived at the oral history center's room, greeted the professor with a strong handshake, and, waving a brown envelope, warned us: "Today you will meet *my* family." Photos of his original family were in the envelope: father, mother, and sisters. I wanted to learn about the unusual, specific aspects of his illness and confinement. But he announced that the "in there" (an expression he used when referring to the years in confinement) was not the whole of his life. It was not even the starting point he had elected; it was not the time about which he wanted to start talking. The "in there" was part of a much greater life trajectory. And he insisted: "Calm down, kid, I need to tell you something first." And, curiously, I was not the only one he referred to, as in the first interview. That time, and in the following, his body was mostly facing Professor Hermeto. Because she was a senior researcher? Maybe. Because she was not his granddaughter? Maybe too. Maybe for both reasons.

It was intriguing to note the transformation in the interviewee's body language. Even if for some moments he still manifested reluctance when faced with certain subjects, especially for the fear he felt of the stigma weighing over his children—what could happen if people learned their parents had been/were "lepers"? But, as the great narrator he was, João moved forward. As a matter of fact, we had to request him to wait while we prepared the recorder and recorded the session's header, such was his urge to talk. A few minutes later, it was his turn to raise his index finger and clarify what he was doing there: he placed the photos he had brought with him on the table, as well as a note to his late wife Guiomar.

In that interview session, he returned to some of the topics we had discussed in the first one, related to his childhood and youth in Andrelândia, embellishing the accounts about the "out here" and making it clear that this was not the right time to talk about the "in there." By showing the photos, he materialized his narrative in the faces of his relatives and talked about his father with much pride and admiration—his male role model, without a doubt. He then narrated his parents' big expectations for him, the only son of the dentist in a small town, who should follow the steps of that successful self-employed professional and benefactor, owner of a few tracts of farmland that helped with the family income—and also many people from the community, who would turn to him in difficult moments.

In the 1930s, he was the only one of the four children to leave home to study, which was an obligation and right restricted to men in his family culture.

But he was taken aback by his father's death. Aside from having him as his main reference point, he had to take over the father's role of the "man of the house." An adolescent, he found himself unable to continue his studies and started working as an accountant because he was "good with numbers." He would travel around town carrying money for payments, a huge responsibility for his age—both familiar and professional. João narrated stories from this period with the pride of someone who could handle what life had brought him, enjoying himself as he remembered the solutions he had to find at that time.

He continued in this way for a few years, working hard, until someone noticed a bruise on his foot. How long had it been there? Some time—but he did not know how long. But it would not heal. His mother called the doctor who took care of the family and he learned he would have to undergo treatment at a hospital near the capital city, since his town did not have the necessary resources for that illness—whose nature he knew nothing about. His brother-in-law escorted him, by train, to the Roça Grande Leprosarium, in the city of Sabará, five hours away. At the reception desk, a large counter separated the "out here" from the "in there." In his memory narrative, it served as a symbol—which he even drew for us—of this divided world he would have to live with, from then on. He entered, and his brother-in-law left without saying goodbye. Not to make him feel bad, he knew. But maybe for being unable to be the last one to say goodbye, symbolically delivering the news that life "out here" was on hold. Indefinitely.

As he tearfully told us how he came to feel alone and trapped "in there," João perhaps then concluded that the story he had kept from his family during all these years could be known. He said goodbye, adding "And this is my story." He was referring to the pre-confinement story, to the Andrelândia "out here," from the time in which he had been the man his family expected him to be.

"That one died"

The interviews in which João narrated the period of confinement at the Roça Grande Leprosarium were enormously rich. Rich in information, of course, about the evolution of the treatment, the sociability, the relationships marked by the social inequality of the inmates, how they dodged the system. But the interviews also revealed absolutely private affectionate memories: how he met Guiomar and how they dated "in there," how he learned new crafts, how he missed his home, and the feeling that life would not resume normally.

My grandfather was true to our initial agreement and narrated his Hansen's disease stories with lively colors. This allowed me to proceed with my research project and continue dealing with oral history topics related to Hansen's disease and the history of diseases.

However, as he told us about the period of remission and cure that allowed him to leave the leper colony, we faced a last unexpected moment. His will to talk about his return home and his social reintegration seemed greater than his will to talk about the confinement period. João did not want to construe himself as a sick person or a victim of society as a result of the forced confinement.

We reached the dimension of this unexpected moment when he grew emotional as he told us about how he prepared to return to the small town of Andrelândia. With the little money he was able to save after he left the leprosarium, working as an electrician (without being one, learning from experience), he purchased a suit so he could arrive home well-dressed, presentable. At one of the stops on the way, he bought a cigarette. No, he did not smoke. But that attitude seemed to him that of a grown man. He inhaled and choked. But he felt mature, ready to face the town.

He got off at the train station and took public transportation. They asked who he was, to which he answered he was the son of *Dona* Maria da Glória. The driver was surprised: "Didn't her son become a leper?" João responded: "That was the other one. That one died." Back in the "out here," he wished to have another existence, even if it was in the same body. And he went on narrating himself, later, as a hardworking man who managed to rebuild his family house, get his single sisters married, and fulfill his mission as "the man of the family." And, mission accomplished, he could marry Guiomar, who, also cured by then, waited, loyal and patient, for him to honor the word he gave his father before they could get with their life.

In the sequence of interviews filled with the unexpected to us researchers, we witnessed *Seu* João, through his clearly expressed moral judgments, enable himself to transit from the empty space of the memory consigned to silence for decades, to the initial zones of production of meanings relating to the past. As a narrator, he brought to life the threads of his personal history: resignifying old ties—lost or abandoned—adopting new perceptions and, at the end, attenuating the perpetuation of resentments in the present time.

When I face my grandfather, now in his nineties, I see him as an old person who, given his accumulated experiences, is not easily surprised. But his life story shows that he has encountered the unexpected with great frequency.

As with *Seu* João, we all store parts of our stories we are afraid to look at, from which we would rather escape. But, in this specific experience, once we initiated the unexpected/interview, we could no longer not look.

He could no longer not speak.

I could no longer not listen.

CHAPTER 5

Florence Richard, Childhood Sexual Violence, and the Unsettling of Local History

Steven High

My interview with Florence Richard did not so much "go wrong" as it did go in an unexpected direction, a direction that raised questions in my mind about the kinds of expectations that oral historians bring into the interview with us. The interview occurred in May 1988, when I was just 20 years old, after I was hired by my hometown museum in Thunder Bay, Ontario, on the isolated North Shore of Lake Superior, to conduct oral history interviews for the summer. I was given an audio recorder, release forms, and a stack of blank analogue cassettes and told to interview old people. There was no training whatsoever and I had free reign to interview who I pleased. Over the next three and a half months, I interviewed 38 people, instinctively adopting what I now know to be the life story interview method.

Given my own interests and working-class background, many of those whom I interviewed were able to speak of the city's trade union and labor history, but I also interviewed business people, professionals, politicians, and others. One woman, a member of the charity Imperial Order of the Daughters of the Empire (IODE), told me how she worked in an armaments plant in World War I. There were also two former German prisoners of war interned in Northern Ontario during World War II who returned to the area after being repatriated at war's end. Another interviewee, a retired teacher, had taught in

---

S. High (✉)
Centre for Oral History and Digital Storytelling, Concordia University, Montreal, QC, Canada
e-mail: steven.high@concordia.ca

© The Author(s), under exclusive license to Springer Nature Switzerland AG 2023
R. Santhiago, M. Hermeto (eds.), *The Unexpected in Oral History*, Palgrave Studies in Oral History,
https://doi.org/10.1007/978-3-031-17749-1_5

a railway school car during the Great Depression. These were all great stories, teaching me much about the history of my hometown. It was the summer that I fell in love with oral history as a way of learning about the past, launching me on my professional journey.

While I found the unexpected in almost every interview that I conducted that summer, my interview with Florence Richard stood out. It was the second interview that I ever conducted, undertaken only a few days after I started the job. I knew Florence and her husband Norman slightly, and had heard them speak of their political radicalism and labor organizing during the 1930s and 1940s. I wanted to know more. Thunder Bay has a vibrant history of left-wing activism. But what made the interview stand out was not so much her memories of being a Communist Party activist, though there were fascinating glimpses into the lived interior of radical politics, was her experience with childhood sexual violence. The horrors of her youth left a profound imprint on Florence Richard's life and her sense of her own life story. As I remembered it, Florence volunteered to be interviewed in order to put her childhood experience of sexual violence on the local record.

Had she been in distress I would have had no idea what to do. As this was a seemingly innocuous "local history" project, nobody thought it necessary to develop a list of emotional or psychological support resources or to provide any training. Thankfully, Florence was very much in control, but the experience taught me an important lesson—hard stories can surface where you least expect them in oral history interviews. Indeed, the risks might be greatest when it is unexpected. It is also a story that I have shared, without naming names, dozens of times in oral history training workshops and seminars, as it raises questions about group "vulnerability," a standard feature of ethics review in Canada, or where we recognize or expect danger. Life story interviewing unsettles many of these assumptions.

When invited to contribute to this volume on "unexpected interviews," I thought it would be a good opportunity to revisit this experience in more depth. In fact, it is the first time that I have listened to this interview recording since that summer. As my interviews are archived at the Thunder Bay Historical Museum, I had to write to get a digital copy sent. Time was also a factor, as Florence Richard had opted to close her interview for 20 years. It has therefore only been publicly accessible for a dozen years at this point. I also draw from my personal diary from that summer, the last year I maintained one. The diary entries include brief descriptions of my very first encounters with oral history—a methodology that is now central to my professional identity. And yet, unexpectedly, both the interview and the diary reveal a somewhat different story than the one I remembered, prompting me to reflect further on my relationship to the childhood story that Florence Richard shared with me so many years ago.

The Diary

In reading my diary entries from that summer, I was surprised, and a little disappointed if truth be told, to discover no effusive comments about oral history. This runs counter to how I regularly represent that summer to my students: as an epiphany that set me on the road to where I am today. In many ways, the summer of 1988 has come to anchor my origin story as an oral historian. My diary reminded me, however, that this was a minimum wage job. My employment as an oral historian would therefore not be nearly enough to pay for my university tuition and accommodation costs at the University of Ottawa for the coming year. I therefore took a second job that summer, working in a kitchen in a home for the aged most evenings and on weekends. This was a union job, and paid far more. Despite my 60-hour work weeks that summer, my diary was also filled with my social life, as I reconnected with friends after eight months away at university. In short, only a small proportion of the diary during these months was dedicated to my practice as an oral historian. Most of my comments related to the logistics of interviewing, or in quick judgments on what I thought about what I heard. I usually wrote two or three sentences about each interview.

That said, the diary entries do reveal a great deal about the context of interviewing. I had seen the job posting for an "Oral Historian" at the employment office. When I called, I was interviewed the next day, and started the job the day after that. Much as I remembered it, there was no training whatsoever, except for a few "how to interview" pamphlets. This was before the internet of course. At first, I felt "abandoned" by the museum, as I was left to my own devices. Another staff member told me that two others had been hired before me, only to quit a few days later. The wages of $4.15 per hour were indeed miserable. Yet, I decided to approach the interviewing holistically, using the life story approach, where we would work along the life course. I also organized a pre-interview in most cases. Moreover, many of the interviews spanned over multiple sessions and many audio tapes. This was all surprisingly robust given my lack of guidance or training, but it seemed to make sense to my 20-year-old self. Not everything went so well: I learned the hard way not to mistakenly flip the same audio tape a second time. One had to keep track.

In rereading my diary entries, I was startled to learn that I started interviewing just three days into the job. A few days after that, on May 18th, I interviewed Florence Richard in her home. Remarkably, my entry for that day fails to mention Florence's experience with childhood sexual violence, and instead focuses on her early political activism. It was a surprisingly upbeat hot take: "I interviewed Florence Richard. I must admit it went very smoothly. It was also fascinating!! She was an organizer for the Communist Party of Canada in the 30's and 40's. She was from Hurkitt [sic]. FASCINATING!" And that was it. I like to think that I didn't mention the violence as she had opted to close the interview for 20 years. Indeed, I know now that I should not have written anything down in my diary about a closed interview. More likely, the focus of my diary entry reflects my own core interests—after all, listening is as subjective as storytelling. What we hear depends very much on how we are positioned in relation to wider structures of societal power, and the project framing or purpose of our interviewing.

But, in writing this paper, I wonder if my silence does not also have something to do with my own ill-ease with the subject given my own experience of childhood sexual violence, perpetrated by an uncle of a childhood friend at their summer camp, at about the same young age as Florence's own experience. I hesitate to share this here, as it is not an experience that I have ever shared before, beyond my immediate family. As a child and teenager, I felt deeply ashamed by what happened and it took many, many years before I told my parents about it. In fact, it was probably around the time of the 1988 interview, or a year or two later, that I finally did so. I do remember reflecting on my own experience while Florence Richard recounted hers. As we will see, when faced with an initial description of her childhood as marvelous and beautiful on the one hand and a horror on the other, my own experience likely prompted me to ask a follow-up question about these childhood horrors. It may also be this personal connection that, decades later, led me to return to this interview again and again in my work as an oral history teacher.

The Interview Recording

In relistening to the relatively short 1 hour and 13-minute interview so many years later, it is clear to me that the heart of the interview was not Florence Richard's account of her Communist Party activism during the 1930s and 1940s, a part of her life that she consistently minimizes or discounts as the "loony left" during the interview, but rather the horror of her childhood. Her experience of childhood violence profoundly shaped her life, as she now understands it.

Born in 1918 in Winnipeg, Florence Richard (I don't know her maiden name—as I didn't ask) moved with her parents to Hurkett—a rural area east of Thunder Bay, the following year. Her father had got free land to homestead and farm. I asked her if her family lived in a log house, to which she replied that they had but it was "spread out" with all the additions built over time. Just two and a half minutes into the interview, Florence unexpectedly spoke of the horrors of her childhood. Here is this initial exchange:

FR: So I had two brothers and five sisters. I went through all of the horrors of childhood that a lot of children endure. I can't say it was entirely bad. It was absolutely marvelous, beautiful, I mean living on a farm in the backwoods. I think every kid should have such an experience. It was wonderful. We lived in the forest. And, we played in it.
SH: What were some of the horrors?
FR: Being molested at the age of eight by old men. This sort of thing, which is not unusual, amongst particularly female children. It is not unusual at

all. In fact, I am amazed that it is only coming out now, being spoken of. But this has been going on of course for hundreds of years. These kinds of horrors shut you off to the beauties of life around you because all you can only think of is the horror. So that was my childhood.

If I was interviewing Florence today, I would have been much more circumspect in directly asking about the violence. By ending this initial disclosure with "So this was my childhood", I can now see that she was inviting me to move on. Staying with her childhood, I then asked if her home in Hurkett was isolated. She replied that they were in a way as there were few cars in those days and they lived a mile from the main road. There were many other families "seeking out a living the same as we did," but almost nobody farms there anymore, the land is too marginal. I then asked if they were relatively self-sufficient, which prompted Florence to speak of the poverty but she circled back to the horrors of her childhood saying that the poverty in no way justified the violence:

FR: Actually, the poverty part, I don't think was anything that children were so much aware of. When we went to school of course, yes, we were aware of our clothes and all this. But I mean all of the kids were pretty much in the same boat. None of us had anything special. We just had what was absolutely needed to go to school. So, there was no case of being ostracized because you weren't dressed. But of course, we all wanted nicer things, which we never got. I think the main thing was the hang-ups of people that created the difficulty, rather than the poverty. The poverty, wasn't hard to bear. Of course, a lot of people are going say that I am crazy to say this but it is a fact as far as I am concerned. The poverty I wouldn't have noticed if it hadn't been the attitudes of people. And like I say the hang-ups, the perversions. Of course, this is very strong in my memory because I am one of those who was abused. I think it happens to all female children.

SH: Did you feel angry?

FR: Oh well [exclamation], I had to bury the whole thing because I didn't bear to tell anybody. In those days, you didn't mention anything below the navel. And my mother would have been [pause]... I ... I just couldn't have told my mother because you didn't talk about anything. And we children were frowned upon if we even said 'darn' in the house, you know. But somehow, she seemed to realize that that she couldn't hold that kind of sway over the barnyard and the men's area where my brothers worked with father and my father was one of the most violent men that you could imagine with his family. But I will say this, he was not a molester or a child abuser in that way. But he was violent. And he was violent with my mother and with my brothers. More with the tongue, but with my mother, no it got into, I mean, there was a regular [pause]sort of [searching for the right word] foofaraw every once in a while, in the house for absolutely no reason that anybody could pin down. As I have figured it out in the years since, I realized that it's the whole arrogance of the male of the species simply because for hundreds of years they have never been curbed. They have never been made to understand that that sort of thing is unacceptable. Whereas the women have been on the other end of it and they have known always that they couldn't do that sort of thing. This is what we were living with. Whenever a man felt like throwing his weight around, or being absolutely violent, whatever, he just did it. Nobody questioned it.

SH: So, it was very common then.

FR: Oh, ya. Amongst those men that were inclined to be that way. And my father was one of them. However, we had a neighbor, not far from us, he was an old Swedish man. And that man I don't think ever even raised his voice to any one of his family, at any time. In later years, I had all of this to contend with. This backlog of horror that I had to live with. Because it does not go away, by itself. Time does not do anything to help the situation. You still bear that. So, in later years, in fact at the age of 57, is when I started primal therapy and that I would say is the one thing that made a complete change in my life. Although I had tried to get along as best I could, but I had to live with all those horrors.

In hindsight, my first follow-up question about anger probably reveals as much about my own feelings about what I experienced as it does what I was hearing from Florence in the moment. Her mention of primal therapy then prompted me to ask her about that too, which turned out to be foundational to her sense of recovered self. Her older sister had recommended a book by Arthur Janov, undoubtedly *The Primal Scream,* given this was the mid-1970s, who developed the idea that the repression of childhood trauma can lead to neurosis. It can be resolved, however, by meeting it directly by revisiting it in psychotherapy. The patient is encouraged to express their repressed feelings by screaming or angry shouts. Primal therapy was popular in North America during the early 1970s, but has not achieved acceptance in mainstream psychology. It is today largely discredited, as most believe that it places too much faith in cathartic discharge and, most controversially, can produce false memories of early childhood. But for Florence Richard, it was foundational to her sense of self at the time of the interview: "What it amounts to is that, instead of trying to push down the dreadful feeling of what happened to you, you live them, you relive them, you scream out the horrors. And once you have done that, you have expediated the problem. And then you don't have it anymore, are not frightened anymore."

Altogether, this exchange took up 12 of the first 15 minutes of the interview. But it structured the rest of her oral narrative in important ways. The horrors of her childhood deeply affected her, instilling a deep-seated fear of men. This fear surfaced repeatedly during the interview. She went to grade 8 in a rural school, but her family had no money to send their children to high school in the city. It was only after she was 40 that she was able to access adult education. When asked about schooling, Florence recounted the many fine women teachers that she had, saying they "did not make me feel terrified. But men teachers, I had a terrible time with having had the experience of my father being a violent man, and generally being terrified of men. And they were arrogant, because that was the thing that men could be. They knew that they could get away with and so they did it." Again, in her own words, she was "terrified of them, always." She got married when she wasn't quite 16 years old, explaining that "in those days, it was the natural thing to do." As she "never had a father that I could relate to," her first marriage proved to be another bad situation. They lived on poor relief and bounced from house to house. Her fear of men in authority also surfaced during her recounting of her work in a canteen on the lake boats, identifying one male superior in particular.

The only place where her fear of men was not evident in the interview, at least before her discovery of primal therapy, was when she described her activism within the Communist Party. Her father and grandfather were very involved; she thus "naturally inherited my politics and my atheism." Unexpectedly, this radical political space even made her represent her father in a much more favorable light than she had previously. She recalled, with some pride, how her father taught Marxist political economy around the dining room table for groups of young people in the area. She still considers them to be "damned good" teachings, and as relevant in 1988 as they were in the 1930s. As a teenager, she sat in on meetings and picked blueberries to raise money for the Communist Party candidate locally. As her politics in 1988 were no longer what they were, she regularly apologized for or dismissed her communist activism. Despite my many questions on the topic, her answers were often curt and she felt much more at ease, or even present, when talking about the ways that gendered violence shaped her life.

Conclusion

To be honest, when I sat down to write this chapter, I had no intention of revealing my own experience of childhood sexual violence. But once I revisited the audio-recording, and transcribed key parts, I realized that I could not proceed otherwise. As someone who regularly invites others to share their stories with me, I resolved to include this personal context to help us understand the underlying dynamic of our interview conversation. My own memory of this interview differs substantially from my May 1988 diary entry and the interview recording. I am no longer sure that Florence Richard volunteered to be interviewed with the idea of putting her childhood experience of sexual violence on the local record. It may have been the case, but it is more likely that this experience was simply foundational to how she understood her life. The fact that she broached the topic herself is suggestive, as is the fact that she then returned to it repeatedly over the course of the interview. But in asking follow-up questions that prompted her to expand on her initial disclosure of childhood sexual violence, I likely contributed to its centrality in the unfolding conversation. This realization, and Florence's decision to keep the interview closed for 20 years, now raises the question of whether or not I should identify her by name in this article. Florence died many years ago, as has her husband, so I can't go back and ask her permission again. Thirty-two years have slipped by. In the end, I decided to name her as this is what she explicitly consented to at the time. To do otherwise, would be to render her invisible and imply that this experience was shameful.

The interview also raises intriguing questions about the ways that expectations and the unexpected shape, and sometimes distort, the oral history interview. The framing of an oral history project informs and structures our expectations, shaping who is recruited and what questions are asked. But the life story method is predisposed to the unexpected given its open-endedness. The same is true of the ethos of sharing authority that asks oral historians to ensure that the interviewee has the space to lead the conversation in a direction they feel is important. There is no telling where that goes. There is therefore a certain amount of tension between project framing—in this case the history of a locality—and the agency of interviewees who might take the interviewer to other places. Even more important, perhaps, is the positionality of the interviewer and what experiences they bring to the conversation. My interest in left-wing politics led me to interview Florence Richard and, later that summer, her husband Norman Richard, but it was my own childhood experience with sexual violence that probably led me to ask follow-up questions about the horrors of her youth. This darkness can lurk in any life story, not simply amongst groups of people who are already recognized as "vulnerable," or in places where "danger" or "difficult knowledge" is most evident. I for one am glad that Florence Richard put this on the record, thereby unsettling the essential goodness of local history.

CHAPTER 6

An Unexpected Gift: Oral History and the Documentation of Michfest

Ann Cvetkovich

My story of an unexpected interview emerges from my ongoing, but mostly thus far incomplete, efforts to document my experiences as a worker at the Michigan Womyn's Music Festival, a lesbian feminist cultural institution that ended after 40 years in 2015.[1] I worked at the festival for over 20 years, arriving in the early 1990s as a queer theorist who was initially skeptical of lesbian feminist women's culture and back to the land politics. My assumptions were turned upside down, however, by the everyday reality of the festival, especially the worker's community, which I found it to be a very rich and very queer culture that defied stereotypes as it wrestled with racism, accessibility, sex positivity, children, shifting music styles, care of the land, butch-femme identities, trans-inclusion, and more. I came to see Michfest not only as an exemplary case of lesbian feminist culture, whose survival was something of a miracle, but also as an experiment in intentional community that deserves its place in queer subcultural and world-making history alongside cruising, performance, and other utopian practices.

---

[1] With many thanks to Lisa Vogel for her willingness to let me use her words in this way and for making the Michigan Womyn's Music Festival her life's work.
See www.michfest.com. There is some documentation of the festival in the films *Radical Harmonies* (Dee Mosbacher 2002), and *Rise Up: Songs of the Women's Movement* (PBS 2020).

A. Cvetkovich (✉)
Feminist Institute of Social Transformation, Carleton University,
Ottawa, ON, Canada
e-mail: anncvetkovich@cunet.carleton.ca

© The Author(s), under exclusive license to Springer Nature Switzerland AG 2023
R. Santhiago, M. Hermeto (eds.), *The Unexpected in Oral History*, Palgrave Studies in Oral History,
https://doi.org/10.1007/978-3-031-17749-1_6

Like many newcomers and converts to festival life, I was immediately gripped by archive fever and felt an intense desire to document what I saw, particularly in my case because of its implications for queer and feminist theory, which has often been dismissive of lesbian feminism as man-hating, essentialist, anti-sex, humorless, pc, goddess-worshipping, and trans-exclusive, just to name a few of the stereotypes in circulation. But I was also overwhelmed by the huge task of capturing the festival's sprawling multiplicity, especially given the ethical injunctions within my scholarly circles about speaking for others.[2] Oral history seemed like an ideal method for documenting Michfest—in recognition that there are as many realities as there are women who have walked the land—workers as well as festies, outsiders as well as insiders, enthusiasts as well as critics. The interview has thus figured prominently in my efforts to document or archive my experiences, whether with the larger goal of using them as a resource for further analysis and writing, or just as a record of some kind.

But it has also been a research method fraught with contradictions and ambivalence for me. One of my earliest efforts began as an informal conversation with the festival producer Lisa Vogel. Along with my folklorist friend, Kay Turner, who was also a new worker at the festival, we approached her with our earnest and urgent conviction that there should be more information available about this wondrous event and its herstory. But to our surprise—in a version of the "unexpected interview"—Vogel expressed a wariness about documentation, suggesting that the festival was a closed and intimate ritual space that couldn't really be translated to outsiders, especially given how many people might not want their experiences made public. That conversation has always served as a cautionary note, and I've tried to retain an epistemic humility in my dreams of making Michfest visible, especially for the scholarly audiences that are my primary ones.

But I also kept trying. Over the years, I've published short articles and a group interview with workers, delivered academic papers, and also accumulated a lot of unpublished manuscript material, most of it on work and performance at Michfest.[3] I've also watched with interest as others have documented

---

[2] See Madeline Davis and Elizabeth Lapovsky Kennedy, *Boots of Leather, Slippers of Gold: The Making of A Lesbian Community* (New York: Routledge, 1993, 2014), which has been a major influence on my thinking about the ethics of oral history and respect for narrators/interviewees. See also eds. Nan Alamilla Boyd and Horacio N. Roque Ramirez, *Bodies of Evidence: The Practice of Queer Oral History* (New York: Oxford University Press, 2012). Feminist theory's caution about speaking for others is exemplified by Gayatri Chakravorty Spivak, "Can the Subaltern Speak?"

[3] See Ann Cvetkovich (*An Archive of Feelings: Trauma, Sexuality, and Lesbian Public Cultures*. Durham: Duke University Press, 2003) which includes an account of Tribe 8's performance at the 1994 festival, and also Cvetkovich and Sel Wahng (Don't Stop the Music. *GLQ* 7 (1): 131–151, 2001) and Cvetkovich (Gal's Salon. *Sinister Wisdom* 103: 152–154, 2017).

the festival, including their use of interviews or the voices of others.[4] Having worked on a large activist oral history project before, I was daunted in advance by what it would mean to try to incorporate interviews into my writing in a way that respects people's stories.[5] But over the years I continued to do interviews of various kinds, mostly informal ones, mostly with other workers, and I also kept copious field notes, thinking of my method, including the practice of the interview or conversation, as that of the embedded ethnographer. My mixed method, including the combining of memoir and interview, my own story and that of others, seeks to capture the intensity of doing research while working and the experience of immersive and intimate conversation that wouldn't be the same as an interview in a bounded setting outside the festival.

The challenge of documenting Michfest has been immeasurably complicated by the criticism of the festival for not being trans-inclusive because of its stated intention of being a space centered on the experiences of "womyn-born womyn." The visible and vocal presence of Camp Trans, a counter-festival set up in protest outside the festival gates in the late 1990s and early 2000s, and calls, especially in its final years, for boycotts of the festival and sometimes its performers, have shadowed its reputation and legacy. In some cases, any mention of having attended or any talk of it is shunned. As someone who was supportive of trans-inclusion but also wanted to hear from those who felt otherwise, I have been disturbed by the silence around the festival herstory, especially because my version of the festival is very continuous with queer and trans cultures—and their overlap with lesbian feminist ones. The festival has much to offer to understandings of women-only space, women's music, anti-racist feminisms, transfeminisms, and the sex wars, and, even if the goal is critical reflection, it is important to document and discuss this history.

This publication seemed like an interesting way to approach my ongoing struggle with how to write about Michfest and for what audience, which has been shadowed by the fear of failure—whether failure to capture the truth, failure to represent others accurately, or failure to navigate the conflicts around the festival's history. I initially conceived of this essay as a kind of methodological preamble to my work so far and envisioned it as an opportunity to explore the question of method, and especially my uncertainties about the role of oral

---

[4] See *Welcome Home* (Self-published, 2009), a book of photographs by Angela Jimenez from her experience as a worker; *Voices from the Land* (Self-published, 2015), a collection of first-person accounts edited and self-published by Sara St Martin Lynn; special issue of the lesbian feminist journal *Sinister Wisdom* on "Celebrating the Michigan Womyn's Music Festival" (1999), edited by eds. Allison L. Ricket, Amy Washburn, Angela Martin, Brynn Warriner, Shawn(ta) Smith-Cruz; and Bonnie Morris, *Eden Built by Eves: The Culture of Women's Music Festivals* (Boston: Alyson Press, 2000). One year the artists Daniela Sea and Eden Bakti, in consultation with Lisa Vogel, interviewed people throughout the festival in a dedicated space on the land—a kind of testimonial station called The Archive Project. To the best of my knowledge, the interviews exist in the archive but have never been shared publicly. The papers of the MWMF are housed at Michigan State University in Lansing MI.

[5] See *An Archive of Feelings*, which includes a discussion of oral histories with lesbian AIDS activists, within the context of discussion of the genre of testimony and the role of affect and sex and intimacy in oral history interviews.

history in documenting the festival. When I initially agreed to write it, I planned to use the rubric of the unexpected interview to imagine an interview with Lisa Vogel, with whom I have been trying to connect since the festival ended in order to discuss different ways, including oral history, to preserve its history. And then the unexpected happened… the Covid-19 pandemic. And, with it, a version of an interview with Vogel that far exceeded my dreams.

Virtual Fire Circles in a Time of Pandemic

As the pandemic led people to gather online in all kinds of new ways, Vogel announced that she would share, via Facebook livestream, some of the yet unpublished stories that she has been writing about the festival. She began on a Sunday afternoon in early April 2020, about four weeks into lockdown, acting on an idea to go public with her writing that came to her while cleaning her lemon tree the day before. Despite various technical difficulties, the first date was so successful that she continued it for eight weeks, reading three stories each week.[6] Opening the circle 20 minutes ahead for people to connect via the Facebook comment feed, she began by lighting a fire in her living room, conjuring the fire pits on the land that often served as the site of informal oral storytelling circles. She worked in dialogue with comedian and long-time Michfest performer and worker, Elvira Kurt, who served as emcee, comic relief, interlocutor, and witness to help bring the stories forth and make the internet interface more human and alive. Elvira recreated her top 10 lists, a regular genre from her festival performances, drawing some favorites from the archive—such as the top 10 ways to spot an infiltrator—and introducing some new ones, such as the top 10 ways to have a festival during the Covid-19 pandemic. There were two ASL interpreters for deaf womyn, which added to the technical challenges but also reflected the culture of accessibility central to the festival's values. While Facebook might seem like an unlikely place to gather, since it has been the site of many bitter flame wars about festival culture, 500 women regularly showed up, and the comment stream was a way for them to connect in real time though a shared experience that resembled that of live performance.

Over the weeks, Vogel seemed to grow more confident, and even to thrive, in this new medium, especially with the encouragement in the feed and the dialogue with Elvira between stories. Vogel was drawing on material developed in workshops with lesbian feminist poet Judy Grahn, and the stories had clearly been carefully crafted. But as the weeks went by, she also wrote to the occasion and to her audience's eager interest, including more stories about the festival's infrastructure. By the end of the series, there were 24 stories and close to 16 hours of recordings—far more than most oral history interviews, even a lengthy

[6] Fire Circles, 1–8, April 5 to May 24 on Lisa Vogel's Facebook page. She left the recordings up for a couple of months, but they are no longer publicly available and are thus, like a live performance, ephemeral.

life history, would provide. Moreover, by drawing on her written accounts, Vogel was able to tell the story in her own way, perhaps far better than even the most empathetic interviewer could elicit. At the same time, the back and forth conversation with Elvira and the obvious interest of the live listeners allowed for some of the active listening that can also make oral history and the interview format so powerful. Vogel was careful to position herself as just one writer of the festival's many stories, but as someone who has known the festival since its inception and as its producer, her testimony is very special. I would argue that the stories occupied an important space between the oral and the written—with the written word coming alive through the oral delivery, including the sense of a listening audience, and also grounded in many oral storytellings before being put on paper.

I consider the Fire Circles to be a form of unexpected interview because they allowed Vogel to use the live performance for an audience to show her own vulnerability while also maintaining a kind of control over her narrative that she might fear would not be possible in an interview, especially because of her experience with critical, and even hostile, interviewers.

As might be expected there were many stories about the lore of the festival's early years—the improbable story of dykes with very little production experience seeking to set up a festival in rural Michigan in 1976. Their efforts to realize the dream of lesbian feminist culture that would bring down the patriarchy—to find land, build stages, bring in performers, and serve food, all in a potentially hostile rural setting, yields many stories of wild adventures and encounters. It is an improbable triumph over the odds, especially since after that first year, they thought never again. What emerges is a story of resourcefulness and feistiness—Vogel is proud of her Michigan working-class roots and, countering the stereotype of the man-hating lesbian, talks about the men in the surrounding area with whom she built long-term relationships, those that made it possible to sustain women-only space. It is a feminist victory because the women who built stages and put on shows were doing work they were often not thought to be capable of. There were also important stories about the festival's dream of accessibility. Through her stories, Vogel sought to capture the behind-the-scenes labor but also the magic of building such a lavish spectacle.

Let's Talk About Sex

An entire week of stories devoted to the topic of sex (May 3, Week 5) provides a powerful example of how Vogel addresses areas of conflict that have been the site of misrepresentation both within and outside the festival. This arc of three stories covered both the skirmishes around BDSM in the sex wars of the 1980s and the story of how the festival came under scrutiny in 2001 by the state of Michigan when the AFA (American Family Association), a Christian right organization, filed a complaint about exposure of children to public sex. Their case drew on discussions of a female ejaculation workshop from bulletin boards on Michfest's own website, an early form of social media presence that raised the festival's profile for critics, whether transgender activists or the Christian right. The stories for that day culminated in Vogel's powerful account of a visit from the county sheriff and representatives from the state attorney general's office, with whom she had to tour the land in order to show the layout of the workshop spaces in relation to the childcare areas.

In laying the groundwork for these stories and clearing a path to be able to tell them from her point of view, Vogel takes up stereotypes about lesbian feminists and the festival's reputation for having been anti-sex and hence hostile to BDSM and other kinds of radical sex cultures. She describes the frequent representation of the festival as the opposite of the lived reality, with debates about sex an especially spectacular example of that problem. So whereas, especially in the context of the sex wars, lesbian feminist culture gets cast as "anti-sex," Vogel emphasizes that there was a lot of sex on the land, which was often "one big tent swap," guided by a feminist politics of "loving and sexing with other women" as "a revolutionary act," where "we were building community (…) one fuck buddy at a time." Sexual freedom was just one aspect of a liberation of the body that the festival made possible—as women "walked more in our bodies" and "felt more sexy, sensual, alive" (Fire Circle 5, Sunday, May 3, 2020).

This commitment to the festival as a place of sexual freedom includes the presence of an evolving BDSM culture. Without downplaying conflicts or differences of perspective, Vogel presents a complex picture of how the sex wars played out at Michfest, including the challenges with sex scenes in public that led to the creation of the Twilight Zone, a play space on the outskirts of the land that welcomed visitors. She focuses, for example, on the moment when pro-sex flyers were dropped from a plane not only on festival land but throughout the area, which she sees as a "myopic" rather than radical act because of how it exposed the festival and those who attended it to scrutiny and harassment. Through these complicated stories, Vogel seeks to show how the festival made space for pro-sex cultures while also setting boundaries, and how what was sometimes seen as anti-sex or policing were efforts to protect the festival from scrutiny.

The ejaculation workshop that made its way to the bulletin boards, where there were also discussions about the tensions around the inclusion of children in a community also dedicated to sexual freedom, is also a reminder of the ways in which internal disputes become fodder for misinterpretation beyond the community, and hence the difficulty of representation that Vogel's stories are aiming to navigate. As the stereotype of "granola dykes" shifts to that of a "den of debauchery," she has to negotiate the festival's image with outsiders, which interferes with her capacity to describe its sexual cultures on her own terms. Although the live audience for the Fire Circle stories were sympathetic insiders, the stories reveal the challenges of writing for and about them.

Thus, the third story in that day's cycle dwelt at length on an image that also closed out the second story—that of Vogel dressing up in femme drag in order to tour the county sheriff and representatives from the state attorney general's office through the land. The details of Vogel wearing a Banana Republic blouse with a purse slung over her shoulder and putting on eyeshadow and earrings conjure a vivid image of a painful and tender performance of normativity that is necessary in order to keep the festival from being shut down. This account of what she does to try to protect the festival from scrutiny is a reminder of the vulnerability of her own position as festival producer who must answer to many different audiences—and not to capitulate to outside control. This is a powerful story not only as a record of Vogel's own vulnerability and fraught experience—but for ways of thinking about the festival as having to fight off the same policing of public sex that has been fought by gay male culture or queer youth of color. Its stereotypical depiction as anti-sex, both within and outside lesbian and queer communities, precludes the possibility of seeing it as an important site of radical sex cultures.

OTHERWORLDLY

Vogel closed out the series with an important story called "How We Bought the Land," which she herself admitted was difficult to read because of her fears of being criticized for having chosen private over collective ownership and for benefiting financially from the sale of the land to a collective who are seeking to maintain it as space for girls and women. In a coda that also smoothed out the challenges of telling it, Vogel repeated a story from Week 3 that had been interrupted numerous times by technical difficulties. "Otherwordly" addresses spiritual practices on the land—and was worth repeating because it so beautifully captures the spirit of the land—and also because it acts as a healing balm for the rifts and tensions about the purchase of the land. It begins with the story of how she consulted a healer in the wake of her breakup with her co-producer, with whom she had shared ownership of the land—thus putting the festival into a precarious position in the mid-1990s. The healer sees angels and encourages her to continue—and the story closes with Vogel's vision of angels in the night stage bowl. The story tracks different moments in Vogel's ambivalent relation to spiritual practices and goddess culture on the land—what we came to call with affection "the woo." She finally came to a different understanding through her relationship with Kay Gardner, who led sacred singing on the land and suggested the closing candlelight ceremony, which became a popular event at twilight on the final Sunday evening of festival.

Even more powerful than visions of angels, though, is the sense of "otherworldliness" that is daily life on the land. Vogel eloquently describes the "porous relationship to time and space" that was laughingly called "land time." As she puts it, "the veil that held time blew wild in those woods—and completely flexible, it sped up or slowed down to a crawl not uncommonly at the same time. It was like we had never left for the 51 weeks between festivals." (Hence the use of the term "area 51" for the world outside the festival.) She describes the land itself as sacred space with an "absolute abundance of spirit, the shimmering energy, the sweetness of life, the source of at least some of the grace that looked after our group of ragtag Amazons through all of our journeys, every one of our potential dangers, all of our political trials." Ultimately, what matters most for Lisa is the spirit that women brought to their work on the land. "Each and every one of us strove to bring our best to the tribe. And our growth individually and as a group blossomed from that one primary commitment—our best, our kindest, our most helpful, our most willing, our courage to change." "We did our work with reverence whether we were cooking food, digging a ditch, caring for another sister's child, or building a stage. Every piece of what we did was spirit driven—and fueled our connection with our labor, our love for each other and the land that held us. We created ritual out of everyday life and all of our efforts became sacred" (Fire Circle 8, Sunday, May 24, 2020).

I too have felt the power of hands at work on a task, especially in partnership with others, many times in my own experience as a worker at festival. We practice ritual every day not only in putting on shows, but in making food and caring for others. Across the eight weeks of Fire Circles, Lisa Vogel found ways to bring the lived reality of this magical and ephemeral space into the circle. Part oral history and part memoir, she used this extended documentary forum to offer testimony, and we were witnesses to something sacred, and sometimes fraught with conflict, that revealed the complexity of telling the story of both what the festival was and what it meant, even for those who participated in it. Vogel found ways to tell the story of the festival on her own terms—rather than doing so as a defense against skepticism, criticism, legal scrutiny, or what she calls the "diminishment" of lesbian lives. Forged out of the unusual conditions of the pandemic, which catalyzed the creation of online forms of community, we received the unexpected and surprising gift of getting to hear Lisa Vogel's version of some of Michfest's many, and still largely untold, stories.

CHAPTER 7

Commentary: The Elaboration of What Has Been Lived

Ana Maria Mauad

TWO BRIEF STORIES TO BEGIN WITH

In 1980, during my doctoral research, I began to work with oral history without realizing that oral history was what I was doing. My doctoral dissertation, *Sob o signo da imagem: a produção da fotografia e o controle dos códigos de representação social pela classe dominante na cidade do Rio de Janeiro (1900–1950)* [Under the sign of the image: photographic production and the control of social representation codes by the dominant class of the city of Rio de Janeiro (1900–1950)], had as its object of study the embourgeoisement of *carioca* society (*carioca* being the native of the city of Rio de Janeiro), based on the circulation of photographs from the private realm to the visual public space of illustrated magazines. The family in question was my own: my grandmother, like a guardian of memory, stored in boxes and more boxes a significant photographic collection, extending from the arrival of her parents from Lebanon in the late nineteenth century to their achievement of places of distinction and power in the city in the years when Rio de Janeiro was the Federal Capital (which it remained until 1960, when the capital was transferred to the planned and recently constructed city of Brasília).

My research began in the mid-1980s and was completed in 1990, when I defended the dissertation. Throughout those years of research and study, I

A. M. Mauad (✉)
Universidade Federal Fluminense (UFF), Rio de Janeiro, Brazil
e-mail: anamauad@id.uff.br

spent considerable time in the development of an analytical method that could adopt photography as a valid historical document, as support for social relations—of the middle class in this case—while also acting as an element of distinction in the construction of class hegemony. Inspired by semiotic analysis, my method assumed photography as a visual message that communicated to the social world how class cultures took root.

Perhaps because of my great efforts to comprehend the cultural structure and its developments, ideological discourses, and hegemonic processes, I did not make myself aware of the memory work involved in the hours and hours of interviews with my grandmother that I recorded during the routine organization and description of her photographic collection. Despite the contact I had with the seminal book by social psychologist Ecléa Bosi, *Memória e sociedade: Lembranças de velhos* [Memory and society: Recollections of the elderly] (1979), a study based on narratives by elderly laborers considered to be one the first milestones in oral history in Brazil, my attention turned to the power of social structures in historical analyses.

Memory as a historiographical issue is not present in my doctoral work defended in December 1990, but it appeared in my articles published in the following years. It makes sense, considering that it was only in the 1990s that memory emerged as an important subject for historical studies in Brazil, with a collection of publications that deal with the subject (Meneses 1992, Pollak 1989, 1992; Nora 1993, to list only the classics).

The interviews with my grandmother were recovered and properly dealt with in light of the relations between memory and photography. A new field of study that connects words, images, and archives was being opened at the time, forcing us into significant theoretical-methodological efforts. These efforts benefited from conferences sponsored by the Brazilian Oral History Association, founded in 1994, as an "ecumenical" space for debate. The recognition and consolidation of oral history in Brazil in the past 30 years have allowed for the further development of debates about the uses of the past, the appreciation of memory as an object of history, and the subjective dimension of the knowledge produced with living subjects. These challenges transform oral history activity into a source of the unexpected. As much as we are cautious in an interview, the unusual may and does emerge.

Back to grandma. All the memory work promoted by organizing her photographs in talks with me, her granddaughter, created quite a thrill. She was contributing to my doctoral dissertation at the same time as we encountered memories that had been well hidden for years. During this process, she invited me for a car ride. We drove up to the top of the Jardim Botânico neighborhood and she asked me to stop the car as we reached a quiet street, held my hand, and asked for forgiveness. I was surprised and asked what the reason for such a request was. She answered, "For loving who I should not love." An off-the-record confession, which clarified many other stories that involved familiar sensitivities, an unexpected revelation that brought us even closer together.

Putting aside the family recollections, my work turned to the trajectories of an innovative generation of Brazilian photojournalism, which had incorporated political discourse into photography, transforming images into syntheses of events. Among the photographers I interviewed, I highlight the meeting in 2003 with Erno Schneider, creator of a famous photo of Brazilian president Jânio Quadros, for the coverage of an encounter with the then-Argentinian president Arturo Frondizi. The photograph showing Quadros with his legs twisted in an unusual off-balance pose became one of the most significant photos in twentieth-century Brazil, and was awarded Brazil's top photojournalism prize in 1962.

After being introduced to Schneider by researcher and photographer Silvana Louzada, who had worked with him, we scheduled an interview at 3 pm, at his apartment in Copacabana, a friendly penthouse in an old building in front of the famous Copacabana Palace hotel. Joined by Louzada, we arrived at the place and were met by Schneider, who initially seemed quite reticent, unwilling to talk much. We sat at the table on a small balcony with many plants, and I began to explain the project and the purposes of a professional career interview. I presented the interview script, divided into parts that ranged from his youth to his current situation. He consented and we began the talk around 3:30 pm. The interview gathered pace and time went by without us realizing it. Schneider requested a pause, we opened a few beers and resumed work at an even greater pace. The interview turned into a chat that lasted until 3 am at a bar. I, who had left home saying I was going to work, arrived swearing my lateness was the fault of oral history.

During Schneider's interview, we came to know that the famous picture that was awarded the prize in 1962 hadn't been published on the first page, as historical memory had established. In fact, it's not even published in *Jornal do Brasil*, the newspaper where Erno Schneider worked at that time. However, it had been part of a press photography exhibit in airport lobbies throughout Brazil. Schneider's photo, exposed, was photographed and only then was able to run for the award, since it had been published in the culture section of the newspaper. The unexpected was to discover how the story of this famous photo unfolded.

The anecdotes could multiply because chance, the unexpected, and frequently the unusual, may occur in an encounter, as much as we rely on protocols—and that leads us to rely on creativity and to value the subjective dimension of knowledge based on memories. The three chapters that comprise the first part of this book deal with the unexpected that surround this sort of encounter, anticipated as work situations ruled by methodological principles, but that surprise us with the possibilities they open to knowledge, both about ourselves and about the study objects/subjects we embrace.

Possible Pasts

The three chapters feature multiple paths, corroborating the idea that there is no single track connecting past to future. Time, the craft material of historians, has long broken the compromise it established with the teleological march of humanity. What emerges, in the debris from the 1990s alleged "end of history" (Fukuyama 1992), is the understanding that the relation between past and future is plural and processed by the senses of distance, estrangement, difference, anachronism, traditional chronology—but also by the sense of the unexpected. Thus, in each situation recounted, the unexpected emerges as a trigger to help rebuild the past.

Steven High's article discusses the emergence of the unexpected in the midst of the predictability of local history. The idealizing of characters who are part of a community for its entire life leads to expectations over what is worth telling. The public image shaped by the relation between the greater history of worthy social struggles, of revolutionary activism, and the hidden story of common people and the disturbing secrets they conceal under the shadow of established narratives.

The connection between interviewer and interviewee allowed for a location familiar to both to become disturbing and even sinister, due to the coincidence of traumatic situations of sexual abuse in childhood that had occurred there. Both stories intersect and a new access is created. The expectation to hear about the interviewee's activist background is redirected into a sensitive listening, a sharing of feelings and affections. Despite being from distinct genders and generations, High and his interviewee Florence Richard establish a dialogue where whoever listens can perfectly understand what is being told, because they share the unspoken, the underground memories that rise to surface, sometimes in the form of, as she recounts, a primal scream.

It is also worth considering the reunion that High, in his article, promotes with his past and his professional career. Memories are always built over a present situation, and it led us to an unsettling aspect of remembrance processes: the presence of our subjectivity as an unavoidable factor in the sort of knowledge we produce, a feature that oral historians have been paying attention to for more than 40 years. The implications of this aspect have already absorbed countless hours of debate in meetings, seminars, and conferences in our field; still, High shows how it continues to disturb us when we are faced with a concrete situation that goes beyond theoretical propositions. Memory, as a dialectic image, transforms into a current presence events that occurred in the past. Through narrative work, we elevate what is experienced and turn it into a report to be shared, into an experience to be denounced—perhaps that is where Florence Richard's revolutionary dimension resides.

How many plots are woven into family histories? João, the grandfather, and Luiza Porto, the granddaughter, demonstrate confidence that contacts were successfully established between generations, resting upon the value and authority that lived life and life to be lived embody.

The Austrian sociologist Michael Pollak (1992) wrote that social memory is the result of work, and that past experiences of suffering are often silenced or set aside in order not to hurt and allow life to proceed. *Seu* João did so: he rebuilt his life based on a new beginning. A man of spirit, he overcame stigma by "reincarnating" in the same body. The opportunity to repair brings forth the experience preserved deep in the soul—yet another challenge to be overcome, this time in maturity.

Porto, on the other hand, found in the discovery of a secret the possibility of telling a story. She extended her practice as a historian to a meeting with her family, and provided an opportunity for *Seu* João to carry out, with all safety protocols in place, his work of memory. The encounter between the researcher granddaughter and the narrator grandfather allows for a safe framing of lived stories into a narrative that made sense to the narrator, and paved the way for the scrutiny of historiographic analysis. Both have gained from the encounter. In familial terms, they strengthened the emotional bonds between granddaughter and grandfather, but also guaranteed that the experience of such a stigmatized illness as Hansen's disease would be reported as a historical reality that opened a horizon of expectation (Koselleck 2006), reshaping *Seu* João's social role, once again by recognizing the value in overcoming a succession of random events.

From a historiographic point of view, Porto, the young researcher, goes through an unexpected academic initiation ritual, while carefully complying with the methodology of a guided scientific research project. As a result, she turns her grandfather's personal history into a stepping stone of an essential inquiry for oral history studies, where the private realm itself is part of the problem to be analyzed. Nothing more unpredicted than to witness the rarest fruit spring up in our own backyard. Long live *Seu* João!

Ann Cvetkovich shares in her text a surprising experience, resulting from the objective conditions of the Covid-19 pandemic. Thanks to that, which was not expected in the project, the surprising results lead to an innovative focus in her oral history practice.

A narrative web is woven around the trajectory of the Michigan Womyn's Music Festival, a lesbian and feminist cultural institution that ended in 2015, after 40 years. At first, Cvetkovich's objective was to document the festival drawing on oral history interviews, but the shaky ground of the roles at stake in the festival's cultural scene raises questions that are often difficult to face. Cvetkovich's own involvement in the organization of the festival and the procedures for conducting oral history interviews were guiding her to the possibility of interviewing the festival manager, Lisa Vogel.

The expectation of a biographical interview with Lisa was frustrated by the health emergency. However, what emerged as an alternative was perhaps more interesting and significant, and it is on this alternative that Cvetkovich focuses her discussion. As early as April 2020, at the beginning of social distancing, Lisa scheduled sessions of "Virtual Fire Circles" on Facebook, in which she planned to tell stories about the festival. The experience of sharing those stories through livestreams went beyond expectation, gathering an audience of approximately 500 people. Those were not public interviews, but performances where the stories about the festival were narrated and shared, emphasizing the sense of belonging to a community in difficult and challenging times.

Ann Cvetkovich reflects on the complexity of an experience carried forward through eight weeks of "Fire Circles": memory performances that appear as situations in which history is ritualized through recollection and enunciation procedures. In his reflection about "how societies remember," the English anthropologist Paul Connerton (1989) refers to this ritual power in recollection methods. In this unique context experienced during the pandemic, Lisa Vogel's stories were, we could say, "enacted" in ritualistic sessions, in which she told and described situations which, for the most part, had not been shared before by those involved in the undertaking of organizing Michfest. Vogel's narrative power resides both in her authority as a Michfest organizer and in how she extends this authority to all *womyn* who helped produce the festival.

We can observe that social distancing did not prevent the establishment of the necessary conditions for the ritualistic creation of a magical recognition circle. Lisa Vogel's performances on Facebook, according to Cvetkovich, were not made further available, emphasizing the ephemeral nature of the live streams, which leads one to believe and to hope that the Michfest documentation, based on oral history interviews, is still to come.

The Impossible Recovery of Memory

The term "recovery" is often employed in relation to memory. When this association is made, two actions are involved: the first concerns an attitude related to removing social groups from oblivion, and, through research, "giving them voice;" the second is related to the understanding that memory may be "trapped" in the past and that it is possible to "rescue" it from this prison, setting it free. In both cases, the assumption leads to strategic errors in research with communities and/or individuals. This because the issue is not one of "giving voice," but rather of how to learn to listen, implicating the acknowledgment of the methods used by individuals to elaborate their past experiences routinely. Furthermore, recollection methods rely also on social operations in memory processes, in which the construction and/or reconstruction of past experiences is processed in an ever-present time. Although memory may be nurtured by past material, it does not become present through mere recovery but through the actualized narrative.

In the stories presented in the three preceding chapters, the memory work actualizes itself through a sort of trigger: unexpected events propel situations that redirect the rememorating process into a story that has not yet been elaborated. Experiences which were not communicated—or which were silenced for some reason—come alive because of the unexpected. Michael Pollak (1989), again, offers instrumental concepts to understand the relation between memory and the role of oral history as a strategy to deal with the experienced testimony.

His line of argument relies on the constructivist view of memory, in which memory is not conceived as an objective construct but as the result of a process. In the second part of his 1989 essay, a section named "Memory in dispute," Pollak presents three examples where "underground memories" of critical historical moments emerge: de-Stalinization; Nazi persecution and deportation; and the forced enlistment during the beginning of World War II in Alsace-Lorraine. His examples of how underground memories erupt into the political arena led to conceptualize the term 'unspoken': things that were not forgotten and await the opportunity to cast themselves as enunciated. Pollak also argues that the correlation of underground memories would involve the process of memory framing, carried out to give sense and depth to the identity-based experience of social groups with distinct sizes and institutional presence—ranging from nation to family to clubs and associations. Finally, the author recognizes the challenges in remembering and how agency emerges through oral history memory work.

Returning to Pollak's ideas allowed me to think of a question that seems to be central for this book: to what extent does the unexpected in interview scenarios respond for the opening of opportunities for the emergence of the "untold"? We learned about the act of sharing sensitive experiences in Steven High's story, in which he recognizes the memories silenced during the research process. We learned about the pandemic context that allows Ann Cvetkovich to elaborate her recollections during Vogel's memory performances. Finally, we learned about Luiza Porto's rite of passage as an oral history researcher, providing safe conditions for her grandfather to elaborate his personal and family memories. In all three cases, what we observe is the very formulation of experience into narrative—and, thus, the framing of recollections that once were, but are not anymore, silenced.

References

Bosi, Ecléa. 1979. *Memória e sociedade: Lembrança de velhos.* São Paulo: T.A. Editor.
Connerton, Paul. 1989. *How Societies Remember.* Cambridge: Cambridge University Press.
Fukuyama, Francis. 1992. *The End of History and the Last Man.* New York: Free Press.
Koselleck, Reinhart. 2006. *Futuro/passado: Contribuição a semántica dos tempos históricos.* Rio de Janeiro: Contraponto/Editora PUC-Rio.
Meneses, Ulpiano Toledo Bezerra de. 1992. História, cativa da memória: para um mapeamento da memória no campo das Ciências Sociais. *Revista do IEB* 34: 9–24.
Nora, Pierre. 1993. Entre memória e História: a problemática dos lugares. *Projeto História* 19: 7–28.
Pollak, Michael. 1989. Memória, esquecimento, silêncio. *Estudos Históricos* 2 (3): 3–15.
———. 1992. Memória e identidade social. *Estudos Históricos* 5 (10): 200–212.

PART II

Between Lies and Half-Truths:
The Unexpected as Falsification

CHAPTER 8

Introduction to Part II

Miriam Hermeto and Ricardo Santhiago

We have long learned, either from first-hand experience or from fellow oral historians, that the people we interview in order to produce oral sources (and, unfortunately, not only people in those situations) are prone to lie, to create their own versions of themselves, to exaggerate, to favor their agency in historical events, to embellish their tales, to celebrate their personal role models, to induce the researcher to pay more attention to realities they consider to be important. Whether they do it deliberately or not, truth thus becomes a problem that accompanies oral history obstinately. Precisely for this reason, researchers in the humanities and social sciences—such as historians and sociologists, heirs to the nineteenth-century scientific imperative of objectivity—have, in the past, argued against the legitimacy and reliability of oral history interviews as a serious instrument for producing knowledge. In that view, the encounter between subjectivities and everything it implied was not a *research problem* but a *problem for researchers*. Under this prism, oral sources—susceptible to all sorts of falsification—would be indelibly marked by an original sin.

The view from inside was, obviously, different. Even those who primarily resorted to oral history in search of factual information would insist that interviews were valid and irreplaceable sources. Strategies to assess their reliability were sought, based on standard historiographical rules of source criticism, as

M. Hermeto
Universidade Federal de Minas Gerais (UFMG), Belo Horizonte, Brazil

R. Santhiago (✉)
Universidade Federal de São Paulo (Unifesp), São Paulo, Brazil
e-mail: ricardo.santhiago@unifesp.br

Paul Thompson's classic *The Voice of the Past: Oral History* demonstrates. According to Peter Burke (1984), such efforts had repercussions in the historical field as a whole, not only for contemporary historians: even a Middle Ages specialist would benefit from them. Years later, Marieta de Moraes Ferreira (2002) would develop a similar line of thinking, arguing that oral history's challenges make it a kind of compass for all historical knowledge, highlighting the need for permanent vigilance in dealing with sources, which historians in all specializations should respect.

In the 1960s and 70s, yet another aspect of the relationship between truth and lies in oral history, now highly political rather than epistemological, emerged. Official renderings of the past that, because of social power relations, erased certain experiences of subaltern groups, came to be considered necessarily suspect. In this case, the vectors between lies and the oral history method were inverted: doing oral history would be praised as a means to pierce the bubble of the officially sanctioned lies—the "official framing of memory," as Michael Pollak puts it. A recent line from the world-famous oral historian Svetlana Aleksiévitch echoes such an inversion: "[In my work] I am dealing with a two-sided lie: the lie of totalitarianism, and the lie of history as a science that scrubs life clean, resulting in the passionless paragraphs of history textbooks" (Quintero and Vasilevich 2018, 17).

By contrast, along a more meaningful and productive line, oral history has looked to the diversity and complexity of the human condition, which implied perceiving and comprehending (in both meanings of the word) a miscellany of ways of life, representations, values, cultures, perceptions. One-sided conceptions of the "lie" gained depth, thanks to the constellation and tension between theory and practice, as much as to external pressures from individuals and institutions. Especially from the 1980s onwards, when memory—in its social and individual dynamics, along with the operations of power that constitute it and operate with it—came to the center of the field, "lies" stopped being a deal-breaker and became instead a riveting object of inquiry, requiring oral historians to engage in dialogues with other sets of sources and disciplines such as narrative theory, discourse analysis, and psychology, among others. The broader revitalization of qualitative research in the social sciences, and the social demands for memory and representation, especially in the Southern Cone, clamoring for the "truth of experience," were also integral elements that facilitated this requalification.

"The Great Liar," the essay by Janaína Amado we mentioned in the introduction as the primary inspiration for this volume, deals with lies in more than one dimension. Not only does the piece grow out of an interview recovered long after it was recorded (because it was initially discarded when Amado learned that the narrator had lied), but Amado also invites us to think carefully about how to react when we are listening to an outright lie. In a conversation with Carla Mühlhaus about his interviews as a journalist, Joel Silveira laughed over having once said to an interviewee, after discovering his lie, "But the other answer you gave is a very good one, isn't it?" (Mühlhaus 2007, 184). An oral historian would hardly allow himself such an ironic response as the one given by Silveira, but the writings in our field offer a number of tricks and techniques for circumventing, or peacefully accepting, what is a blatant distortion.

But what to do, in with an interview filled with "lies"? Commonly, falsification is read as misrepresentation and distortion, in the sense of an act fueled by the narrator's ill intent. But in oral history, is the meaning of this term necessarily negative? Does it always originate in clear intentions of falsification? Is it necessarily devoid of sincerity? In this field where subjectivities are the matrix of knowledge, at the same time as they are the plasma of narratives, the finesse with which a researcher must analyze the character of unforeseen falsification in an interview is enormous.

The five texts that make up Part II of this book, by Heliana de Barros Conde Rodrigues, Lívia Nascimento Monteiro, Miriam Hermeto, Ricardo Santhiago, and Luciana Kind, offer quite different reflections on the problem of falsification in oral history interviews. These are five examinations of the trajectories of different flights that resulted in a landing among unforeseen distortions that the researchers encountered. Situations in which lying, dubiousness, denial, and manipulation were frustrating from the information-mining point of view became highly significant for reading the subjective and intersubjective processes at work in oral history.

Miriam Hermeto analyses an interview conducted a decade ago, which she considered at the time to be a failure: her interviewee, Fábio, mingled disparate facts involving 1970s Brazilian culture when narrating his experience (which may not even have happened) of watching a famous theater production whose reception the author was investigating. His were distortions without bad faith, it seems. However, when revisiting the context of the interview, Hermeto found a possible root of his inventiveness in her own way of approaching her narrators.

Lívia Nascimento Monteiro reconsiders old interviews about folkloric Afro-Brazilian parades, the *congados*, in her own small town. She faces intentional silences in Dona Elmira, and counterfeits and memory lapses in Dona Afonsina—falsifications that are not mere effects of the subjects' acts, but effects also of the culture and time. Drawing on the distorted narratives of her interviewees, who are incidentally her great-aunts, Monteiro not only revisits racial segregation in local history but also reviews her own position as a white woman discussing that topic.

Heliana de Barros Conde Rodrigues embraces her interest in "honest lies" as a research direction: she met falsification in an informal conversation that took place months after a structured interview with a distinguished scholar in a sub-field of psychology—a field she was investigating and writing about, as her interlocutor knew. Her unexpected event emerged outside the oral history setting, prolonging it: a good-natured anecdote during a social lunch, now analyzed in the light of the mechanics of remembering and the narrator's need to make (or reinforce) a point.

Ricardo Santhiago shares the intensity of reliving the pain of singer and composer Miriam Batucada, whose biography he is writing: Valdina, mentioned by many other interviewees as Batucada's great love, declared herself to be no more than a soulmate, a friend. She may be betraying her own past, but she—now in her late 70s—is loyal to the social persona she adopted for herself during and after those years of same-sex love. This is a falsification that amplifies, in the present, the many layers of silence covering the life, death, and work of Batucada, an important but now quasi-forgotten artist.

These are distortions and misrepresentations that Luciana Kind illuminates by treating the chapters as occasions to uncover new meanings in remnants of old research. She sees them as pieces that alleviate the asymmetry often found in oral history work, in which the interviews take center stage and the process (rather than the products) tends to be far less visible. Commenting on the texts, Kind invites us to enter the noisy kitchen that is almost always forgotten once delicacies are brought to the table.

References

Amado, Janaína. 1995. O grande mentiroso: Tradição, veracidade e imaginação em história oral. *História* 14: 125–136.

Burke, Peter. 1984. Commentary. *New Literary History* 16 (1): 199–203.

Ferreira, Marieta de Moraes. 2002. Historia oral: una brújula para los desafíos de la historia. *Historia, Antropología y Fuentes Orales* 28: 141–152.

Mühlhaus, Carla. 2007. *Por trás da entrevista*. Rio de Janeiro: Record.

Quintero, Natalia, and Elena Vasilevich. 2018. *Entrevista—Svetlana Aleksiévitch. As últimas testemunhas*. Porto Alegre, RS: TAG Livros.

CHAPTER 9

The Must-See Play that so Many People Staged: A Mosaic of (False) Memories

Miriam Hermeto

The interview experience on which I base this reflection is one of two that were the source of this book. Until Ricardo Santhiago and I arrived at this idea, I had considered the interview in quite simple terms: I did not listen to it again; I did not go on to transcribe it; I abandoned it in the hard drive of my personal computer, together with others from the same series, but with an invisible seal that labeled it: "frustrated occasion." The interview was so buried that I had never used it up to this moment, not even to check if it was of value for the methodological reflection taking shape in our discussions as we were developing this volume.

When I decided to go back to it to write this reflection, what I had considered "unexpected" was the fact that my interviewee—let's call him Fábio—did not seem to have actually lived the experiences about which he was willing to talk, as we shall see. During the conversation, he went through a mosaic of memories and built a narrative collage of recollections about different events that had taken place in the same period I was questioning him about. It was like an urban version (and less dependent on a collectivity) of Janaína Amado's "great liar" (1995)—a Brazilian classic when it comes to the oral history field's narrative turn, which adds nuance to the usual polarization of truth vs. lie. In my memory, my interviewee did not lie on purpose, but he also had no memories about what he had agreed to discuss. It seemed he had felt impelled to

M. Hermeto (✉)
Universidade Federal de Minas Gerais (UFMG), Belo Horizonte, Brazil

© The Author(s), under exclusive license to Springer Nature Switzerland AG 2023
R. Santhiago, M. Hermeto (eds.), *The Unexpected in Oral History*, Palgrave Studies in Oral History,
https://doi.org/10.1007/978-3-031-17749-1_9

recollect something that was iconic for his generation, something that he "certainly" had to have participated in when he was young. However, I did not deal with this complexity when I was carrying out the interview, because I stopped with the first question: why does somebody spontaneously agree to give an interview on a subject he is not familiar with?

These first impressions were confirmed when I listened again to this interview, recorded almost ten years ago. But, as only happens when we (finally!) allow ourselves to be surprised by our own research, these impressions were insufficient to explain the mnemonical operations that the narrator developed in our brief dialogue. Aside from the big unexpected element that I had already identified in the interview, I found another, similar to what songwriters Herbert Vianna and Thedy Corrêa wrote in their song *Um pequeno imprevisto* [A Small Unexpected Thing]: "I wanted to see the future / repairing the past / calculating the risks / slowly, considerately / perfectly calibrated // Until one day / I saw something had changed / different names on the streets / and people with new faces / in the sky were nine moons / and I never found my way home."

And, after seeing "the nine moons in my sky," writing this text became an attempt to find my way home again—an epistemological home in which convictions are dangerous and comfort lies in questioning and in self-reflexivity.

Before the Unexpected, the Starting Point

It was 2009, and I was working on my doctoral research in history at the Federal University of Minas Gerais. I was investigating the social impact of the important play *Gota D'Água* [The Last Straw], an adaptation of the Greek tragedy *Medea*, written by composer Chico Buarque and playwright Paulo Pontes. The play is set in mid-1970s Brazil—a period of economic crisis after the so-called "golden years" of the military dictatorship, but also the beginning of a political "opening" that would finally end the authoritarian regime a decade later. In my study, I often found strong evidence of the impact of the play on Brazilian society and culture both in the press and in informal conversations about the recollections of those who had seen the play at the time it was first staged.

The *Gota D'Água* project was launched and developed in the second half of the 1970s. The drama circulated in three different formats: a book, a play, and a vinyl record album. The left-wing publisher Civilização Brasileira published the book in December 1975, the same month that the play was staged publicly for the first time in Rio de Janeiro, in a major production with almost 50 artists. The play was widely acclaimed by the public and critics, with audience attendance of almost 200,000 in the first year in several runs in Rio de Janeiro. In 1977, it was taken to São Paulo, where it was also performed frequently, and it commemorated its 500th presentation in September of that year. The music company RCA Victor released the album at this time with some of the songs and dialogue recited by lead actress Bibi Ferreira, one of the most prestigious and well-known artists in the country. In 1980, the play, after not being performed for a while, was taken on a national tour. During this whole process, *Gota D'Água* appeared in the pages of both the alternative and mainstream press; its name was used by student movements in different states of Brazil; it was scrutinized by federal intelligence and censorship agencies, and it created a social memory still alive today.

Although the play was the core of the *Gota D'Água* project (as the one that generated the most public debates), it did not come down to its presence on the stage. Its dramaturgical text circulated in different forms and was widely embraced by a very diverse public: by the middle class and sectors of the working class, by intellectuals and students, by those involved in political issues, by different left-wing political groups. It discussed controversial, robust topics, such as the role of women in society, the co-optation of the middle class by capitalism in times of authoritarianism, the issue of affordable housing, as well as social and gender inequalities. But it also generated a counterpoint: many people did not consider it "committed art" because it had a strong and very explicit commercial slant, which generated polemical debate and considerable rejection. Balancing between praise and criticism, it remained a public focus during the second half of the 1970s and changed the way of considering and producing committed art in the context of the Brazilian military dictatorship. To this day, it continues to be an important reference point in the artistic-intellectual field and in the social memory relating to the dictatorship.

In my research, I worked with several types of historical sources. There were pieces from the mainstream and alternative press, art critics' opinion pieces, accounts of political and artistic debates, and play programs, among others. I also sourced censorship documents and information from other organs of repression. These included censorship papers that affected the text of the play, the staging, and the music album's tracks, as well as documents on the influence of the play on cultural life in Rio de Janeiro and São Paulo. In terms of oral history, I conducted 36 interviews from June 2008 to August 2010, 29 of them with people willing to share their memories of attending the play between 1975 and 1980. In this way, I sought to bring to reception studies the perspective of public memory of an art object.

In early 2008, I created a digital flyer inviting people who had seen *Gota D'Água* in the 1970s to share their experiences. I circulated it via email and posted it on *Orkut*, the most popular social network in Brazil at that time, when the reach, diversity, and versatility of such platforms were much smaller than it is today, and when we did not have smartphones and instant communication apps. Still, considering that I was looking for interviews about an event that had happened three decades earlier, my campaign was successful. I gathered more than 30 spontaneous responses from audience members in different Brazilian states.

Most of the interviewees remembered *Gota D'Água* because of the play, and all of them mentioned its political aspects, relating it to activism against the military dictatorship—at times as something "forbidden," at times as a triumph for freedom of expression, at times as resistance, at times as an icon of hope on the eve of the political "opening." But very few of them had recollections of specific themes or approaches found in the play or of the situation in Brazil in the period depicted in the play, such as low-cost housing policies or the crisis of the so-called "economic miracle."

These very vibrant recollections led me to formulate a metaphor: in today's social memory, *Gota D'Água* is remembered as "that play by Chico that 'she' starred in." Chico Buarque, a singer, songwriter, poet, playwright who has been active in and central to cultural production in Brazil since he began his career in the mid-1960s, was well-known and reputed by then. The public and the media considered him to be one of the "most censored" artists during the military dictatorship due to his "resistance" music and confrontation of the authorities. This image has persevered in social memory, as my research concluded.

However, the same social memory retained few marks of Paulo Pontes, the play's co-author, who was a key political and cultural articulator at that time, a historical communist. On the other hand, the social memory retained a strong impression of "her," of the way "she" performed it—"she" being the famous actress Bibi Ferreira, the "Brazilian Medea," and, at the time, wife of Pontes. She was a strong figure in Brazilian theater from her childhood in the 1920s (his mother was a dancer who was part of a theater company) until her death in 2019. In *Gota D'Água*, her presence was so strong that it overpowered the collective dimension of the production, central for the show that counted on dozens of other people: actors, producers, technicians, musicians, and directors. The prevalent recollection of the public was of "her": her hands, her voice, her strength, her expression, her pain. In general terms, the feminine tragedy prevailed over the dramatic text. For most of the spectators, the political dimension was related to either the work of Chico Buarque, seen as an artist of the resistance, or to the very act of going to the theater to watch the play.

However, this was not what Fábio remembered. Not even a little, with the result that I did not even consider using his interview in my dissertation.

"Chico's Play that He Staged Himself"

Fábio, who had worked as a journalist covering culture, first sent me a message responding to the invitation that I had posted online almost two years before we finally set a date for the interview at a café. In March 2010, I contacted him again and received this emailed response: "Hi, Miriam. I am thinking about the interview about Chico tomorrow, Thursday, at 6 pm downtown. What do you think? Hugs."

I confess that it is only now, as I reread the documents related to the interview, that I notice that his response already indicated his narrative inclination: he was willing to talk "about Chico." Chico, that's all.

Our conversation began and, as I noted the date and time as the interview's header, I joked, "It's April Fool's Day and I am taping an interview with Fábio—this is not a lie!" Immediately, he set the tone for our conversation:

"April first is the anniversary of the dictatorship, right? How awful!" The interview, then, would probably be not just about Chico, but about Chico during the dictatorship. He spoke a little more about this, and eventually, I asked him if he recalled how he heard about my research. "I remember, sure, that someone forwarded me your email, saying that if I would be interested in talking about *Gota D'Água* I should get in touch with you. Chico Buarque is Chico Buarque, right? So, let's get to it!"

Up to that point, what was going on was not much different from the other narrations about "Chico's play." The particular aspects of Fábio's (non)memories would soon become evident.

I asked him what he remembered about that production that he had confirmed, in response to my call, to have seen in the late 1970s. Peremptorily, my interlocutor answered: "It was held at the Marília [theater], as I remember." But it had not been. The play took place at another place, the Palácio das Artes, the largest theater in the city, with a stage big enough to hold the large scenery of *Gota D'Água*. I turned away from this subject, asking him if he was a journalist specialized in culture, and where he worked at the time. Fábio repeated his previous statement before answering the new question: "I recall it was at the Marília. And I worked at...." I became a little more uncomfortable but did not return to this subject.

We continued. I asked if he had worked only in culture, and that was the clue for his flow: yes, he said, and, used to "see [art performances] often—I remember that I saw mainly concerts."

Fábio began to share his impressions of different performers. And he talked about Elis Regina, a well-known singer from the 1970s. He said nothing related to *Gota D'Água*, opting instead to recall details of her musical career and of her love life in the 1960s. He enthusiastically praised her interpretation and the outfit she wore in a concert he had gone to, alluding to her hippie style. His narrative was a mix of cultural tendencies, artistic jargon, and artists' public and private lives. He even made comments comparing the position of Elis Regina in Brazilian music to that of Clarice Lispector in Brazilian literature, and feeding the fan rivalry between Elis and the bossa nova icon Nara Leão—clearly asserting his preference for the former. He then talked about the marriage and separation of Elis and the pianist César Camargo Mariano in the 1980s; he mentioned a live interview that Elis had given to Tutti Maravilha, a famous radio broadcaster in Rio, and remembered that Elis and Tutti had been such great friends that they would go for walks together in the Municipal Park at night—"you could still walk around there at that hour"—and that later he was invited to be the godfather for one of her children.

"So, this was the kind of thing that I used to watch." I took advantage of his pause: "So, theater was not exactly your focus?" As he confirmed my impression, we continued our dialogue about this:

MH: So why did you go see *Gota D'Água* then?
Fábio: First, because of Chico. And for Pena. It was a difficult play, because "it's coming [to town]," "it's not coming [to town]," it ended...

MH: It had this anticipation?

Fábio: I don't know if it was a marketing ploy, but it worked. I got there, I went and bought my ticket in advance, I watched it and it was wonderful. Some artists are very famous but don't speak well on stage, they don't speak clearly, they don't sing clearly, it is very complicated. Chico, no—he is traditional. He sings well in live performances, perfect. Some singers only are good on records, and others on records and on stage, which is his case. So, I wanted to be sure to watch it. (…)

MH: And Bibi?

Fábio: Huh?

MH: And Bibi Ferreira?

Fábio: Oh yeah, at that time, I think that it was not Bibi who was starring, no… I don't remember well. I remember him there and all… the songs, four or five songs that he launched in the play… Isn't that it?

MH: He was there? You remember seeing him?

Fábio: Yes, it was him, singing and acting. I don't remember, for example, who else was there. Bibi, I did finally see—yes, I saw her—but it was later at the Palácio das Artes. Bibi, she has an amazing guttural voice! (…)

MH: You remember seeing Chico in the play? In *Gota D'Água*?

Fábio: Yes, he was there, he… He was not actually on stage, of course. When he was traveling [on his tours] there was just the troupe: Paulo… Paulo Fontes, right? But he, he… he was in it. There are so many plays, so many shows, that he had to spread himself out. (…)

MH: Do you remember why the subject of *Gota D'Água* interested you?

Fábio: The content is based on Medea, which is a classical play, that he [Chico] transposed for the situation in Brazil, so that the central character, Joana, I think it is Joana (…) Well, it was very Brazilian. (…) The [playwright] Oduvaldo Viana Filho is the one who gave him the idea, but Oduvaldo, a little later, died. So then it was him and Antônio Paulo Pontes, and… and he… Chico is fairly dramatic, too, at times (…) and the songs, then…

MH: Do you remember the songs?

Fábio: I don't remember. I remember [only] four of them… I know that one is… about the land, how does it go?! It is the theme song of *O Que Será* [What Will Be]. His *O Que Será* has three versions…. It is *Flor da Terra* [Earth's Flower]! I think it's *Flor da Terra*, that is *O Que Será*, that is the main theme. And another four [songs] that, later, were diluted in his recordings. But it was a musical with few songs—more story than music. But it is very interesting. Now the fact that… Well, Sábato Magaldi, who is the theater director from Minas Gerais, from Belo Horizonte here (…)

At this point, Fábio picked up the thread of stories about miscellaneous people in the world of Brazilian culture in the 1970s—from the American singer Sarah Vaughan to the composer from Rio de Janeiro, Marcos Valle. For about another 20 minutes, he talked about many other such topics, only returning to the topic of the interview to state that "Medea, no—it had nothing to do with politics." And a few more times, to comment on Chico Buarque: "he is phenomenal," "there was no one who didn't like him," "everyone waited for his new works skewering the dictatorship."

The narrative that Fábio developed about *Gota D'Água* mixed an odd variety of images and references. Contrary to what he says, Chico Buarque was definitely *not* on stage in the performances of *Gota D'Água*—the interviewee's recollections were probably of other concerts he watched. Bibi Ferreira *always* was on stage in the play. The song *O Que Será*, in any of its three versions, was *not* part of the play's soundtrack, which had indeed only a few songs—a detail widely available in texts on the play available on the internet. The co-author of the play was no more than a name that he tried to recall, trying out various options: "Pena," "Paulo Fontes," "Antonio Paulo Pontes." It seemed like he was trying to remember something that he had studied, as when he suddenly mentioned the playwright Oduvaldo Viana Filho, a name that is better known, easier to get right, but who had nothing to do with *Gota D'Água*. Fábio seemed to be narrating recollections of other occasions where he was a spectator of art performances, merged with a recitation of things he had memorized. I had the impression, both during the interview and when I revisited it for this chapter, that he googled on the theme before we met.

Upon relistening and rereading our conversation for this chapter, I revisited the question at the point where I had stopped ten years before: why would someone who does not know anything about a particular topic agree, spontaneously, to talk about it? And three possible answers, which do not exclude one another, led me to understand the unexpected.

Right at the beginning of the interview, Fábio offered me a first clue about his motivations: he had not only received my flyer, but he had been spurred on by the person who forwarded it to him to talk about the theme "if you want to." He did not make the decision so spontaneously: being a former culture journalist, he was provoked to talk about a well-known theater project in this field and probably felt compelled to do it. After all, how could he not have something to say about an event that was so important for his generation?

Second answer: the topic of the narrator and the topic of the researcher did not coincide. *Gota D'Água* was a mere pretext for him. His real theme was Chico Buarque. After all, "it is Chico Buarque, isn't it?" He, Chico, was very important, and it was about him that Fábio had something to say.

And third, being a journalist covering the area of culture and having gone to many concerts, even though he did not remember the specifics about the play, he would have something to say about that ambiance. In his view, not remembering particular facts would probably not be a problem: Fábio probably believed that talking about the cultural backdrop of the epoch would suffice.

"Just a Willingness to Talk"

However, since Fábio felt impelled to talk based on my flyer, another question occurred to me: would it be possible that this provocation had had some role in shaping the wandering conversation that my interviewee took? I had not seen the flyer for more than ten years, and I looked at it, just out of curiosity. And it was there that "nine moons" appeared in my sky—the "small unexpected" that changes the order of things. Or that, looking up then made me realize that they had always been there.

In the flyer I made, a picture of a young Chico Buarque was featured in a watermark. At the top, in blue, red, and black: "*GOTA D'ÁGUA*. Campaign: Memories about the Brazilian theater." Below, in a smaller font, followed by my name and email address, the following text:

> Wanted, for interview for my research for my doctorate research in history at the Federal University of Minas Gerais, people who attended the play *Gota D'Água* in the 1970s.
> There is no need for many recollections... just a willingness to talk.

As I reread this flyer I made, I figure out that the interview with Fábio was not that unexpected. I was the one who had emphasized the figure of Chico Buarque, even more than the play's title. And, although I had emphasized that I was looking specifically for people who had seen the play to give an interview—that is, to have had the "experience," this assumption that is basic for a narrator's legitimacy in oral history—I confirmed, categorically, in crystal words, that "there is no need for many recollections... just a willingness to talk."

This observation, after shocking me for a few minutes, led me to new methodological questioning. First, about what led me to present my call for interviewees in such vague terms. Yes, I remember well: in informal conversations before creating it, people became enthusiastic when they started to share their recollections of seeing the play. But, when I asked if they would like to give a formal interview on the subject, their enthusiasm disappeared: "It was so long ago... I don't know if I remember very well... I only saw it once, I'm not sure if it was like that...." So, when preparing a public call, I tried to make it lighter and more informal. This seemed to be a solution to a methodological problem that we often face in oral history: the fact that scholarly research may inhibit potential interviewees. Urged to talk, faced with a recorder turned on and subject to scrutiny afterwards, many question not only their own memory, but also their legitimacy as agents of history.

In the case of the research I was carrying out, this issue mushroomed. After all, I was inviting people to do a thematic interview about an event that did not have the seal of "historic" Stamped on it. Having watched a play was not something grandiose, nor did it relate to the sphere of politics, strictly speaking. My interviewees seemed to ask me: what could recollections of having seen a play more than 30 years earlier have that is of historical value? In this tacit questioning, they seemed to adhere to an entire traditional imagery of what counts as History with a capital H, its subjects and facts. Thus, what I tried to do with my flyer was get closer to my potential interviewees, even without knowing them, inviting them to a (simple) conversation that would, nevertheless, be essential for scholarly research.

Fábio accepted my invitation. Given the terms in which he received it, he did it in an almost predictable manner. After all, I was the one who was not faithful to the proposal that led to our conversation, labeling his interview as something that did not work. To recognize today this "little unexpected issue" brings me back to the position of a historian of memory: one who investigates the different layers of a story, who inquiries into the very process of dialogue, who tries to understand what were the forces that shaped it. And I think that "I found my way home"—inverting the end of the lyrics I mentioned at the beginning of this text.

Reference

Amado, Janaína. 1995. O grande mentiroso: Tradição, veracidade e imaginação em história oral. *História* 14: 125–136.

CHAPTER 10

New Looks at Old Interviews: Racism and Privilege Around Black Folk Festivities

Lívia Nascimento Monteiro

In June of 2013, on a cold autumn afternoon in the state of Minas Gerais, my interviews with Elmira Monteiro and Afonsina Nascimento were trying to spark memories. The questions I asked them were varied, but the answers I got were not what I had been hoping for. Quite the opposite. They were empty and did not fill the voids presented by my questioning at that time. Hence I thought these narratives were not useful for the project I was developing. I believed both interviewees were avoiding the topics of the questions I was posing and were not answering properly because they knew little about what I was looking for. Thus, my choice at that time was to discard those interviews.

In May, the "Congada and Moçambique Month" comes alive in Piedade do Rio Grande, a small town in the hills of Minas Gerais. It is a Black festivity whose political meaning has been reaffirmed for the past 90 years in parts of the state that used to be segregated by racism. Congadas, Reinados, and feasts of Rosário—festivities that involve folk culture and processions of faith—take place all over the state. Congado kings and queens take over the streets with parades, dances, music, and devotion to different Catholic saints that are mixed with elements rooted in Afro-Brazilian religions.

From 2012 to 2014, I carried out more than 30 interviews for my doctoral dissertation, in which I sought to analyze the past and present of these

L. N. Monteiro (✉)
Universidade Federal de Alfenas (Unifal), Alfenas, Brazil

festivities in the small town of Piedade, my birthplace (Monteiro 2019). During the second year of investigation, I decided to interview the former secretary of the ex-president of the Our Lady of Rosário and Our Lady of Mercy Congada and Moçambique Association, Ms. Elmira, and his sister, Ms. Afonsina. Both women were teachers, white and retired, and were 82 and 79 years old, respectively, at the time.

I chose them because I had found letters in the Association documents that had been written by Afonsina's brother, Darci Nascimento (who, at the time of my research, had already died) and Elmira. These letters had been sent to the Minas Gerais Folklore Commission during the 1980s, calling on the Commission to get to know the best and most "traditional"—as Darci and Elmira had written—Congada festivity in the state of Minas Gerais.

In my list of questions and in the oral exchange with Elmira and Afonsina, I asked more and more questions about the role of the Association's secretary and president at that time, about their relationship with the *congadeiros-moçambiqueiros*,[1] the rituals, dances and past festivals, and especially if they knew the first, early captains (I will explain more later) and their family histories, which are woven into the reports about past festivities. I expected to hear stories about the *congadeiros-moçambiqueiros* as, from what I read in the letters, these women seemed to have known them.

While my interviews with members of the Black *congadeiro-moçambiqueiro* families were full of talk, connections, and stories, and lasted from two to three hours each, the interviews with these two women lasted a little more than half an hour, including long silences. I had expected to hear more stories, memories, and details of the history of the Association. Instead, silences and partial memories took up most of the interviews. Thus, I thought that the women had been vague, shallow, and silent, and that they had not responded to my questions because they did not know as much as I had supposed about what I was looking for.

As Alessandro Portelli well points out, aside from that dialogical relationship between the researcher and the narrator maintained during the interview and in the production of oral sources, we do not always know how to deal with the unexpected because "historians generally do not know that there are areas of unexpected experience that they should explore" (2016, 15). Such unexpected aspects surprised me in 2013, but I did not explore them in my dissertation. This text is the occasion to do so.

---

[1] The dancers and members of the Congada and Moçambique Association of Piedade do Rio Grande, called *congadeiros-moçambiqueiros*, are men who belong to the two groups (Congada and Moçambique) that make up the Association and who carry out the festivities.

Who Did Elmira Remember?

The interviewees, Elmira and Afonsina, are also my great-aunts. Elmira is the sister of my paternal grandmother, and Afonsina of my maternal grandfather. Since the nineteenth century, our families have lived in the small town of Piedade do Rio Grande—whose population today comes to about five thousand—and owned the main slave plantations in the region. By revisiting the interviews, seven years later, for this chapter, I was able to rethink the racial relations between the white, former slave-owning families of the city, and the Black *congadeiros* and their families who have been keeping the festivals alive for over 90 years.

My interviewees spent most of their interviews telling stories about the landowning families. This was especially the case of Elmira. She repeated several times that the best person who could provide me with the information I was seeking on the background of the first *congadeiro-moçambiqueiro* captains (the "royal procession," composed of the Congo king and queen, princes and princesses, is escorted by *congadeiro-moçambiqueiro* dancers, led by the captains) was the so-called "Murilo":

LNM: I am trying to find the name of the parents of João Lotera [second captain] in the documents.
Elmira: Go ask Murilo… Have you talked to him?
LNM: Which Murilo?
Elmira: Maria Angélica's Murilo.
LNM: José Murilo de Carvalho?
Elmira: That's him. On the internet, he can find all that you're asking for.
LNM: It's hard to find…
Elmira: But Murilo must remember.

This Murilo is the respected historian and sociologist José Murilo de Carvalho, author of dozens of books and member of the Brazilian Academy of Letters; he is from Piedade do Rio Grande and is mentioned several times in this interview by Elmira as responsible for "finding on the internet" the answers for which I was seeking. When I ask more questions on the ancestors of the *congadeiros-moçambiqueiros*, and on where they lived in the rural zone of Piedade, Elmira cuts off the discussion on the family of captain João Manoel da Cruz (known as João Lotera):

LNM: Where does he live? Over in [the neighborhood of] Arião?
Elmira: Yes, near Jardim. But you have to ask Murilo to make a family tree for the Ribeiro family [his family] for us. His godfather was my baptism godfather.
LNM: He made a family tree for Cecília, do you remember her?
Elmira: I do. Now you should ask him to make us one of his family.

Elmira is asking for the histories of the white, ex-slave-holding families, written as family trees crossing generations in this small town going back to the nineteenth century. My discomfort and, I confess, irritation with Elmira's insistence on this request made me ask her if she remembered Cecília and, thereafter, Maria das Dores. It was an attempt to show her, in some way, that José Murilo de Carvalho, together with his sisters Maria Selma de Carvalho and Ana Emília de Carvalho, had written a book that provided parts of the family tree of Maria Cecília de Jesus and Maria das Dores Alves. These were Black women, laundresses, residents of the Santa Cruz farm where he and his family had spent their childhood (Carvalho et al. 2011). In the book *Histórias que a Cecília contava* [Stories that Cecília Used to Tell], José Murilo and his sisters published 22 tales recorded at the end of the 1970s along with stories told by Cecília and Maria das Dores, in addition to the reconstruction of parts of Cecília's genealogy.

Not knowing how to deal with her insistence and with this unexpected situation—I had expected her to know the histories of the *congadeira-moçambiqueira* families—I tried, with this follow-up question, to tell her that he had already written a family tree. But I was also adding that it was not for a landholding family, and that this is quite significant. However, the break in Elmira's narrative was even more brusque: she noted that she remembered, but that now he should do the genealogy "of *his* family"—who are related to hers/ours.

At the time, I believed that little or almost nothing had been narrated. So, when I finished the interviews, which I considered lacked data, I also judged that their stores added almost nothing to my doctoral research. After talking to my advisor, I decided that my focus now should be on interviewing only the very *congadeiros-moçambiqueiros*, the keepers of the memories I wanted so much to hear. And so I did.

But revisiting the interviews years later showed me that I was wrong about the "lack" of information. When I asked whom Elmira remembered among the *congadeiros-moçambiqueiros* and she replied she remembered only a few of them, I read aloud the names contained in the minutes of the foundation of the Association, to try, in some way, to reconnect her with the memories. I was insisting on the opposite of what this unexpected response was showing me:

LNM: And who else do you remember?
Elmira: Oh! I remember just a little, because we lived at the Taboão farm [a farm located far from the town, where she had lived as a child]
LNM: And you would come for the festivities in May?
Elmira: When we moved here, we were already going often to the May festivities. I came here when I was six years old.
LNM: And did you participate or watch?
Elmira: No, I just watched.
LNM: The whites never participated?
Elmira: No, at that time no. Just watched.

By responding to my questions about the folk festivities with punchy commentaries about the white, landholding families of the town, and insisting on their genealogies, what Elmira produced were silences. At that moment, I did not practice the true art of listening and did not see myself as part of that interview. During the dialogue, Elmira was not given enough space to elaborate on their views and on the topics she was keen to discuss; after the dialogue, the same thing happened on my side, another way of silencing since I decided to put her interview aside. Today, however, I would do it differently, agreeing with Alessandro Portelli when he writes that "what makes oral sources important and fascinating is precisely the fact that they do not passively record the facts, but elaborate upon them and create meaning through the labor of memory and the filter of language" (Portelli 2016, 18). As he argues, it is the willingness of the interviewee to speak that makes our research possible; however, there must be willingness also coming from us, oral historians, in terms of opening ourselves and the very goals and design of our work.

Who Did Afonsina Forget?

In the other interview, with Afonsina Nascimento, what dominated most of the conversation was her condition of "forgetting," which she mentioned over and over. She began the interview recapitulating her life story. The full names of her parents, grandparents and great grandparents were enunciated in rapidly, without pauses or interruptions. She started the interview by recounting the history of her family. When she was finally questioned about her memories of the *congada* festivities in the town, she replied: "All my life I remember it, because the *congadas* always pass by here. When the kings call the people for the church, they pass by here with the *congada* queens...." But when she was asked what she remembered about the feast dancers and captains, she immediately responded: "Oh, my brain doesn't work very well now! Some of them would even stay overnight. What was their names? Oh! My brain is useless!"

The interview with Afonsina has long silences scattered all through it. Her attempt to remember the names of *congadeiro-moçambiqueiro* ancestors happened during almost the entire interview, with repeated justifications that always referred to her "lack of memory" and "general forgetfulness." One example:

> Well, I don't remember his wife. I remember a Black woman called Gloria, and there was one who moved to [the town of] Barbacena and went to live with [a man named] Adiles. But my brain is so bad... What was her name!... I am trying hard to remember her name... A man who lived over there in [the town of] Vargem. They were brothers... I'm racking my brain here. She had a son who went to the war, during the [former governor Tancredo] Neves years. But I can't remember if he came back here. I only remember [the other man,] Adebaldo.

Afonsina's memory lapses during the interview may well reflect the quality of the memories of elderly individuals and possible neurological obstacles in remembering; but they can be considered also to expose the problem of racial segregation in Piedade, showing the role that most of the white families played in the May festivities. Although they enjoyed, watched, and followed the festivities, these families did not know the celebrants (who are, after all, their neighbors) and their festivities because their experiences did not belong to anyone: they were socially and racially circumscribed. Memories about the festivities are not included in the white people's recollections nor in the town's collective memory; rather, they are relegated to the underground, to use a term important to Michael Pollak (1989). This is why Afonsina could "forget" details about the festivities. In order to survive, the *congadeira-moçambiqueira* memories had to be cultivated from within, driving "their work of subversion in the silence and in an almost imperceptible manner" (Pollak 1989, 12).

Afonsina does not remember these individuals and the specifics of these events simply because they are not part of her personal history. Both Elmira's and her interview result in silences—but the Afonsina's involves nonbelonging to a community, and therefore, the impossibility of remembering, while the first one involves intentional forgetting, the choice not to offer a remembrance. That is particularly true in the case of Elmira, a former teacher publicly acknowledged in the town because of her role as an exemplary professional, who, during her active years, produced knowledge considered worthy of being remembered and registered. At the time of the interview, Elmira knew about the research I was conducting and that is why she urged me to write a genealogy of the local white, landowning families. However, she would also add: the prominent historian José Murilo de Carvalho—and not the poor, Black *congadeiros-moçambiqueiros*—would be the one who was the bearer of such knowledge.

The Oral and the Written

Listening again to the interviews and writing this text has made me relive my position as a white researcher investigating a folk Black festivity in my hometown, in the middle of family relationships that are inherent to the historical processes under analysis. Now I could perceive questions about whiteness, in the term of Grada Kilomba (2019) that were submerged in these interviews that I, in 2013, opted to discard.

When we contrast the 2010s interviews with the letters written by Elmira in the 1980s, found in the documents of the Piedade Congada and Moçambique Association, the gap between the intentionality of the oral expression in the present and the writing in the past becomes conspicuous. Because I had read the letters with their information on the festivities that took place in the 1980s (and this was indeed the reason for my deciding to do the interviews with Elmira and Afonsina), I created an expectation that more information and stories could be told about the festivities in Piedade. But I was faced with a difference created by Elmira's attitude: a difference between a written document (a letter) that fulfilled a strictly administrative function at the time, and an interview that fulfilled the task of producing history, of communicating what should or deserves to be told, according to her.

In one of the letters, dated 1981, Elmira, who was the Association's secretary, wrote to a folklorist who lived in Belo Horizonte: "We do not have a written history. It is more a tradition that has been passed on from one generation to the other. Obviously, this is linked to Black culture in our region… The high point of the festivity is when you request the blessing to the priest at the door of the Church. At this moment, there is a song that is sung in a mixture of languages: the captain (head of the group) says: "*Sinhô Padê*" ["Masta, Fatha", Master Father]; and the group continues: "*Damos água benta*" ["Gib us holy water", Give us holy water]".[2]

What Elmira is recounting in the letter is one of the rituals of the festivity, known as the "appeal for holy water." It is an appeal made by the *congadeiros-moçambiqueiros* at the door of the Catholic church, asking for the resident priest to bless them, to sprinkle holy water on their heads—holy water representing blessing and protection for Catholics. In the letter, Elmira writes the words as they are sung and corrects them in parentheses, in an attempt to amend what she often considers to be incorrect language, as though it were necessary to translate for the folklorists she was corresponding with whatever did not correspond to writing standards. That is the case, in this excerpt, with the expressions "*Sinhô Padê*" and "*Damos aguá benta*."

Aside from this, Elmira also authoritatively establishes what would be "the high point of the festivity": the appeal for holy water at the door of the Catholic church. It turns out this is *her* view—her Catholic point of view, which does not represent what the very *congadeiros-moçambiqueiros* defended when the letter was written. At that time, incidentally, no parts of the festivity were allowed inside the Catholic church, and their relationship with the parish was contentious.

Elmira ends her 1981 letter with a series of important information about the festivities, the indumenta, rituals, music, and characteristics of the *congadeiros-moçambiqueiros*. According to her, these "are people of very low income, a low level of culture, many of whom are illiterate or barely literate (…). It is not easy to provide you complete information on our *congado*, as not even the oldest participants have this information. It seems to be a curious secret maintained by the members of the group, all of dark color. What would be the deepest essence of their rite? This is an open question for those who study our folklore."

In the interview, I asked Elmira about the information contained in these letters. She replied that she wrote in this way, "increasing the historical value" and even making up some parts, to try to get more funding for the group.

---

[2] Letter of the president of the Our Lady of Rosário Congada, José Darci Nascimento, to Lúcia Helena P. Campos, 1981. Archives of the Piedade do Rio Grande Congada and Moçambique Association, Minas Gerais.

Moreover, she said, "as a teacher of Portuguese language, I wrote in loud and good Portuguese so that anyone would trust in the importance of those histories." Along with her silences and prejudices, Elmira insists, at the end of the interview, that her admiration and respect for the captains is great, even though she did not know their histories or know how to tell them.

Ends and Trails

The interviews with Elmira and Afonsina were put aside for several years. I only remembered them amid the Covid-19 pandemic, when I had other distinct experiences with the Congada and Moçambique festivities during the period of social distancing. Notwithstanding the lack of physical presence and body contact, some festive rituals took place in 2020 and were broadcast live on Facebook and by local radio stations.

Listening to the interviews again to write this chapter reconfigured my researcher *ethos*, because now I can inquire what was left unspoken. In 2013, even equipped with all the oral history methodological procedures, I had not understood that these interviews that had "gone wrong" possessed strong subjective dimensions, and that their meanings involved my relationship as interviewer/researcher with narrators who were my great-aunts. At that time, I was faced with the urge to write genealogies of the former landholding families, the intentional omissions, the relationship between the letters they wrote and what they really thought—but I did not fully comprehend their meaning as an attempt to hold on to the many privileges that our families still maintain in the small town of Piedade. It reflects, on a small scale, how we still live in Brazil in the twenty-first century—with the scars of racial segregation and social legacy of slavery and a racist social structure that still prevails here, and where whiteness and white privilege still dominate the main spheres of power.

At the moment of my field research and writing of my dissertation, I opted to listen and to tell the stories of the *congadeiros-moçambiqueiros* only. I did problematize my subject position, or my "speech place," as the Brazilian philosopher Djamila Ribeiro (2017) teaches us, by asking for permission from the enslaved ancestors of my family's old slave plantations and from all the *congadeiros-moçambiqueiros* to tell parts of their life stories and to try to find the lost links as a form of reparation for the past.

But now, revisiting the recordings that were left aside, I was able to face again the unexpected in my interviews—with their silences, partial recollections, prejudices, and memory lapses. Surprises in the oral history work are, as this experience has shown again, especially prone to raise—not necessarily solve—meaningful questions, as Janaína Amado and Marieta de Moraes Ferreira (2006) wrote. The relationship between scholarly work with Black cultural movements, their identitarian strategies, and the reparations needed in the present to compensate for Brazil's slave-owning past are challenges that impact the public dimension of our oral history work.

REFERENCES

Amado, Janaína, and Marieta de Moraes Ferreira, eds. 2006. *Usos & abusos da história oral*. 8th ed. Rio de Janeiro: Editora FGV.
Carvalho, Maria Selma de, José Murilo de Carvalho, and Ana Emília de Carvalho. 2011. *Histórias que a Cecília contava [Contadas por Maria Cecília de Jesus e Maria das Dores Alves]*. Belo Horizonte: Editora UFMG.
Kilomba, Grada. 2019. *Memórias da plantação: episódios de racismo cotidiano*. Rio de Janeiro: Cobogó.
Monteiro, Lívia Nascimento. 2019. *"A Congada é do mundo e da raça negra": memórias da escravidão e da liberdade nas festas de Congada e Moçambique de Piedade do Rio Grande-MG (1873–2015)*. Doctoral dissertation. Universidade Federal Fluminense.
Pollak, Michael. 1989. Memória, esquecimento, silêncio. *Estudos Históricos* 2 (3): 3–15.
Portelli, Alessandro. 2016. *História oral como arte da escuta*. São Paulo: Letra e Voz.
Ribeiro, Djamila. 2017. *O que é lugar de fala?* Belo Horizonte: Letramento.

CHAPTER 11

"Sincere Lies Interest Me": The Power of Falsehood in Oral History

Heliana de Barros Conde Rodrigues

I first heard about oral history when I was starting my research for my doctorate. During a meeting with colleagues interested in "psy" types of knowledge, where I presented my project on the History of Institutional Analysis in Brazil, someone suggested: "Since you're working on a relatively recent field, why not use oral history?" As a "sorcerer's apprentice"—I am not a historian, I am a psychologist—and, rather embarrassed, I asked: "But... what are you talking about?" I remember hearing murmurs about Michael Pollak, concentration camps, and, mainly, "recorded interviews," which left me uneasy and curious.

Although I am convinced that historians, whether apprentices or masters at their craft, should not predefine their research subject but rather build it by means of the actual investigation carried out, there is no way to proceed without a minimum of information about Institutional Analysis (or IA, an acronym used by the "initiated"). The paradigm of IA, at times ignored in some parts of Brazil, includes concepts and practices described in the French postwar context by writers from various fields, such as René Lourau (a sociologist), Georges Lapassade (a psycho-sociologist), Gilles Deleuze (a philosopher), and Felix Guattari (a knowledge bootlegger, said to be a psychoanalyst by the academic patrols). Critical of institutions (such as school, family, medicine, psychiatry, capitalism, etc.), which they understand as forms of life that are enfranchised but are also susceptible to transformations and historical waning, these writers became tools for the thought/action of some Brazilian agents beginning in the

H. de B. C. Rodrigues (✉)
Universidade Estadual do Rio de Janeiro (UERJ), Rio de Janeiro, Brazil

© The Author(s), under exclusive license to Springer Nature Switzerland AG 2023
R. Santhiago, M. Hermeto (eds.), *The Unexpected in Oral History*, Palgrave Studies in Oral History,
https://doi.org/10.1007/978-3-031-17749-1_11

1960s and 1970s, as part of the resistance movement against the civilian-military dictatorship. Argentines and Italians also contributed to our native IA. The former, through exiled Argentine psychoanalysts linked to the Grupo Plataforma, who broke away from the International Psychoanalytical Association (IPA) and whose members were persecuted by the military dictatorship. The latter, through the theories and practices of Italian Democratic Psychiatry, inspired by Franco Basaglia, who renounced the social mandate of psychiatry and revolutionized the treatment for madness there. Brazilian IA became a patchwork of knowledge and practices from many places, incorporating also activities such as group action, alternative education, Marxist or anarchist criticism of the State, self-managing practices, etc.

I have just rambled on, when I meant to be brief—something inevitable with definitions that abandon, even partially, historical context. But let me recall that it was exactly to avoid this grim consequence that I developed a project on the history of IA in Brazil and presented it to my colleagues, who then suggested… that I use oral history!

As I anticipated, I became uneasy and curious. Why uneasy? Well, psychologists are accustomed to the techniques of "interviewing"—for everything, we interview! However, we are almost always moved by a *desire for the truth* that denies creativity, invention, or fiction. Upon learning that oral historians used taped interviews, I was struck by the fear that, if I grew closer to the institutional analysts, asking them to tell the stories of their lives, I would run into this sad form of veridiction. As many of them were "psy," I ironically imagined narratives that began in their mothers' uteruses, in the admirable intention of characterizing *true* subjects of a *true* psycho-*logic*. I was also haunted by the specter of producing research analogous to some I was familiar with (and hated), in which the words of the interviewees were transcribed with intolerable fidelity—every "ah" and "um" duly noted—in order, I believed, to exhibit proof, but that merely illustrated what the interviewer already believed.

Not only am I ironic, but I am also quite curious, and the question/suggestion—"Why not oral history?"—kept echoing in my head. First step: explore some texts to discover what else there was, aside from interviews, in this oral history. I chose the Brazilian anthology *Usos & abusos da história oral* [Uses and Abuses of Oral History] (Amado and Ferreira 1996), a pioneering volume that assembled texts from authors in various parts of the world on this method. I would not say it was disappointing: some articles were very problematic, others literally provocative, others even humorous. But as a whole, it could not avoid a certain repudiation of Nietzschean "power of the illusion." For example, it got caught up in discussions of whether oral history is a discipline, method or technique; of the most adequate techniques for transcribing tapes; of ways to assure the veracity of the "depositions" (a term I had adopted that today horrifies me, given its police-ish tone); or if the perfect moment to interrupt the "data collection" had been reached.

Then, everything changed: the translation of Alessandro Portelli's article "The Massacre at Civitella Val di Chiana (Tuscany, June 29, 1944): Myth and

Politics, Mourning and Common Sense" led me to note, in the margins, "very smart author." This adjective does not begin to describe my experience, but it was what I came up with then. I decided then to consider oral history simply as a "procedure," avoiding the hierarchical arguments, and so was "hooked" by its fictional drift, which would soon multiply.

A few words about that article: it promotes a history writing that is like a movie script, shifting, through the use of interposed planes and flashbacks, over a period of about 50 years—from the 1990s, when it was written/redirected, to the day in 1944 when the Nazis massacred all of the men of a Tuscan village. By using these resources, Portelli questions if the recollections of Civitella are just a "divided memory" between the "official" version characterized by the praise of the heroism of the *partisans*, and the "spontaneous" recollections of those who witnessed the massacre, who saw it as retribution for the so-called unnecessary assassination of two German soldiers by the Resistance. The text stems from Portelli's participation as a debater at the European Conference on the Memory of Nazi Crimes and reactivates recollections gathered at different times—from the postwar (1946) to the post-cold war (1993 and 1994). He illustrates, based on both the "memory of the Resistance" and the "town's memory," a multiplicity of accounts: the differences and inflections presented go way beyond reductive binary opposition ("divided memory") and/or excluding totalities ("collective memories"). Portelli's intervention dispels all that seemed solid: mixing, among other aspects, critical analysis (but never disqualifying) of political myths (such as the "good German" who refused to shoot civilians), recollections compared according to the circumstances in which they were gathered (resentment against the Resistance was rare in the postwar period but has been growing since the 1980s, fanned by the right-wing parties) and debates on what is considered to be a legitimate component of the public sphere (those who are qualified to speak in the name of the people varies over time, but the exclusion of peasants is almost permanent).

Tensions from the field preserved in the writing, sharing with the reader the political conflict inherent in the events, a narrative that intervenes in the present: such aspects led me to order everything I could by this Italian scholar whose work is (or was) more easily accessible in English. Another peculiarity: the French language of the Annales School historians, also the first language of IA, the focus of my attention, loses its primacy when one refuses to compete for documents with mice and opts for cultivating dialogues that not rarely are confrontational. I would also add that the title of the first collection of Portelli's articles (1991) that I could get my hands on, *The Death of Luigi Trastulli and Other Stories*, reminded me of a collection of murder mysteries—a subject to be taken up again later.

"Hooked" by this Italian author who has no appetite for the "true truth" (Trastulli, his infamous man, gains paradoxical emphasis because old Terni workers report his death in the wrong year and under suspicious circumstances) but starving for ethical-esthetic-political experiences, I soon found him again in the pages of the Brazilian journal *Projeto História*. There I discovered a new perturbing oral historian, the Brazilian documentary filmmaker Eduardo Coutinho (1997) (author of innumerable films that develop what he calls "cinema of conversation"), as well as the Australian oral historian Alistair Thomson (1997), brave enough to break with thoughts that do not harm anyone, showing himself to be capable of challenging warrior heroisms that, by silencing differences, engender abjection. From Coutinho, I retain this mantra for oral history research: instead of "filming the truth," present/discuss the "truth of filming." From Thomson, I take the idea of composure, which invites one to create levels of consistency for what is hegemonically silenced—a conduct that challenges those who inhabit what Primo Levi (1988) called the "gray zone," stretching into the present, by the way, like this untreatable pandemic.

But what definitely attracted me to oral history was, without a doubt, the vicissitudes of the interview process. All that happened in Buenos Aires, for example, I can sum up in a chat I had with a taxi driver who, upon learning of my interest in the history of psychology, exclaimed: "In Buenos Aires, you throw out a seed, a psychologist blossoms!" In the Brazilian cities of Rio de Janeiro, São Paulo, and Belo Horizonte, my research with orality often became an adventure full of stumbles (and parallel enthusiasms). The initial invitation I used to make—"Please, tell me about your life in its relationship to institutional practices"—could not always be maintained: "But why do you want to interview me?" they would reply. Their trust, at times, was gained with difficulty. "Now turn off the tape recorder, because I am going to talk about people who were fighting clandestinely at that time," was a request that was only withdrawn after I talked a little about my own life. Some interviewees fought bravely against the forces of forgetfulness in search of precise information that I had not even asked for; others chose to tell a good story, faithful or not to the supposed facts. Some moved closer, involving me in stories beyond the intended script; others treated me as an annoying researcher for whom they would open up their library for unguided consultation. And most disturbing: some spoke to me about circumstances in which I had also participated, with details and interpretations that were different from my recollections or understanding—cases in which, never neutral, I found myself arguing.

In the midst of these adventures in the field, my reading continued. It was only in 2003, after my thesis was finished, that I discovered "O grande mentiroso" [The Great Liar] by Janaína Amado (1995), an essay that became required reading in the oral history courses I came to teach at Rio de Janeiro State University. And it was so appreciated by the students that one group, upon exploring "A culpa nossa de cada dia" [Our Daily Guilt], another work by Amado (1997), now about ethics in oral history, doubted that they were dealing with the "same author"—which tangled up my foucaltianism, so critical of the "authorship" category (after all, "does it matter who is speaking?"). But I cannot deny, once again disturbing the coherence of such criticism, that Portelli was, and is, for me a kind of "muse." His contributions, emphasizing what makes oral history different—the very (and not always obvious) orality of the sources, its narrative forms, the presence of subjectivity, the "singular credibility," never absent, of the memory, the decisive importance of the relationship between interviewer and interviewee—forge my *interviewer-body*.

Notwithstanding, these contributions would have remained mere academic pleasures if it were not for my fieldwork, during which unexpected interviews turned them into, to use a Deleuze-Foucaultian expression, a "toolbox." I could present here innumerable narratives that would, still using the words of my "muse," convey good and/or beautiful stories, which, strictly true to the facts or not, are vital for the existence of the sense and, consequently, for the truth itself. I gave literary titles to these narratives: "The Turtle Man," "Kiss of Lacan," "Why I Murdered My Wife." They occurred to me due to associations with fields of knowledge or practice that, let us say, favor a critical appreciation of narratives. Only the second story, "Kiss of Lacan," comes from an actual interview, the other two being the result, respectively, of an informal encounter and of what could be called a "self-interview," as I myself am part of the field of knowledge/practice whose history I was investigating. For reasons of space, it is not advisable to write/transcribe these three quasi-stories that make three different points; so, I decided to choose the first, which merits a reasonably detailed analysis, to expose how much "sincere lies interest me," as the Brazilian rock star Cazuza said in one of his famous songs.

The Turtle Man

We were lazing after lunch at the hotel bar where we were staying during the conference. I had just devoured Emílio Rodrigué's autobiography, *El Libro de las Separaciones* [The Book of Separations] (2000), which Gregório Baremblitt, who was present at that lunch, had not yet read. Both of them were members of the Grupo Plataforma and were exiled in Brazil—Rodrigué in Salvador, the capital of the northeastern Brazilian state of Bahia, and Baremblitt in Rio de Janeiro. They are both deceased now; Baremblitt passed away more recently, in Belo Horizonte, where he had been living and working.

Other persons at the table had links to the topic: a research project on psychoanalysis in Bahia, a particular interest in the Grupo Plataforma, and so on. Baremblitt then states that he is not fascinated by what he calls Rodrigué's hippiness: he prefers *Plenipotencias*, an old selection of his stories, rather than his writings after *El Antiyoyo*. But Baremblitt is well aware of my doctorate research, as well as of the fact that it converts me into an audience. "This should interest you," he says, emphatically, grabbing the attention of everyone around him. He begins by stating that although Rodrigué had already occupied all of the important positions that a psychoanalyst could aspire to, he never held on to any of them: "This is his good side, perhaps the good side of his hippiness." Then he begins to reminisce about the day in which he and his own analyst got up together from "the couch and the armchair," respectively, and wrote the manifesto that split off the Grupo Plataforma from the International Psychoanalytical Association (IPA). He knows that I know the details, as he had already told me about it in our formal interview in Belo Horizonte, which he seemed to prolong in this informal moment. So, as a clear high point, he mentions that even when recently returned from London as a "great Kleinian," Rodrigué had immense good humor.

He goes on to tell a fabulous story: "I am lying on the couch, facing the garden at Rodrigué's office, during one of those heavy, terrible sessions... when, all of a sudden, I see two immense turtles... humping!" One woman at the table who had been silent finally could not resist: "And... how do turtles hump?" Baremblitt replies briefly, "Carefully." But then he adds, to avoid losing the impact: "Surprised, but maintaining the formality that we still used at that time, I asked: 'Doctor, I am seeing two turtles in the garden... humping?!?' And Rodrigué replies: 'Certainly, Doctor. What did you think it was? The primal scene?'" The table explodes in laughter.

* * *

The Turtle Man story was not recorded, obviously, but I remember it as if it happened today. Among other aspects, the story shows that oral sources unfold over time, always different, invariably changers/changing, according to the circumstances in which they emerge. In this case, they can even be compared to written documents—namely, to Emílio Rodrigué's autobiographical texts, as he is a character in Baremblitt's story. Like Portelli, I do not think that written sources have a monopoly on trustworthiness; however, following him closely, I recognize that they provide a backdrop for appreciating oral sources (and vice versa).

Phillipe Lejeune (1975) calls an "autobiographical pact" the discursive performance that establishes a meeting between the author, the narrator, and the character, and he contrasts it with the novel, in which the "I" becomes mobile, making the author unreal. However, the autobiographical pact is frequently broken, which mitigates this opposition and even allows one to speak of "autofictions." In Rodrigué's dedication of his autobiography, we see such a multiplication of the "I": "I dedicate this book to the creative, brave and a little hysterical Argentine psychoanalyst called Emílio Rodrigué." In an earlier writing, he had also stressed: "whoever thinks I am writing a biography is mistaken. It is something else, subtly opposite. It is as if my life were an autobiography of my autobiography (…), a fiction of fiction."

Earlier, I compared *The Death of Luigi Trastulli and Other Stories* to a collection of murder mysteries. Along this line, it should be noted that oral history could be related to micro-history—in turn associated, via Carlo Ginzburg, with what we could call the *murder mystery pact*—due to at least two aspects: the reduction of scale (emphasis on particular fates, through intensely examined clues) and innovations in the manner of exposition (experiences that lead the reader to share with the researcher the methods used and the results progressively obtained). Let's go back to Baremblitt's story: Rodrigué intervenes, giving precedence to empirical data (two turtles that, to all effects, are humping in the garden) instead of psychopathologizing (Baremblitt is afraid that he is hallucinating) or psychoanalyzing (Baremblitt may imagine it due to his patient's fantasies linked to the copulation of his parents or "primal scene"[1]). One could hypothesize, intensifying the existent clues, that the clinical actions of the future member of Plataforma is already going back to the matter of unconscious desire, even before their break with IPA, in a manner less established than that of official psychoanalysis—which, obligatorily, would interpret everything based on the Oedipus complex. While Baremblitt does not mention it, it seems to be a continuation of the observations he had just made on Rodrigué's lack of enchantment when he returned from London as the beloved disciple of Melanie Klein, by the power conferred by the IPA. It is as if the phrase the analyst spoke, upon emphasizing the empiricism of the sexual relations between the turtles in the garden, had this subtext: "There are many more things in life, Dr. Baremblitt, than Freudian lucubrations!"

Rodrigué's autobiographical writings are full of these kinds of nonconformist details. These include his disagreements with his first analyst, culminating in an existential adventure in postwar London; his return to Buenos Aires followed soon after by his passion for the wife of a colleague in the Argentine Psychoanalytical Association (APA); his departure for the United States with the intention to study analytics with Suzanne Langer, but which led to incursions into work with Therapeutic Community; his return to Buenos Aires as a teacher, then as president of APA and, soon after, ties to Plataforma. There were also his literary experiments, his rupture with official psychoanalysis, his exile in Brazil, his approximation to the Californian practices of human potential, his new adventures in fiction ("autobiographical"), his marriages and separations, his connections to Candomblé, etc. Rodrigué says about part of this: "I joined Plataforma, which was a scandalous group. Or we can look at a more recent case: my marriage at the [*candomblé* grounds] Axé Opô Afonjá; a turbulent wedding... Having had four marriages is, in itself, an upheaval... Since *El Antiyoyo*, my books have become scabrous... I am astute and innocent at the same time. In this, I am Exu."

Considerations Not at All Final

As conceived by some of its practitioners, oral history also brings us to the whims of the *orisha* Exu, who is seen both as a divine trickster and an opener of the doors, the messenger of the gods: it offers us the *innocence* to adhere to the truths of our interviewees (that which they believe they know, want to be, like to tell, etc.) and the *astuteness* to reinvent their forms of composition (multiplicity of the social production of memory, effects of the present on the

---

[1] In his article "Freud, the Wolf-man, and the Werewolves," Carlo Ginzburg (1989) compares the Freudian interpretation of a dream about wolves—signs seen or heard by the patient of his parents having sexual relations, or "the primal scene"—with other kinds of signs, taken from folklore and Russian literature, a connection between birth with a caulnand becoming a werewolf, that would allow one to seize on it as having an initiatory nature.

evocation of the past, singular contingencies in the encounter of the interviewee with the researcher, etc.). Scavenging in this line, I take the risk of hypothesizing, in the dialogue between the oral source (Baremblitt's story) and the written source (Rodrigué's autobiographies), the existence of paradoxal fidelity/disagreement:

Multiple effects of the written and lived experiences on the oral narrative: in Rodrigué's writings, there are references to a garden next to his office in Buenos Aires, linked to a story about the canary Gargantua, who served as inspiration for describing the fates of Plataforma; Baremblitt and Rodrigué met again in Brazil, where Rodrigué had for a time a turtle in the garden of his house in Salvador; the parables that Rodrigué uses in his texts to try to explain certain experiences are often constructed based on the behavior of animals;

Consequences of the interview situation and the target audience of the narrator: at the moment of the focalized informal story, Rodrigué had just released his autobiography in Buenos Aires; Baremblitt presumed, as he had said in our formal interview earlier, that his own stories would probably not be published in Argentina due to the embarrassment that they could cause to certain psychoanalysts; he knew that I, at that time, was writing a thesis in which he was an important character and that Rodrigué had reactivated links with psychoanalysis, now Lacanian; he then tells me a good/beautiful story that he believes will be disseminated containing the vicissitudes of the life of an Emílio Rodrigué always fighting *alongside*, but equally (and preferably) *against*, psychoanalysis.

After these exchanges between oral and written clues, two hypotheses can be raised. First, no matter how factually true it is, what matters for oral history is the version of the narrators—in this line of thinking, the scene symbolizes the perception of Baremblitt of his old didactic analyst. Second, the scene should be appreciated through the exclusive perspective of the history of memory: it is a changing/changeable recollection, in constant re-composition, demanding an inventory of public accounts that condition it.

Both of these hypotheses are relevant, and I do not aspire to an eventual synthesis. I prefer to conclude this brief (autobiographical?) essay by emphasizing that no matter what analytical perspective is adopted by an oral historian, it cannot be forged independently of the manner of the history writing. As often said by Portelli, with whom I share this "lesson" that I have tried to explore—I'm not sure if successfully—throughout the text, the decisive aspect is always the taking of a position when it comes to oral history as a genre: "The way in which the narrator's voices are included in the historian's book (...) depends on whether the effect that the book is striving for is one of material factuality, or whether the aesthetic value of a good story, invented or not, is taken as a sign of cultural or individual subjectivity, and whether the historian attempts to convey to the reader also some of the aesthetic revelations or pleasures experienced in listening to oral history" (1997, 20).

References

Amado, Janaína. 1995. O grande mentiroso: Tradição, veracidade e imaginação em história oral. *História* 14: 125–136.
———. 1997. A culpa nossa de cada dia. *Projeto História* 15: 145–156.
Amado, Janaina, and Marieta de Moraes Ferreira, eds. 1996. *Usos & abusos da história oral*. Rio de Janeiro: Editora FGV.
Coutinho, Eduardo. 1997. O cinema documentário e a escuta sensível da alteridade. *Projeto História* 15: 165–191.
Ginzburg, Carlo. 1989. *Mitos, emblemas, sinais: Morfologia e história*. São Paulo: Companhia das Letras.
Lejeune, Philippe. 1975. *Le pacte autobiographique*. Paris: Seuil.
Levi, Primo. 1988. *The Drowned and the Saved*. New York: Random House.
Portelli, Alessandro. 1991. *The Death of Luigi Trastulli and Other Stories*. Albany, NY: State University of New York Press.
———. 1997. Oral History as Genre. In *The Battle of Valle Giulia: Oral History and the Art of Dialogue*, 3–23. Madison: University of Wisconsin Press.
Rodrigué, Emilio. 2000. *El libro de las separaciones*. Buenos Aires: Sudamericana.
Thomson, Alistair. 1997. Recompondo a memória: Questões sobre a relação entre história oral e as memórias. *Projeto História* 15: 51–84.

CHAPTER 12

A Love Story That Never Happened

Ricardo Santhiago

A couple of years ago, I began a biographical research project on Miriam Batucada, a Brazilian singer and composer from the late 1960s who became quite famous—literally overnight—after appearing on a show on a leading TV channel, which was, at the time, a breeding ground for some of Brazil's greatest musical talents. Her success was as striking as it was ephemeral. Working intensely between 1966 and 1971, Miriam thereafter endured an uneven career, from the perspective of job opportunities and public recognition. From her first appearance to her early death in 1994, she recorded only two solo albums—a measure, among others, of the imbalance between her scarce public achievements and her enormous talent as a singer, composer, comedian, and rhythmist.

Born in the city of São Paulo in the Italian-influenced neighborhood of Mooca—where I too was born and raised—Miriam was a persistent but hazy reference in my personal set of musical preferences. I knew her as the aberrant "Wonder Woman" knockoff who appeared, wearing glasses and with her hands on her hips, on the cover of an album titled *Sociedade da Grã-Ordem Kavernista Apresenta Sessão das 10* [Society of the Kavernist Grand Order Presents the 10 pm Show], which she recorded in 1971 with three other musicians (Raul Seixas, Sérgio Sampaio, and Edy Star). The disc is considered a kind of Brazilian *Sgt. Pepper's Lonely Hearts Club Band*—in this case, being a thematic project, an alter ego of its creators, filled with multiple style influences.

R. Santhiago (✉)
Universidade Federal de São Paulo (Unifesp), São Paulo, Brazil
e-mail: ricardo.santhiago@unifesp.br

© The Author(s), under exclusive license to Springer Nature Switzerland AG 2023
R. Santhiago, M. Hermeto (eds.), *The Unexpected in Oral History*, Palgrave Studies in Oral History,
https://doi.org/10.1007/978-3-031-17749-1_12

In addition to my appreciation of this collective album, I was also fascinated by Miriam Batucada's unusual talent for drumming with her hands (hence her artistic name, *Batucada*, slang for "drumming") and her notably Italian accent. I had a vague memory of watching her on a few popular TV shows. I also knew about the tragic endpoint of her history, a sort of collective trauma among artists of her generation, for drawing a picture of a possible horizon for many of them: she died alone from a massive heart attack, and her body was only discovered 20 days later.

Miriam was, to me, that and nothing else—after all there were not many sources to resort to. Captivating, sassy, innovative: she represented a field day for a Brazilian popular music researcher. But it took three events for me to reach closer to my neighbor. The first, institutional: the will to study the path of artists from São Paulo's East Side (where Mooca is located), as I started working at a campus in the area. The second, political: the urge to treasure experiences seen as sexually deviant, with the recent arrival of a homophobic government in 2018. The third, personal: the equally early death of my stepfather, Luiz, a little over 50 years old, which made me think further about abruptly interrupted lives, assailed by the mysteries of the human body and the impetuosity of the end.

This all took place in 2018; in January 2019, I purchased my one-way ticket to Maringá, the third largest city in the state of Paraná, in southern Brazil, where Mirna Lavecchia has been living since 1987. With no particular purpose in mind, I went there to visit Miriam's only family member still alive: her older sister. We spent pleasant days together. Mirna told me her own story as one of Brazilian TV's first poster children and, later, as a successful entrepreneur. At the age of 79, divorced, with no children or living siblings, Mirna ended up entrusting me with proprietary rights over Miriam Batucada's production and collection. I discovered in Mirna's speech and in the evidence donated by her a much more complex and uneasy character than I expected to find. I was intrigued by the power of her experience and proceeded to work on the production of an album with some of the unreleased songs left by Miriam, the organization and publicizing of her personal papers, and—the most predictable result of all—a book, somewhere between a biographical profile and a traditional biography.

Since then, I have conducted a few dozen short interviews (personally or by phone) with friends, colleagues, family members, employers, admirers, and even antagonists, of Miriam Batucada. I also conducted a few long interviews with people closest to her, in São Paulo and Rio de Janeiro, as well as in Maringá. The latter are, undoubtedly, oral history interviews, in which Miriam's persona inspired the narrators to extensively recollect their own lives during the time they spent together. The first ones are definitely not. They consist of thematic reports varying in length from ten minutes to one hour. Their significance to a biographical project does not, however, depend on their duration: some interviewees speak very little, presenting crucial data or corroborating information from other sources, still under scrutiny. They are, indeed, examples of a more traditional journalistic "investigation," where "every detail is relevant": "Sometimes, an apparently insignificant detail gains dimension as new revelations are gathered. Additionally, as details are brought together into a mass of data, the interpretation of facts is made easier," writes Eduardo Belo (2006, 91), about research for non-fiction books.

Although inconvenient from the perspective of traditional historical research, these interviews—short, accurate, conducted over the phone, with no release forms—were not at all unexpected to me. I was aware that, by preparing a biography of a highly popular character, I would have to transform my methodology and morph somewhat into a documentary reporter—the person most of my interviewees were expecting to meet. To not compromise with such morphing would mean abdicating almost everything that brings meaning to my research; without this documental flexibility, I would end up with nothing but dry reporting and lifeless writing.

Among these concessions is the use of off-the-record statements—not as information that can't be publicized, but in the sense of preserving source confidentiality. Rather than requesting, my interviewees *implied* this possibility, which became evident when, as they mentioned certain passages or information, they would say something like, "for this, you can reveal I'm the source."

I am well aware that these less formal testimonies tend to be seen as spurious in historical research. However, they may be justified by context: biographical research on the history of Brazilian popular music is mostly conducted by journalists, who not only accept off-the-record confidences as an integral part of their job but often assign them greater reliability, since the source is not focused on controlling their own public image. Nor did the community of subjects I reached out to understand source protection as an antithesis to the general goal to which they signed onto when they agreed to talk to me: to participate in a clearly shared assembling of a biographical profile.

I recently noted with interest that Igea Troiani (2019) claimed, in her work on architectural historiography, that the off-the-record information provided to her was also fundamental, as it offered insight into professional politics and clashes within the job. For Troiani, these data are useful in critical histories for many reasons: they register stories other than mainstream ones; they highlight battles, losses, and mistakes, instead of glorifying individuals and projects; they depict the relationship between socializing and professional success. Without the off-the-record statements, this dimension would be irretrievably lost.

In my work about Miriam Batucada, I too accepted off-the-record statements, giving up one of the principles of historical research (the clear indication of each and every source) in order to respect an even higher principle: committing to a diversified and reasoned research with an interpretive complexity on a par with the subject. My readers are invited to trust my testimony—in the epistemological sense—and I hope they do. Following this research trail, it was precisely after gathering so much significant data that I met *her* and, believing I would register an extraordinary life history interview, my unexpected.

The Great Liar

Suppose her name is Valdina and that we met, let's say, at a French restaurant in the upscale neighborhood of Jardins. That's where Valdina is staying. I know she lives by herself in Rio de Janeiro and is in São Paulo for business. I've been trying to meet her for months, but fate meant us to meet only now. When I reached her for the first time, I knew she had been a very close friend of Miriam between the late 1960s and early 1970s, encouraging her and even providing help in her early career. I insisted on talking to her because she was an irreplaceable "witness": the main reference outside the family, who followed Miriam's move from São Paulo to Rio, in 1967.

Between my first e-mail to Valdina and our first and only in-person meeting, more than eight months have passed. She asks for more information about me and my research; provides me with her phone number but prefers to communicate through text messages. She is evasive. I tell her I will travel to Rio to meet her, and she indicates interest, but warns me her professional schedule is unpredictable. I take the risk. We set up a meeting in the evening; she lost her voice and couldn't come. On a second trip, we reschedule, now in a nice café; she writes me a few hours before telling me she suffered a minor accident and "ripped her tongue." Symptomatically, both circumstances prevented her from speaking, even if she wished to.

Being consistently courteous, Valdina offers me reasons not to give up and I keep the communication channels open until, at a certain point, we set up a third meeting. I knew she was coming to São Paulo and reminded her I was all ears. I invite her for dinner at my place. Who knows if passing by Mooca, on the way to my home in Belenzinho, wouldn't spark memories? She tells me she has very little time and suggests a place closer to where she is staying. She guarantees it is comfortable, silent, intimate. We arrive together, meet at the sidewalk, and enter the establishment.

I mentally welcome Valdina's former cancellations. The eight months that separated our first contact and our glass of wine have allowed me to learn more about her relationship with Miriam. Almost two dozen people told me they were not just friends; they were more than friends, more than close friends and that they, quite discreetly, intensely loved and helped each other. They faced together a moving to a city they had never been to, rebuilt their subjectivity claiming an unprecedented sexual freedom; they lived as a couple without ever proclaiming their sexual and emotional condition, which nonetheless was betrayed by mannerisms and costumes identified as deviant; they adored each other for about five years until love wore out.

At least half of those two-dozen people added to the outcome fewer noble details: Valdina, upon realizing Miriam hadn't succeeded as a popular and commercial artist, would have started an affair with a beautiful rising actress. The betrayal would have been a hard hit to Miriam's already fragile self-esteem—who, adoring Valdina, would have accepted becoming a close friend to the new couple, even if it meant keeping only a bit of the affection of the former, once devout, partner.

Wine and sparkling water served, Valdina asks whether I will record or take notes. I request permission to turn on the recorder and she agrees, relieved: "This way we can talk with fewer concerns, right?" As I always do, I remind Valdina of my project. I tell her I have questions (and I, in fact, bring three pages with very specific questions), but that I would like her to feel free to start by telling me about her history with Miriam, even going back a little, so I could get a better picture of this character who was so important to my subject's life. Valdina accepts the oral history invitation; she guides me through her student years; to the cafés and soirees she attended in the 1960s with artist friends; to the unpretentious university music festival she helped organize when she studied architecture; to her tours at the magical Record Theater, where the *crème de la crème* performed at the peak of Brazilian popular music's golden generation. But, all of a sudden, the smooth tannins from the malbec grapes give way to an unwelcome taste.

A Taste of *Bouchonnée*

I admit I almost doubted myself when Valdina offered me her bumpy narrative, which didn't even come close to what I had heard from a dozen other people. Although their stories were entirely solid (even in the details), I was facing *her*: not a witness, but the protagonist of a love story. Well-versed in the challenges of oral history; accustomed to interviewees who embellish, distort, invent their past (and that of others); experienced in analyzing interviews in the light of the context of their production; an avid reader of Alessandro Portelli, Luisa Passerini and all that was produced after them, even so, I came close to doubting myself, and not Valdina, when she told me her, well, version.

Version: a popular term in the early days of oral history, when it was touted as an instrument that could allow different groups to register their—precisely—specific versions of a greater history. Currently falling into disuse for decreasing an interview's ability to document past experiences in multiple legitimate ways, as suggested by Verena Alberti (2012), I resort to it in the face of how stunned I felt when faced with that which is, almost, an alternate history. I do it against my will, aware that the narration instigated by oral history isn't the rendering of an existing reality, but a work of language (Alberti 2004) and memory (Bosi 1994).

According to Valdina, Miriam and she met in São Paulo. Valdina had already watched Miriam perform on TV and was charmed by her percussion. Filling in for a journalist friend on vacation, she went to the friendly villa where Miriam lived, in Mooca, to interview the artist who was then emerging. The two of them connected right away and became friends. They would go to the movies together, attend soirees, enjoy themselves at the Italian Sunday lunches organized by both their families. When Miriam moved to Rio de Janeiro (which at the time competed against São Paulo for the title of Brazil's cultural capital, and where many of the mainstream music venues and labels were located), looking for more job opportunities, their friendship remained fairly alive, but the intensity of their encounters died down.

Stunned, I heard Valdina talk for over 20 minutes about what consisted of everything she allegedly knew about Miriam's life in Rio de Janeiro: essentially a professional chronology offered by any quick search on Wikipedia. During one of her breaks, I equipped myself with all the subtlety I could muster to inquire of a woman born in the 1940s, whom I had never met before, about her sexuality: "Valdina, I'm sorry to interrupt, but until now I was under the impression your relationship was of a different nature, or was much closer at the least." Valdina didn't flinch. She wasn't appalled. She wasn't shocked nor did she curse my effrontery. She didn't hold her face between the palms of her hands. She calmly smiled and asked: "And why would you say that?"

I went on to name the many public situations in which the two would have been together, to which Valdina blamed her memories: "I can't remember," "I admit I don't remember," "It's been a while," "If it did happen, it wasn't striking." I mentioned Miriam's works in which Valdina may have collaborated: "Miriam did that all by herself, I never did this." I recalled the importance of her testimony as being the person closest to Miriam in her first years in Rio: "Not at all. Carla [fictional name] was the most closely linked to her." About the vast written data that places Miriam and Valdina countless times in the same setting, Valdina said: "We became friends, but we didn't get together regularly, because there was too much work, we were both much in demand." About the substantial statements that they were a couple of very, very intimate friends, Valdina pitched in: "I don't know where you got that from."

Disappointed, but still hopeful for a breach in the narrative wall built by Valdina, I was as kind as I could be as I turned off the recorder and mumbled something like: "I had, in fact, a series of questions … but that … I will reconsider in the light of what you are telling me. Because everything pointed to you and Miriam being very close…"

Instead of opening up—the deactivated recorder letting her know whatever she said would be off-the-record—Valdina grew stiff. My interviewee, who had been peaceful and elegant until then, asked me quite harshly: "What path is your work going to take?" I reiterated my purpose—a biography focused on Miriam Batucada's professional and personal history—and Valdina became relentless: "You're not taking a nice path. You shouldn't go for the personal stuff. You should approach the innovative part: the music, the stories she told … That's what's cool." Valdina discredited the people I had talked to, whose names I didn't reveal: "I don't know who would make this up. I don't know who could have said this." She distrusted my written sources: "I think you have too much unsubstantiated information. Newspaper columns, gossip … you didn't do good research." She put my interpretive work under suspicion: "You didn't reach for the essence of who Miriam was. You went for the edges, superficial stuff." And, as some kind of narrative Judas, who betrays love's memory with a gesture of affection, she concluded:

> I consider Miriam to be one of my best friends in life. A soul mate, a friend in the full sense of trusting someone, admiring someone. Trust, admiration... Friendship. Nothing beyond this word, that is so beautiful and far-reaching. This is what existed between Miriam and I. Between Miriam and many other nice people. It's very important not to distort reality. The testimony of who lived it is very important. So I tell you: what I had for Miriam and what Miriam had for me was a beautiful friendship. That's what counts.

I ask if I can turn the recorder back on. "Is it recording? You may record," she says harshly, after nodding her head. And, without me asking, Valdina proceeds. She tells me, and to whomever may listen to her through my recorder, towards which she keeps on glancing: "We never had an affair. If I had some kind of relationship with Miriam, I would tell you, I have no reason to hide it. But it's not true."

Faced with the inconvenient question, Valdina doesn't think twice before describing her "soul mate" as being "quite masculine." Nor from saying Miriam "even" dated a famous Brazilian cartoonist, whose name she pronounces without hesitation: previously worried about the "essence" of people, my narrator now exposes an almost 90-year-old man, still alive, married all his life (who did, in fact, have a short and secret extramarital romance with Miriam). "And I met other boyfriends of Miriam's [in Rio de Janeiro]. Nice guys, very fun. At least two of them, but there must have been more," she guarantees, even if it had been when, living in Rio, Miriam and she had not seen each other much. Valdina knew them very well but doesn't recall their names, of course.

Watch Out, Boy!

During the two hours we were together, I dedicated all my comprehension and respect to Valdina—even when faced with her warning, by the end of our meeting, that there could be "legal consequences" when someone writes "things that never happened." Now, when I listen to or read Valdina's interview, I can feel nothing but sadness. Many interviewees had told me that, seeking the spotlight, she had abandoned Miriam after years of a beautiful relationship. Far from judging her for that, I felt truly disturbed as I realized this abandonment also takes place (or repeats itself) in the narrative.

To Valdina, my appearance was probably unexpected; a threat to the image she built and preserves (and I have always been willing to respect, as I will continue to do, her intimate life). With her version, Valdina redoubled the erasure suffered by Miriam. I *dreamt* of hearing from her lips the love story of a couple filled with friendship and companionship, discovering themselves and freedom. I would *understand* and accept without reservations a silence intended to protect, if that was its aim, the parts in an unusual relationship, still in the late 1960s. What I didn't *expect* was to live and feel in the research—because we too feel while doing research—something parallel to the abandonment my character experienced 50 years back.

Some would say that artists, as they create, struggle against their own death—and I may add that biographers struggle against the death of their subjects. Disillusioned by the many levels of obliterations in Miriam's life and legacy, I admit my discomfort when faced with the narrative of someone who, being able to resort to an off-the-record statement, or anonymity, or simply to silence, chose to narrate a version that not only denies a love story but increases the distance from an accurate factual report about one of the most significant stages of Miriam's life as an artist, of which Valdina was the main witness.

From this point of view, Valdina's interview was a blow to my writing: some information gaps only she could fill, small significant questions no other interviewee answered. However, the methodology serves as a sort of refuge: facing Valdina and her version taught me much. But also "un-taught." A few months later, I visited Rio de Janeiro to conduct research for a smaller biographical piece of another fantastic female singer and composer, also homosexual, contemporary of Miriam. I met with her main musical (and life) partner—a woman. At some point, as we approached the inevitable moment where she would have to narrate the time they lived together as a couple, the period in which they were more than friends, more than close friends, and, quite discretely, intensely loved and helped each other, I turned off my recorder. She smiled: "Why did you do that? I am very proud of this love story." I apologized. And smiled too.

References

Alberti, Verena. 2004. Além das versões: Possibilidades da narrativa em entrevistas de história oral. In *Ouvir contar: Textos em história oral*, 77–90. Rio de Janeiro: Editora FGV.

———. 2012. De versão a narrativa no Manual de história oral. *História Oral* 15 (2): 159–166.

Belo, Eduardo. 2006. *Livro-reportagem*. São Paulo: Contexto.

Bosi, Ecléa. 1994. *Memória e sociedade: Lembranças de velhos*. São Paulo: Companhia das Letras.

Troiani, Igea. 2019. Spoken-not-spoken, Written-not-written: From Gossip and Rumor to Architectural History Between Margin and Center. In *Speaking of Buildings: Oral History in Architectural Research*, ed. Janina Gosseye, Naomi Stead, and Deborah van der Plaat, 235–251. New York: Princeton Architectural Press.

CHAPTER 13

Commentary: Leftovers, Their Unexpected Forms, and the Act of Gleaning: Re-encounters with Interviews

Luciana Kind

> *I play the role of a plump, garrulous old lady who talks about her life. However, it is others that really interest me and that I like to film. Others intrigue me, motivate me, challenge me, disconcert me, make me fall in love. This time, speaking for myself, I thought: if we open people up, we would find landscapes. As for me, if they open me up, they will find beaches.*
> —Agnès Varda (2017, 0:00:12)

> *My garden is bigger than the world.*
> *I am a catcher of waste.*
> *I love leftovers.*
> —Manoel de Barros (*2018*, 18)

First-person narration is a component one expects to find in films by Agnès Varda, as is the presence of the unexpected that blossoms from her encounters with the people she films. In *The Beaches of Agnès*, one of her last films, she lets us see a little more of herself as she weaves the encounters she had had during her prolific career as a screenwriter. As I read the chapters by Miriam Hermeto, Heliana de Barros Conde Rodrigues, Lívia Nascimento Monteiro, and Ricardo Santhiago, I felt that I was facing something similar. The texts reveal these

---

L. Kind (✉)
Pontifícia Universidade Católica de Minas Gerais (PUC Minas),
Belo Horizonte, Brazil

researchers whom I have admired for a long time. The texts are less retrospective and encompassing than in the case of Varda, because their topics here are specific. They are not presenting an extensive review of their careers as the filmmaker was. Even so, they do not leave you seeing less. Rodrigues even reveals within parentheses (with wariness, perhaps?) that her writing is by nature autobiographical.

Between this project to share interviews that would seem to have somehow gone wrong and what we are presented with, the authors return to one of the fundamental elements of qualitative research, that is, the willingness to hear stories from other people. There are always (at least) two people on the scene, in asymmetrical positions, in general weighted on the side of the one who has all the research paraphernalia (voice recorder, interview script, terms of consent, etc.). However, the details of the negotiations inherent in this unique relationship between researchers and the *other participants* in their research are not always registered. My italics showcase the argument that I want to develop using the wonderful contributions of my colleagues. We don't usually allow ourselves to be seen with so much wealth of detail in conventional research reports. In our articles, books, and chapters, we tend to maintain a certain authorial distance from the scenes where the interviews occur. The main act in this performance is to hide ourselves in the smoothness of a well-written report, giving center stage to the stories that we heard from the participants while being faithful to the goals of the investigation. But the relationship between researchers and the people invited to participate in our studies is fragile, "always subject to negotiation," as suggested by Jean Clandinin and F. Michael Connelly (2015).

In my colleagues' reports, I read fragments of their negotiations with the participants in their research. There is an assumption that oral history interviews are considered dialogue. Often called the "art of listening" (Portelli 2016) or a disposition to "sensitive listening" (Patai 2010), this reflection is almost always directed toward the history of others, not toward our own. That is why I turn to Varda's screenplay for inspiration and a path to reflection in this venture. The interest in others and their surroundings is also an invitation to see oneself differently. In one of her most emblematic films about encounters with herself and with others, Varda allows herself to be fascinated by the act of filming one of her hands while she is holding a digital camera in the other. The film is *Les Glaneurs et la Glaneuse* [The Gleaners and I]. Among her interpretations of this extraordinary act is that of harvesting herself, of projecting herself, or intermingling herself in the stories of the gleaners she met on the road and who find life and survival in unexpected debris. With potato gleaners, she notices that vegetables in shapes considered undesirable for commercialization (among them, tubers shaped like a heart) are discarded. The form of the heart, so unexpected in potatoes, awakens a new appreciation for that which is rejected. As she holds and admires the potato-heart, Varda (2000) explores her hand and herself while also appreciating the method used to capture it, the portability of the digital camera.

From the preceding chapters, I will gather points that caught my attention, situations that are well explained, others that are incomplete, and I also harvest a few adjectives—they are so abundant!—that my colleagues use to qualify their interviews, their interviewees, and themselves. Walter Benjamin (1936/2012, 221) used to say, "the more the listener forgets himself, the deeper he engraves in himself what is heard." This reunion of reports about interviews and their deviations reflects, I believe, some of that indelible register. Interviews are, above all, dialogue. I see our authors as gleaners of extraordinary leftovers. Their exercise, like Varda's, is based on taking an analytical view of a story told at another moment in their trajectories, re-encountering themselves in the act of carrying out their research. I will leave the filmmaker aside for now, to follow the movements of my colleagues more closely.

To Relive and Re-encounter the In-Between of the Stories

Clandinin and Connelly (2015) invite us to consider that when doing research, the moments of encounter always take place as an in-between. We come to this encounter with others in the midst of our own lives, of our own histories. The participants, in turn, are also living their histories. The encounter takes place in this movement between the histories that we bring, those that we would like to hear, and those that the interviewees are living. Among other things that we bring to an interview is a subject position of ourselves as researchers interested in a particular topic. It is expected that we prepare ourselves for this encounter based on that position, taking care to have proper equipment to record the interview, media for our notes, documents approved by ethical review boards, and so on. But this preparation precedes the moment of the interview.

Santhiago's report and his making himself into Miriam Batucada's biographer is a good example of how the negotiations needed for a moment of an interview to occur are composed of anticipation, hope, and the interviewee's acceptance of the terms proposed. He tells us how much he hoped for this meeting and how he expected, imbued as he was with the task of a biographer, that it would be "The" interview with a capital T. Santhiago entered Valdina's landscape eight months after his first attempt to contact her. In contrast to the generic version that she offers him, Santhiago still tries to create a "crack in the narrative wall" to make a detour in what Valdina wants to tell him. Santhiago sought confirmation of Valdina and Miriam Batucada's love story, but she insists that the path he take not be their personal life. She denied what Santhiago, as a researcher, had already heard in other interviews he had conducted. Valdina insisted that what she had to say was the truth, asserting her authority as someone who was there, in the past which so interested the researcher-biographer, saying: "It is very important to not distort reality. It is very important in the declaration of one who lived it."

In another publication about his biographical research on Batucada, Santhiago explains his commitment: "She was a homosexual artist, lesbian, who had a very strong, very pronounced conflict, with the understanding and exercise of her sexuality" (Carvalho Neto et al. 2020). The conclusion that he reached is perfectly understandable, since he was facing the erasure of an important part of her history. This erasure, under threat of judicial consequences should he choose to make the story public, came from someone from whom Santhiago expected the opposite. In the interview that he gave to *Epígrafe* magazine (Carvalho Neto et al. 2020), he defended the biography as a form of public history in which the political dimension of an individual's life is emphasized. In the case of Batucada, who died as a complete outcast, Valdina was clear in choosing her "Wikipedia version." The tension described in his account invites us to side with the researcher, for anyone who has never been disappointed with a research interview may cast the first stone. And yet, this made me pensive.

Given Santhiago's expectations, after seeing Valdina it seems as if the whole biography is compromised. Is it? I hope not. The analogy of the title of one of the essay's parts, "That Bouchonné Taste," is timely. I take the liberty to expand upon it. Tasting mold when you expect a meticulously chosen vintage would be the perfect comparison. Since it is not possible to call the sommelier to switch out the spoiled wine, I hope that, in fact, the unsuccessful tasting serves as a lesson for all of us researchers who are interested in stories. It seems to me there was as much predisposition for "The" listening as for "The" narration. They were not coincidental and, for both parties, were also non-negotiable. As this interview has become public, it teaches us much about the expectations of the researcher-biographer. His indignation is also made public. One must have the courage to accept the deviations from an outcome so hoped for and, when revealing the acidity of the interview, to question the fragile and difficult course of asserting a romantic relationship in what was lived strictly in private. Fortunately for us, almost two dozen other people confirmed the romance between Miriam Batucada and Valdina.

Unexpected or Unusual?

The preceding authors' writings tell us about (dis)encounters. There are similarities, but also specific displacements in each of the reports. At the time she interviewed Fábio, Miriam Hermeto was surprised at his lack of knowledge as compared to what she hoped to hear. "The theme of the narrator was not the theme of the researcher," Hermeto synthesized. The unusualness of facing a non-narrator-of-what-one-wished-to-hear resulted in her not seizing on the interview when writing her thesis, for which it had been conducted. She already had 36 interviews and many other sources about the reception of the iconic play *Gota D'Água*; so, that one was just residue, simply disposable.

Hermeto contends that what was really unexpected, the turning point in her own narrative, her *patate-coeur*, was the public call for interviewees she had made for distribution on *Orkut*. This established an asynchronous dialogue with her potential research participants, not only because of how she presented her objective but mainly because of the opening that was created by the phrase "no need for many recollections (…), just your willingness to talk." The light tone of the message was also an invitation to the unusual encounter with Fábio. Faithful to the invitation extended to him, Fábio has few memories to accompany his desire to throw himself into the conversation. Between the unexpected, because unanticipated, aspect of their face-to-face meeting, and the surprise of her re-encounter with herself where previously nothing had made sense, Hermeto invites herself to a renewed flirtation with her research and takes us with her.

What a beautiful look at herself! Recognizing herself as "bowled over," Hermeto guides us through her exercise of self-reflection. She modifies herself as a researcher, revisiting and invaluably questioning both her research and the act of researching. She takes an active role in the narration and searches for the intersection between the stories she needs to hear for the goal of her research, and what the participant has to tell. Thus, it is surprising when someone responds to a call for participation in a study and does not know how to talk about the central theme, as Hermeto tells us. Alessandro Portelli alerts us to the possible divergences in the researcher's and the narrator's agendas. He reminds us that an "*inter-view* has to do with two people looking at each other" (Portelli 2016, 35, author's italics). What the researcher wants to know—or assumes that the participant knows, as is also the case in the essays of Santhiago and Monteiro—will not always be guided by the narrator.

In a different way, Lívia Monteiro also encountered someone she did not expect. Unlike Hermeto, her interviewees were not unknown to her. Her quest for the history of the traditional *Congada* and *Moçambique* festivities in the town of Piedade do Rio Grande in the state of Minas Gerais could have been a "meeting with her own home." Elmira and Afonsina are presented to us as former teachers, white, retired, and, respectively, the secretary and the sister of the ex-president of the Our Lady of Rosário and Our Lady of Mercy Congada and Moçambique Association. A little further into the text, Monteiro tells us that they were, by chance, her great-aunts. I do not use "chance" lightly. Chance is a serious thing. I invoke here the definition translated from the French of Varda, *par hazard*, as luck, destiny, fortune. The filmmaker, in many interviews, mentions this unusual surprising aspect, like the "heart-shaped leftovers" (Varda 2015).

Monteiro went to the meeting with her great-aunts seeking their memories of the Congada festivities. Well cultured, for the standards of their time, professionally responsible, and authors of important documents related to the topic of Monteiro's study, Elmira and Afonsina seemed to be the lucky find of any researcher who has reflexivity on their side. But, at the time of the interviews, Monteiro found herself uncomfortable and irritated with what she had gathered. Elmira wanted to remember other things. In her role as interviewed-great-aunt, she asked her great-niece to put together the glorious history of their white families and not the history of the *congadeiros-moçambiqueiros* that interested Monteiro so much. With unmatched agendas, it remained to the researcher, if she wished, to ask an illustrious academic to help "find on the internet" what she needs. But Elmira did remember the festivities. She could have offered Monteiro the "memories that I so wanted to hear." Afonsina, on the other side, presented another kind of unexpected, as she struggled with her memory. In a way, ironically, Monteiro also struggled, insisted, grasped for memories that through silencing or forgetting could not be found there with her great-aunt-interviewees. Initially, she considered that she did not perform "the art of listening" with her interviewees.

As she revisits these interviews, that had been put aside, Monteiro re-encounters her whiteness. She sees herself, then, through a racialized lens. What was unspoken in the interviews is reinterpreted in this new light, with the symbolic privilege accumulated in the normalization of the histories of whites who, for her interviewees, deserved to be remembered and registered appropriately. To see herself as a white woman, a member of that family and with their incumbent privileges of race and class, helps position Monteiro within her place. I understand her considerations as those of a white researcher who, upon "discovering" her whiteness, transformed it in a theme for a just self-reflexivity. The responsibility of understanding experiences lived in a racialized manner is an experience that also affects me. Like Monteiro, I struggle with my whiteness.

What Is There, If Not the Unexpected-Unusual?

Another struggle of mine is daring to encourage dialogues that cross disciplinary boundaries. Listening, recording, composing stories during research has fascinated me for more than a decade. Like Rodrigues, I am a psychologist by training. And just like her, I choose "muses" from other areas; among them, we share the oral historian Alessandro Portelli and the filmmaker Eduardo Coutinho. As she labels them, they are inspiring, perturbing, and visionary.

Different from the reflections of Hermeto, Monteiro and Santhiago, Rodrigues' reflections are not guided by a typical interview scenario. Her "interviewee" summoned her in the middle of a larger audience, in a *par hazard* encounter in which friends were hanging out together at a hotel bar. Being prone to audiences and storytelling, Gregório Baremblitt turns a casual situation into a public interview, calling upon Rodrigues to occupy her position of doctoral candidate. The anecdote that Gregório tells about his ex-analyst, *The Turtle Man*, was not taped. The audience and the informality of this narrative contrasted with the autobiographical writing of Emílio Rodrigué. Based on these records, Rodrigues problematizes aspects of orality and writing as sources of memory; the innocence of one and the astuteness of the other; the faithfulness-disagreement found in both forms of producing "true truths," always open to the interpolation of the basic principle that the stories presuppose relation. Also different from the interviews described by the other authors in this section, Rodrigues invites us to think about the unexpectedness of being challenged as researchers in the necessary but improbable task of pursuing *a* truth. Paths and routes we design when producing the traces of our research bring us closer to the "truth of filming," which Rodrigues turns to in the work of Eduardo Coutinho. As I share her fondness for cinematographic analogies, I return to Varda, our "plump, garrulous old lady," documentarist and inventor of cinematographic languages in foreign lands.

Coutinho started his career in television journalism. For Varda, it was photography and painting. The way they encountered their respective "others,' however, was quite different. If Coutinho plays with the "truth of filming,' in many interviews that she gave, Varda emphasizes editing as an important stage in the construction of an "outside of oneself" narrative, as Yakhni noted (2014). With *Les Glaneurs et la Glaneuse*, Varda becomes enchanted with her profession in a different way. She had already affirmed herself as a documentarist and essayist in previous films. Her intuition for chancing upon what is quotidian and banal but also surprising had already been registered in *Daguerreotype*, of 1976, as one of the possible examples. So, what is new, if not unexpected, but also surprising about the *patates-coeurs* (yes, in the plural, because she went on to collect them)? Experts on her work, such as Yakhni (2014) and Conway (2015), emphasize the act of filming herself as a new mechanism. The digital camera—portable, light, and not depending on complex production logistics—presents Varda to herself and to her audience in a renewed manner. As she experiments with this new technique and is moved by the leftovers' picking project, she sees herself as a gleaner. Looking at the veins in her hands and, in other sections, filming her white hair, lead her to perceive her own aging. She is surprised: "I am getting old, and I am still a gleaner, I am still a filmmaker, I am still loving what I do" (Varda 2015, 184). The filmmaker used herself and those she filmed as components of a poetic, ethical, and aesthetic experience to show that what she gleaned was beautiful and trenchant in ideas, images, and emotions. But there was little spontaneity in the final montage that she would present to us. She used editing as a key point of her narrative. In her words, "a documentary is subjective and, by editing what people say, you can make them appear different (…) When I cut what they have to say… it involves a choice" (Varda 2015, 185).

Let us bring Varda's reflection to the research process. I imagine asking myself and you, the reader, what is there in qualitative research if not the unexpected? And does what we read in the reports of Hermeto, Rodrigues, Monteiro, and Santhiago not resemble the work of editing to which Agnès Varda refers? Does going back to your own work of interviews and unusual encounters in your research not reveal more of yourselves than of the people that were thought of as participants, like Agnès in her beaches?

When first told to Hermeto, Rodrigues, Monteiro, and Santhiago, the stories of Fábio, Gregório, Elmira, Afonsina, and Valdina seemed out of place.

The bewilderment of this in-between of stories, those of my colleagues and those of the people they encountered, can be seen in this "retelling." This time, they arrive as pairs. By narrating the unexpected experiences in their work as researchers, my colleagues spin and (re)weave the stories that were told to them. They needed to be told again, as Benjamin invites us to do. This time, they interwove themselves.

I follow the work of a colleague, an odontologist who wants to record stories from his patients after they "reconquered their smiles." We have talked for a long time about narrative interviews, the patience of listening and, mainly, about how we enter into the stories. On one occasion when he interviewed a particular patient, he told me: "The interview was terrible!" My first reaction was to tell him that I do not believe in the existence of terrible interviews. The reports of Hermeto, Rodrigues, Monteiro, and Santhiago reinforce my old intuition. Understood as dialogue and the in-between of stories, it is almost always possible to take another look to glean potato-hearts. All the stories my colleagues told, especially those about revisiting their participation, discomfort, and frustrations, show the prep kitchen work behind the research, which usually does not make it into more conventional research texts. However, these are the reports that we should tell first. If not in academic journals that adore showcasing research as if it were a fancy party—with everything arranged, the table set with impeccable candlesticks, linen, and china—then in projects that re-edit what look like divergences in the processes that we effectively live.

With a language different from that of Agnès Varda (2000), the Brazilian poet Manoel de Barros—cited in the epigraph of this commentary—dedicated himself to what is unimportant. Working in different art forms, both were tired of words and their excesses of information. Hermeto, Rodrigues, Monteiro, and Santhiago, taking similar paths that led them to the unusual, also made themselves into gleaners. Like the filmmaker, they saw in others someone beyond themselves. Like the poet, they narrated to themselves like harvesters of waste, lovers of residue.

References

Barros, Manoel de. 2018. *Memórias inventadas*. Rio de Janeiro: Alfaguara.
Benjamin, Walter. 2012. 'O narrador' [1936]. In *Magia e técnica, arte e política: Ensaios sobre literatura e história da cultura*, 8th ed. rev. São Paulo: Brasiliense.
Carvalho Neto, Pedro José de, Matheus P. de Silva, and Letícia Fernandes. 2020. A história pública que queremos: entrevista com Ricardo Santhiago. *Epígrafe* 8 (8): 283–331.
Clandinin, D. Jean, and F. Michael Connelly. 2015. *Pesquisa narrativa: experiências e história na pesquisa qualitativa*. 2nd ed. Uberlândia, MG: EDUFU.
Conway, Kelly. 2015. *Agnès Varda*. Champaign, IL: University of Illinois Press.
Patai, Daphne. 2010. *História oral, feminismo e política*. São Paulo: Letra e Voz.
Portelli, Alessandro. 2016. *História oral como a arte da escuta*. São Paulo: Letra e Voz.
Varda, Agnès. 2000. *Os catadores e eu* [*Les Glaneurs et la Glaneuse*]. [Film]. Cine Tamaris.

Varda, Agnès. 2015. The Gleaners and I by Agnès Varda / Julie Rigg (2005). In *Agnès Varda: Interviews*, ed. Jefferson T. Kline, 183–190. Jackson, MS: University of Mississippi Press.

Yahkni, Sarah. 2014. *Cinensaios de Agnès Varda: O documentário como escrita para além de si*. São Paulo: Hucitec / Fapesp.

PART III

Deviating Routes:
The Unexpected as a Mnemonic Device

Introduction to Part III

Miriam Hermeto and Ricardo Santhiago

Guardar na memória is a phrase whose literal meaning in Portuguese is to store something in memory: a kind of medicine "against" forgetting (an opposition that does not take into account its intimate relationship with remembering). But the beauty of the verb *guardar*—a cognate of the archaic English verb *to ward*—resides in its polysemy, which reveals much about the multifarious mnemonic operations that oral historians face when producing and analyzing their sources.

First, *guardar* can mean "to keep hidden" whatever one does not want to make public, locking it in a safe. As the philosopher Jeanne Marie Gagnebin puts it, it is "a turning of the page, a non-permanence in resentment and complaint" (Gagnebin 2006, 8). *Guardar* also can mean "to protect," to ward against the pain that specific acts of remembering, such as those that involve trauma, may imply: for Gagnebin, it is a protection that ensures one's "desire to forget," that "natural, happy forgetting, necessary for life" (Gagnebin 2006, 101). But *guardar* can also be the object of attention of poets, and one of them, the Brazilian poet and philosopher Antonio Cícero, once scrutinized the archaic and erudite sense of the word. "To ward a thing is not to hide it or to lock it up. (…) / To ward a thing is to look at it, to gaze at it, to target it for the sake of admiring it, that is, to illuminate it or to be illuminated by it," he

---

M. Hermeto
Universidade Federal de Minas Gerais (UFMG), Belo Horizonte, Brazil

R. Santhiago (✉)
Universidade Federal de São Paulo (Unifesp), São Paulo, Brazil
e-mail: ricardo.santhiago@unifesp.br

wrote (1996). The meaning that Cícero brings to light is opposite to the previous ones: it involves exposure, not enclosure.

In a way, what oral historians do in their work is to be exposed to, to document, and to unravel the mnemonic operations that shelter beneath these metaphors. Consisting in a documentation of the "history of events, history of memory, and history and interpretation of events through memory," as Alessandro Portelli (2016) states, oral history is fertile terrain for inquiring *why* people remember what they remember, rather than *what* is the content of their recollections. While oral history methodology allows for powerful applied uses that do not involve this sort of analysis—including not only documentation as an end in itself but a broad range of public history practices—dissecting the ways in which remembrance is constructed, as well as the forces that affect it, is an intellectual gesture that ennobles the reading of the sources. "The touchstone [of oral history practice] is the critical reading, the faithful interpretation, the search for meanings that transcend that particular biography: this is our work, and it would be beautiful to say, this is our struggle," the pioneering Brazilian psychologist and oral historian Ecléa Bosi wrote (Bosi 2003, 69).

While mnemonical operations are studied by various sciences, our field is concerned with its oral and narrative materialization through individual extraction that is also socially anchored. We rely not on any evanescent form of memory, nor on measuring brain activity, but on the story individuals tell and on their narrative choices. This is the only concrete form through which we can contemplate the mnemonical operations that ground our interpretations and hypotheses: silence, emphasis, lies, repetition, lapses, escapes, reticence, disarticulation, change of subject, the alternation between formal and informal register, between discursive models, between vocabularies and dialects, and so on. Operations (and their oral/narrative garments) that often overflow with surprises in a researcher's findings.

Cognitive psychologist Michael W. Eysenck (2015) made an intriguing review of the elements responsible for impairing the accuracy of witnesses' recall in court cases. Pointing out the imbalance between the belief of judges and jurors in relation to the testimonies and findings of specialized studies (the latter much more suspicious of witnesses, at least until the former are informed by science findings), he names "change blindness," "change blindness blindness," "expectations," and "post-event misformation" as major disabling elements in court testimonies. He also considers the effects of anxiety, stress, reactions to violence, age, production of false memories, and many sorts of biases and unconscious transfers, as influencing factors.

We, oral historians, are moved not by the mission of scrutinizing the degree of reliability of an oral testimony but by the commitment to pay serious attention to the role that elements such as sensoriality, affectivity, and imagination—at the individual level—play in the production of memories. We are inspired by hypotheses such as those raised by Eysenck, from which we can certainly learn, but we arm ourselves with the understanding that one of the keys to arriving at a good understanding of mnemonical operations is their anchoring. The shared (social, professional, cultural, political, etc.) situations in which oral sources are produced and accessed are a pivotal element of this sort of analysis; they help us to better identify which vehicles were chosen by a subject among those communally available, to produce a specific inscription in the collective memory.

In this section, we encounter highly suggestive chapters, which demonstrate the efforts of researchers to make sense of their own perplexity when confronted with unexpected mnemonic operations. Luciana Heymann and Verena Alberti, Daisy Perelmutter, Bernardo Borges Buarque de Hollanda and Raphael Rajão Ribeiro, and Jorge Eduardo Aceves Lozano invite us to join them in traveling along the roads they rebuilt in the company of interviewees (and an interviewer) engaged in different kinds of oral history projects.

Luciana Heymann and Verena Alberti revisit their encounter with the wealthy entrepreneur Mr. Agripino, two decades ago. They were seeking to learn more about the history of the private university he created and were surprised to hear that a dark-skinned Jesus had once magically appeared, stepped into the interviewee's car, and urged him to build a church—to which Agripino insisted on driving his interlocutors. The authors suggest that we think of such "subversions" and "displacements" in narrative situations in terms of content, performance, and interview setting.

Daisy Perelmutter harvests memory's detours in her reanalysis of two interviews drawn from different projects. In the case of a Jewish playwright who was only minimally engaged in his self-narration, she finds new interpretive sparks in a note he sent her along with the revised interview transcript. In the case of a musician who missed the interview appointment and had to be actively sought out by the research team, she moves through his complaints and listens to the cry of indignation that emerges from his resentful and bitter narrative. The plasticity of the oral history process allows Perelmutter to find new meaning in the interviewee's detours.

The interviewer (and not the interview itself or the interviewee) is the unexpected element that Bernardo Buarque de Hollanda and Raphael Rajão Ribeiro face when scrutinizing "second-hand interviews." Analyzing oral histories about football [soccer] archived at the São Paulo Museum of Image and Sound, they hear not so much the narrators' voices as the interviewers' preconceptions. The authors develop the hypothesis that the research leader, a notable sports scholar, exploited the encounters as occasions not to listen, but rather to put to the test his own ideas about Brazilian soccer.

In his commentary, Jorge Eduardo Aceves Lozano emphasizes the richness of autoethnographic processes in oral history praxis after the research is completed and guided by questions and goals distinct from those that originated in the oral sources. Based on the three previous chapters, he ponders how the change of direction in looking at the source reveals tensions in the method, fortifying its ambiguous status as a non-spontaneous practice.

REFERENCES

Bosi, Ecléa. 2003. *O tempo vivo da memória: ensaios de psicologia social.* Cotia: Ateliê.
Cícero, Antonio. 1996. *Guardar.* Rio de Janeiro: Record.
Eysenck, Michael W. 2015. Eyewitness Testimony. In *Memory*, ed. Alan Baddeley, Michael C. Anderson, and Michael W. Eysenck, 2nd ed. London: Psychology Press.
Gagnebin, Jeanne Marie. 2006. *Lembrar escrever esquecer*, 34. São Paulo: Editora.
Portelli, Alessandro. 2016. *História oral como arte da escuta.* São Paulo: Letra e Voz.

CHAPTER 15

"Who rode in my car? Who do you think? Jesus!": Subversion and Displacement in the Rereading of an Interview

Luciana Heymann and Verena Alberti

On a hot afternoon in February 2002, we interviewed Agripino de Oliveira Lima Filho, founder of the University of West São Paulo (Unoeste), and at that time also the mayor of the city of Presidente Prudente in the state of São Paulo. The interview was for a project named Trajectories of Private Universities, an initiative of the Capes Foundation, the Coordination for the Improvement of Higher Education, that sought to understand the growth of the private sector in higher education in Brazil through oral history interviews with the presidents and administrators of fourteen private universities located in different regions of the country.[1] However, rather than talk about the university whose history goes back to 1972 when he and other professors created the Prudentina

---

[1] The project counted on consultation with the Center for Study on Higher Education of the University of Brasília (Nesub/Ceam/UnB) and was coordinated by the two of us when we were still working at the Center for Research and Documentation of the Contemporaneous History of Brazil (CPDOC) of the Getúlio Vargas Foundation. It resulted in the publication of two volumes, with the interviews we carried out and chapters of analysis of the material (Alberti and Heymann 2002), as well as two articles that we presented at oral history conferences (Alberti and Heymann 2001, 2003).

L. Heymann (✉)
Casa de Oswaldo Cruz da Fundação Oswaldo Cruz (Fiocruz), Rio de Janeiro, Brazil

V. Alberti
Universidade do Estado do Rio de Janeiro (UERJ), Rio de Janeiro, Brazil

© The Author(s), under exclusive license to Springer Nature Switzerland AG 2023
R. Santhiago, M. Hermeto (eds.), *The Unexpected in Oral History*, Palgrave Studies in Oral History,
https://doi.org/10.1007/978-3-031-17749-1_15

Education and Culture Association (APEC), Mr. Agripino only wanted to talk about his mystical experience that had resulted in his decision to build a sanctuary in homage to Jesus of Nazareth.

Almost two decades later, we had no doubt we would return to this interview when the opportunity to reflect on an unexpected interview was presented. For both of us, that original interview was outstanding both for the surprises that it had for us and for the hard-to-see dimensions of reality that it helped to illuminate.

In this chapter, we will discuss the unexpected feature of this interview in terms of "subversions" produced by the interviewee in at least three aspects: (a) in content, because he constantly tried to dodge the theme that had led us to interview him, in order to talk about what interested him; (b) in performance, as he insisted, during the whole interview, in demonstrating physically what he had experienced, superimposing physicality over orality even though he knew that we were producing a sound recording; and (c) in the interview setting, given that it ended, as Mr. Agripino possibly desired from the beginning, with our pilgrimage to the sanctuary—an experience that was definitely not in our expectations as interviewers.

Considering the aspect of content, Mr. Agripino's subversion was evident from the beginning of our dialogue, which took place in the City Hall of Presidente Prudente, a city of about 200,000 inhabitants in the interior of the state of São Paulo, where we had arranged to do the recording. Although the reason for the interview had been presented when the meeting was scheduled a few weeks earlier, Mr. Agripino warned us right away: "I have already told the story of this church to more than a thousand people, just as I am going to tell you two about it …. Can you believe that nobody believed the story? Nobody believed it! On October 5, 2000, Jesus of Nazareth rode in my car!" Thus began a long story about a mystical experience filled with characters and "revelations." The interviewee said that in that October, a few days before the end of his second election for mayor of his city—and less than two years before our meeting—he had left the city in great despair, driving his car, going towards Bolivia, due to a family crisis. His encounter with Jesus had taken place in the small town of Bataguassu in the state of Mato Grosso do Sul, in the middle of his journey to Bolivia, where Mr. Agripino had arrived in the early hours of the morning, looking for a place to sleep:

> I got out of the car and was more or less twenty meters from it. Then a young man passed there in front, a dark young man about thirty years old and said: "Agripino, you here?" and I said: 'I'm here. Do you know me?" He said: "I know you. Don't you want a good place to stay?" "I would. Do you know where there is one?" He said: "I do." "Can you take me there?" "I can." He got into my car, I don't remember how he got in—I have already told this story to a thousand people and no one believed me; if you want, you can laugh at me, I don't mind. He said "this way," but I did not look at his face, nor did he look at mine, in the car. I was nervous. When we arrived, he said: "It is here." I stopped and said: "I'll go see if they have a room and I'll come back to park the car." And naturally to thank him. I went in, they had a room, I didn't have my documents, I didn't have

any money. "No problem, you can stay here." I went to park the car and to thank him. When I went to thank him, he was already behind my car, about 40 meters away, walking down the middle of the road. He went just like that, disappearing, I was nervous, not even paying attention.

Mr. Agripino told us that, months after returning home and assuming the duties of mayor, he received a message, supposedly from the young man who had ridden in his car, whose identity was still unknown. The message said that he should build a church, an undertaking to which he was dedicated at the time of our interview. Many incidents later, when the building was underway, a revelation finally identified the young man:

After one month, more or less, at night, I was lying down, reading, and I thought: I sure would like to see that young man again, I already have a clue about him … and when I thought that, my book lowered, I looked in the other bedroom, in a mirror that I had never seen before, at a crucifix on the bed, shining. So, he gave me an answer, didn't he? Who rode in my car? What do you think? Jesus! At that moment, ten months later, he revealed that it was him. Jesus rode in my car. He determined that I would build the church. He chose the place, he chose the name, he chose everything, the project. I am building something marvelous.

The whole interview, which lasted one hour and forty minutes, was controlled by the interviewee, who recounted in detail his relationship with religion, marked by a personal connection to the divine, and not by the institution of the church. Aside from this, he was quite long-winded telling us his life story, emphasizing that he came from a farm, from a very poor family with eleven children, that he went to night school, was a truck driver, bookseller, and built an "empire," of which the university that he owned, Unoeste, was part, as well as some farms.

My life was very difficult, the sweat of my brow. I came from nothing and was a city councilman for ten years here, I was mayor once, I am mayor again, I was a Deputy in the 1988 Federal Constituent Assembly, I was a State Deputy, I founded a university, I was the rector, I built one of the best hospitals in the country, I have built (…) more than 15 enormous farms.[2]

---

[2] Agripino de Oliveira Lima Filho, born in Lençóis Paulista, in the state of São Paulo in 1931, began his political activities in 1972, the year that he and some other professors founded APEC, the sponsor of Unoeste. That year, he was elected city councilman in Presidente Prudente for the National Renewal Alliance Party (Arena), and was re-elected to this position in 1976. He was a representative for the state of São Paulo in the Federal Constituent Assembly (1987–1988) and was a federal deputy representing São Paulo for the Liberal Front Party (PFL) from 1988 to 1991. In 1992, he was elected mayor of Presidente Prudente for the first time; in 1998, state deputy, still in the PFL Party; and, in 2000 and 2004, was again elected mayor. Ana Cardoso Maia de Oliveira Lima, his wife, also one of the founders of APEC and dean of Unoeste when her husband was otherwise occupied, was a city councilwoman in Presidente Prudente. One of her four sons, Paulo Lima, was a federal deputy for the state of São Paulo in the 1990s and the first decade of the 2000s.

To sum up, in the report of Mr. Agripino, the university (the topic that led us to interview him) appeared as just one more thing among many he had done that proved his tenacity and the fact that he is, to a certain extent, blessed. What was supposed to be an interview with the theme of the creation and trajectory of a university was transformed into an autobiography about his deeds and experiences.

"We Can Talk on Our Way There"

Janaína Amado (1995) taught us that instead of throwing an interview away, it is up to us to change the perspective and ask ourselves what that interview documents. If the mystical experience and the narrative of Mr. Agripino tells us little about the creation and trajectory of Unoeste, the interview, on the other hand, demonstrated the overlap between the spheres of politics, of religiosity, and of higher education, all of which are pervaded by the logic of welfare. For our interviewee, the university, like the sanctuary, was one more way to serve the people of Presidente Prudente and, naturally, to maintain and increase his electoral base.

> Look, our school, and my intention as the educator that I was and, as a farm worker, as the day laborer that I was, was always to channel my service, my work, for the common good. Proof of this is that as soon as we began, I wanted to create a bachelor in dentistry that would serve the whole population for free. Dental treatment, fillings, implants. For free. And so we began to treat the poor. After that came the physic therapy [program], all for free. All day long. We saw two thousand people a day in clinics! You don't find this anyplace else in Brazil. The university spends more on health than the town, municipality, state and national governments do together. So, the institution, if it had done absolutely nothing, if all the students who enter had left illiterate, it still would be treating two thousand people a day in its clinics! Poor people, who have no place to go, are welcomed there with five meals a day—five meals a day: breakfast, lunch, afternoon coffee, dinner and at 11:00 pm, tea.

We carried out this process of changing our perspective and reflecting on what the interview told us, despite its gaps, while we were still conducting the research. Mr. Agripino's case seemed to us, at that time, very eloquent in terms of expressing a specific political culture in which his election and that of his family members to different public offices fit. His combining political capital, charitable activity, and Catholic mysticism showed us that "this association was possible and effective in the context of Brazilian society," as we wrote at that time (Alberti and Heymann 2003).

So far in this chapter, we have dealt with the content aspect of the "subversion" of this unexpected interview. But our interviewee also challenged us by his performance, or of what we called the "logic of the concrete." We were surprised during the interview that the interviewee turned to underpinning his narrative with "evidence" or, as we wrote in 2003:

The recurrence with which he complemented his words with concrete, nondiscursive elements, such as standing up to show us a scar on his back, the result of surgery to which he had submitted, or of reproducing the self-conscious walk that, intimidated, he adopted in the corridors of Congress. ... [Aside from this], he felt the need to show us letters he had written to the vice-mayor right after a family conflict, in which he announced that he should assume the mayorship. These letters, stored in a drawer in the cabinet, served as evidence of his actual intention to renounce his office and flee from [the town of Presidente] Prudente.

A number of times during the interview, his performance compelled us to write down what our interviewee insisted on acting out, as the testimony was only recorded in audio. By doing this, Mr. Agripino clarified the limits of orality in expressing his own statements. Moreover, at several moments, the authenticity of his narrative was reinforced by the emotion that his stories provoked in him. Mr. Agripino cried many times, as when he reenacted a dialogue about the name of the church that he was constructing, at the moment when he himself had chosen the name "Jesus," not yet knowing that this choice responded to a higher designation:

> "This person who appeared to you, this dark young man who sent the message, spoke about the name of the church?" "He said, Mr. Agripino." "What name?" "Jesus." Do you see? So, up to then he had already given 80% closing the story. How amazing. When he said this [sobs]—I cry easily—my mouth fell open. The name that I had chosen? Jesus.

His crying not only authenticated what he was narrating but also, in this particular case, attested to his connection with the divine order.

The concrete aspect that marked his narrative reached its highest point when Mr. Agripino decided to end our dialogue at the City Hall and take us to the site where he was building the sanctuary. During the interview, he had already said several times that we needed to visit the sanctuary someday.

> I would like you to go see it, frankly. Let's make a date for you to see the gate that I am building there. I am making a *via crucis* ... Like this: the entrance is here, and here is the church. It is one mile from the entrance, at the highway, to the church. I am making a *via crucis* like this: first station; after 500 feet, the second station; 500 feet, the third station. The characters—all life size. Jesus? 5′11. The cross? 9′10. Mary? 5′2. The centurian? 5′11. I am making such a beautiful thing.

A little after this passage, nevertheless, the suggestion that we visit the sanctuary became imperative and the object of negotiation:

AOLF: I would like you to come with me to see the sanctuary, right now.
LH: We can see. Let me just ask a last little question.
AOLF: The last one.
LH: Or then the second to last?

AOLF: We can go there, talking on the way. One thing I like to do is talk.

Thus was consummated his subversion of the setting aspect of the interview: "we can go there, we can talk on our way there." From the controlled environment of his office at the City Hall, where we had installed ourselves with our papers and a tape recorder, we set out for an unexpected location.

"A Young, Darkish Man Appeared to Me"

The sanctuary is located in a town next to Presidente Prudente, on a lot that belonged to one of the Unoeste campuses. It already had tanks for raising fish for the agronomy bachelor's degree, and there were also plans to have a section for the tourism degree, which would be focused on the faithful who visit the site, as Paulo Lima, Mr. Agripino's son, informed us in another interview carried out for the same project. The overlapping of the higher education activities and religious ones was once more in evidence by this confluence.

Although the recording of the interview had finished at the City Hall, and not having a formal record of the trip to the sanctuary, the surprising nature of this visit impacted our memories. The ride to the sanctuary was made in two cars: in the first held Mr. Agripino, the two of us, and the driver; in the second were three security guards. At that time, it did not escape us that less than three months earlier, our interviewee—the owner of many large landholdings in the region—had blocked a march of about 600 people for the Rural Landless Workers Movement (MST) in the city of Presidente Prudente.

The same two cars followed us at a very low speed as, once there, we walked through the packed earth listening to Mr. Agripino's explanations about the *via crucis* that was being built and the huge church that would be located at the top of the hill. For almost forty minutes, we listened to the details of this project that, according to our interviewee, would become a "second Aparecida do Norte," referring to the city that is the main center for Catholic pilgrimages in all of Latin America, complete with processions, commemorative dates, and religious feasts in devotion to Our Lady of Aparecida, the patron saint of Brazil.

We can still remember our stupefaction at finding ourselves in that situation, as if we were in a movie. The interview with the founder of a university, in the context of a project financed by a federal research agency, was, to a certain extent, supplanted by the immersion in the local political situation and in the religious cosmology of the interviewee.

When, around two decades later, we decided to return to the unexpected interview for this project, we discovered that the body of Mr. Agripino, who had passed away on March 7, 2018, at the age of 86, is entombed in a crypt in the Jesus of Nazareth church and that the Home of God sanctuary is the number one attraction (of two) in its municipality, according to the website TripAdvisor.

We also discovered that returning to the transcript of the interview, in a different context from the original project, allowed us to do an equally unexpected reading. We had not noticed how the interviewee referred to Jesus who rode in his car: "a young, darkish man [*moreninho*] of about 30 years," "a dark skinned [*moreno*] who appeared to me." What was it that Mr. Agripino wanted to say with this qualification that appears four times in the transcript? We did not ask him. Likewise, an undoubtedly racist section of the transcript that we had not included in the interview version edited and published in the book deriving from the project now caught our eyes.

In another of his digressions, Mr. Agripino talked about the contrast between two visits he made to Paris. In the first visit, he was amazed at the city's cleanliness and asked himself how long it would take Brazil to reach that point. In the second, about fifteen years later, during the Mitterrand government (he made a point of mentioning this), the city was very dirty, according to him, because of the immigrants, especially those from Africa:

> So, the second time that I went to Paris, there were colored people there who would crap and have sex in the middle of the street. And another thing: there were negros there with five or six women because every child gets $800 in family wage there. So, the black men had many women and many children, ten, fifteen children, and Mitterrand raised them.

Given the goals of our original project, that was about the trajectory of universities, we did not approach this discussion during the recording, and we eliminated this section when editing the interviews. It is worth remembering that any research project imposes limits, both from the point of view of the questions we favor, and of the scope of the results. In this particular case, we were not discussing the profile of the interviewees, but rather the trajectory of the universities. Moreover, we had to take into consideration the length of the book we would publish.

This returning to Mr. Agripino's story allowed us to update a discussion we had recently had about the re-use of interviews stored in oral history archives (Heymann and Alberti 2018). Oral history interviews are often seen as "dated" or, as we said then, "hostages to the motivations that created them" (14). In this text, by the way, we mentioned our previous paper on the connections between politics, higher education, and religiosity in the interview with Mr. Agripino (Alberti and Heymann 2003) as an example of re-use motivated by topics that the interview prompted, even when such topics were not originally on the agenda of the project.

A second re-use is what we are doing now, in a new historical context, in which the race question has become more urgent and visible, and ideological polarization between the left and right (foreshadowed in Mr. Agripino's criticism of Mitterrand) has become a hot issue. The encouragement to discuss an unexpected interview made it possible to perceive that, aside from the other subversions that occurred when we were recording Mr. Agripino and the visit to the sanctuary, there were layers of his speech that we did not explore and that can still be the object of an unexpected reading of the source.

Both the first and the second re-uses of Mr. Agripino's interview require us to reflect methodically on the oral sources and the conditions of its production. It was helpful that we have access to the raw transcript of the interview—rereading it allowed us to become aware of content that could have been lost. Preserving the original document and its metadata is fundamental for scholarly research. Aside from this, the idea we are defending, of re-using the interviews, calls attention to the importance of producing field notes. In them, details of the meeting and of the interviewers' impressions can gain more relevance within oral history products. If we had prepared this kind of material at the time of our visit to the sanctuary in 2002 and had not had to rely only on our memories, perhaps we could have had still more layers to our discussion here.

It does not escape our notice that the interview that least fit into the project on private universities, the most unexpected one, is the one that provoked the most reflections. Precisely because of its imponderable nature, it challenged the bias of the research and the researchers. Unexpected interviews can, then, raise questions that are not in the original purview of the projects and become memorable moments in the later trajectory of researchers.

References

Alberti, Verena, and Luciana Heymann. 2001. Um segmento heterogêneo: trajetórias de universidades privadas no Brasil. *IV Encontro Regional Sudeste de História Oral. Dimensões da história oral. Rio de Janeiro: Casa Oswaldo Cruz/Fundação Oswaldo Cruz/Associação Brasileira de História Oral.* https://bibliotecadigital.fgv.br/dspace/bitstream/handle/10438/6800/1226.pdf?sequence=1&isAllowed=y.

———, eds. 2002. *Trajetórias da universidade privada no Brasil: depoimentos ao CPDOC-FGV.* Brasília, DF: CAPES / Rio de Janeiro: Fundação Getúlio Vargas/CPDOC.

———. 2003. Jesus de Nazaré andou no meu carro: ensino superior, política e religião em Presidente Prudente. *V Encontro Regional Sudeste de História Oral. Diálogos Contemporâneos: Cultura e Memória.* https://bibliotecadigital.fgv.br/dspace/bitstream/handle/10438/6776/1369.pdf?sequence=1&isAllowed=y.

Amado, Janaína. 1995. O grande mentiroso: Tradição, veracidade e imaginação em história oral. *História* 14: 125–136.

Heymann, Luciana, and Verena Alberti. 2018. Acervos de história oral: um patrimônio silencioso? In *História oral e patrimônio cultural: potencialidades e transformações,* ed. Leticia Bauer and Viviane Trindade Borges, 11–29. São Paulo: Letra e Voz.

CHAPTER 16

Metabolizing the Leftovers of Memory

Daisy Perelmutter

As researchers in the field of oral history, we are enthusiasts of the craft involved in the production of our sources. Aware and zealous of its plasticity, we are both witnesses and agents of the multiple contingencies that affect its construction. Nevertheless, as we share the results of our research and/or help to build public and private archives, the work behind these delicate documents is not always spotlighted or even revealed, reinforcing the phantasmagoria of our theories as a species of "illumination" disassociated from the experience and the empirical data. This volume's challenge, to speak openly about drifting and supposed lack of success in our work, is a unique opportunity to keep breaking with any prudishness that might persist.

Inspired by this provocation, I will share two experiences from different projects, followed by a brief reflection.

Case 1

The first case is an interview carried out during my doctoral research, concluded in 2004, titled *Intérpretes do Desassossego: Memórias sensíveis de artistas brasileiros de ascendência judaica* [Interpreters of Disquiet: Sensitive Memories of Brazilian Artists of Jewish Ancestry]. My objective with this work was to understand the immaterial legacies that formed these subjects, how Jewish heritage was transmitted and inscribed in them, as well as the intensity of its reverberation in the contemporaneous sensitivity of each of my interlocutors.

D. Perelmutter (✉)
Escola de Artes, Ciências e Humanidades da USP (EACH/USP), São Paulo, Brazil

The interviewee in question (among a dozen subjects whom I interviewed on this theme) is a playwright whose professional career is long and greatly respected. He accepts the invitation to cooperate with my research on the condition that the interview takes place in a public place (a restaurant in a shopping center food court!) on day X, when he would be passing through São Paulo, as he did not live in the city. I accept the conditions, obviously, although I am apprehensive about the unfavorable setting for the type of work that we will do together: I will stimulate the narrator to think about his heritage and share the journey constructing his existential patrimony.

The meeting takes place under the terms established and, notwithstanding the expected interferences (noisy, impersonal, and chaotic space), what catches my attention from the beginning is the interviewee's hesitation to recall and rework his Jewish memories. He begins his narrative with a negative, saying that a Jewish heritage practically was not conveyed to him and that his childhood had few such expressions. Not in the way his parents had raised him, not in the schools he attended, not in the secular nature of his family, not in his relationships with his non-Jewish friends in the neighborhood, not in the nonobservance of the holidays, not in the various mixed marriages, and not in his chosen profession. His *nots* were punctuated mechanically in the cadence of his testimony. His "nots" seemed to me less a "no" to his supposed "weak Judaism" and more a sign of his refusal to dig into these formative affects and re-read them based on the present.

His ambivalence to accept the invitation while refusing the revisitation it involved—a hypothesis I elaborated in that context, which gave me the sensation of an ill-fated encounter—took a surprising turn. A few months after the interview, when I sent him the transcription for verification, the interviewee returned it with some corrections in the body of the text. He also included a handwritten note saying that if I were to interview him again, he would certainly be more pertinent and get more involved. The note, sent long after the finalization of the interview, in a way confirmed my interpretation of the interviewee's evasive tone.

His ambivalent relationship with his Jewish heritage, initially expressed as negligible, revealed itself long after the setting. His peremptory "not," attributed to an immobilized past, transformed itself into a "maybe," into a "yes and no," into a past that could be shaken by the present, through a "nomadic particle of difference," alluding to the Philosophy of Difference of Gilles Deleuze and Felix Guattari. Ignoring this interpretive clue—the note—as if it were exogenous to the body of knowledge produced would waste the potential that oral history research has to not relegate an experience to the inertia of its own course, but rather to engender new sparks, new significances, new readings, new tasks, and new utopias. Memory as an ethical act, as affirmed by Agnes Heller (1985): the experience of self-determination in contrast to the condition of being pushed by circumstances.

Case 2

The second case is that of an interview carried out in 1993 with an important Black musician from the "Vanguarda Paulista" [São Paulo Avant-Garde], an underground musical movement of the 1980s in the city of São Paulo that brought together musicians with different styles through their opposition to the dictates of the record industry of the time. This musician was held by his professional colleagues and music critics to be one of the most brilliant of this generation. However, he suffered from his image of "marginality," practically ignored by the big radio and television stations and the record labels. The interview was undertaken for the "Memory of Brazilian Artistic Production" collection developed from 1989 to 1995 by the oral history program of the Museum of Image and Sound (MIS) of São Paulo.

Founded in 1970 as a state museum, MIS, considered a pioneer in the building of oral history archives, was led by a group of prominent artists and intellectuals—among them Rudá de Andrade, son of the modernist writer Oswald de Andrade (1890–1954), one of the principal promoters of the legendary Modern Art Week of 1922. It immediately began an ambitious project on the cultural memory of the city of São Paulo, organizing joint efforts and expeditions to collect disparate cultural manifestations that, according to them, were threatened with extinction. These collections, constructed on an emergency basis with no coordination among them and without methodological rigor, were replaced in 1981 by a program to build a well-structured archive of sound and images. Marked by in-depth research and concerned with the preservation/cataloging/availability of its collections, the initiative gained enormous respectability. The oral history program was well known inside the institution, in the oral history community, and in other public and private cultural entities in the city. Thus, an invitation to give an interview at the MIS, at that time, was, without a doubt, a motive for flattery and jubilation. On these "feast" days when we received our illustrious guests, the invisible and not very glamorous work of the oral history program had its moment of epiphany.

As with almost all institutional projects there was no possibility of carrying out a second talk with the same interviewee due to the limites resources. Our aim, therefore, was to get the most out of the first, and only, encounter. There was no possibility of having a rough draft of the experience. The interview had to "deliver," or we would have lost the opportunity to integrate the report into our archives. It was difficult, then, to temper the expectations of the staff. It was always at high voltage.

The musician in question—iconic composer, lyricist, and singer of the 1980s, brilliant, singular, theatrical, transgressive, and experimental—had been willing to give his statement to the museum in a joint initiative of the music and oral history program. On the arranged day, we waited with all the ceremony (informal but reverential) that he deserved. More than one and a half hours late and after several attempts to contact him, a member of his family alerted us that he was sleeping and that the only possibility of guaranteeing his commitment would be to pick him up at his home in the neighborhood of Penha.

Motivated by the spirit of volunteerism that characterized our work as a team, whose excellence depended greatly on these personal inputs, we used our personal resources to get to this encounter. After traveling the immense distance between the neighborhoods of Jardim Europa in the western part of São Paulo and Penha in the east, we found him lethargic. In response to the mediation of his family and our insistent appeals, we convinced him to accompany us to the museum so that we could register his testimony. We felt that the preamble of our meeting had not revealed itself as promising. As we began our conversation, the pressure cooker of anguish and resentment (which were not uncommon in his public statements and his commentaries on stage) blew its top. None of our questions or stimulation gave him a hook for reflecting on his unquestionably beautiful artistic life and career.

Like one of those old broken records, we repeatedly heard the refrain of the marginality that he had encountered, his frustration about his lack of commercial recognition, the material precarity in which he lived, and the indifference of the famous musicians from Bahia (composers and singers of enormous influence in musical circles, whose seal of approval usually, at that time, corresponded to an almost immediate opening of professional opportunities) in relation to his work. All of these complaints were scattered throughout his conversation.

Once we overcame our sadness at witnessing his pain, we recognized that the catharsis expressed in the context of the interview could be related to his sensation of a present in imminent danger—a crushed present, a present that had no dialogue with the past and no perspective of a future. A somber image of death in life. It was an account very distant from what would be an "exemplary" testimony, for bitterness, conquests, and resilience marked it. Thus, it is, without a doubt, a historical portrait of sentiments that accompanied the artist in the last years of his life, which ended less than ten years later. If oral history, on the one hand, has an ethical commitment to favor and present subjects in their whole extension, then it also has the duty to embrace the indignant scream of those who feel constricted or obstructed, so that this outcry can be heard beyond the walls of their own invisible territory. And if this pain was, without a doubt, very appropriate, it was and still is that of many other Blacks and of many other artists considered marginal or peripheral.

Oral History: Total Listening

In one of his key texts, "Tentando aprender um pouquinho: Algumas reflexões sobre a ética na história oral" [Trying to Learn a Little: Some Reflections on the Ethics of Oral History], Alessandro Portelli (1997) affirms that practically all the people with whom he had the privilege of conversing enriched his experience and surprised him in some measure. Brazilian filmmaker Eduardo Coutinho (1933–2014), no less generous with life and with humanity, stated that all that exists in the world should, in some manner, be observed and worshipped. These two relevant references have served to guide my dialogue with my interviewees.

The creation of a space adequate for dialogue is the *parti pris* of our craft/career/vocation. For the interview setting to function promisingly, incorporating the memories and sensations triggered in the interviewee by the interviewer, objective conditions are important (adequate space, availability of time, silence in the surroundings, temperature of the surroundings, among other prosaic factors). Nevertheless, what cannot be overlooked in the production of oral history interviews are the subjective qualities of the interviewer, innate or developed through practice, such as curiosity and tolerance. The delicate interpellation of the interviewee is not limited to fulfilling the protocol of good manners, a warning consecrated in our field. Without deep understanding of and also continence toward what is being elaborated by our counterpart, there is no freshness in the encounter or knowledge coming from the greater or lesser quality of this connection, absolutely unique and singular.

The musculature gained with practice (maturity, in this context, is definitely an important asset) helps us to modulate our prior expectations in relation to testimonies, developing a profound commitment to the present of that presence we find ourselves confronting. Resilience to the choices made when interviewing does not put into perspective, or even invalidate, the nodal importance of the preparatory work of research. We can only visualize the "leftovers" and the "deviations" generated in/by the interviewees precisely because during our preparation we have created avenues and paths along which we suppose our discussion partner does travel with regularity or will travel, stimulated by our provocation.

There are innumerable oblique ways for interviewees to respond to the interviewers' request for them to remember. They range from a simple inversion of the order of what could be considered the narrative's central refrain (valuing instead adjacent and peripheral issues) to a categorical refusal to consider what is being requested, insisting on some other seemingly sudden key. A parenthesis is needed on this concept of "central" and "peripheral": the invitation to participate in an oral history project is usually justified by the pertinence of the interviewee to a determined group/community/collective/class or by their recognition as an eyewitness to structures/social dynamics/historical period under study.

This is an ingenious art: to identify and collect these "leftovers" that intercept the stories and to articulate them in a way that makes sense with the other data collected. This ability—similar to the perfect pitch with which musicians seem to be blessed—is also useful in our work. To hear noise where there is silence and to identify silence where there is a profusion of sound and noise. And to be aware that the composition nurtured by our provocations and interpellations begins with the first contacts made with the interviewee and concludes (artificially, always) long after the interview as such ends.

Generous with the "leftovers," the oral historian should also do this, equally, with all of the stages of the process of producing oral sources: researching/identify the problem; selecting the network of interviewees; contacting the protagonists; writing the list of questions; producing and scheduling the interview; transcribing/revising the text cross-referenced with the audio; sending the text for corrections and observations by the interviewee; making a final analysis.

If this dynamism and breadth of our field surprise us by revealing new objects and new perspectives for analysis, this plasticity is certainly due to the reverence directed to the expressions/questions that arise in the process of "hoeing" the source of the research. As field researchers, each of us actively participates in the constant refit of our own theoretical edifice. To observe, index, relate, interpret, and diffuse what is configured singularly in our experiences is a form of enriching the epistemological debate on oral history, broadening its reach and its analytical possibilities.

References

Heller, Agnes. 1985. *O cotidiano e a história*. Rio de Janeiro: Paz e Terra.
Portelli, Alessandro. 1997. Tentando aprender um pouquinho: Algumas reflexões sobre a ética na história oral. *Projeto História* 15: 13–49.

CHAPTER 17

The Unexpected in an Archive: Interferences in a Soccer Memory Collection

Bernardo Borges Buarque de Hollanda
and Raphael Rajão Ribeiro

This chapter examines a collection of oral history interviews produced within a particular institutional setting: the "Memories of Soccer" project, carried out by the Museum of Image and Sound (MIS), in São Paulo, in the first half of the 1980s. We will address the possibilities afforded by working with collections of interviews conducted by third parties, decades apart, and the unexpected aspects arising from the use of narratives recorded at a time when oral history was not yet well established and widespread. The chapter also highlights the unexpected conduct of interviewers who imposed their personal research interests and discussions inherent to sports journalism over the public purpose of a project to preserve Brazilians' collective memory of soccer.

When we first accessed the recordings in this collection, our expectations in reusing the materials were to access contents about the life trajectory of players, coaches, and sports columnists. However, a closer examination of the data presented us with other possibilities of usage and analysis, not previously planned by the research, which was initially focused on the interviewees themselves. Notably, we were attracted by the record of the thoughts from a

B. B. B. de Hollanda (✉)
Escola de Ciências Sociais, Centro de Pesquisa e Documentação da Fundação Getúlio Vargas (CPDOC/FGV), Rio de Janeiro, Brazil

R. R. Ribeiro
Fundação de Cultura, Prefeitura Municipal de Belo Horizonte, Belo Horizonte, Brazil

character who initially performed backstage at the Museum, since he was one of the project's managers: José Sebastião Witter (1933–2014), who was a prominent professor at the University of São Paulo (USP).

Strictly speaking, Witter emerged before our incursion into the collection's recordings, when Bernardo, one of the authors of this chapter, interviewed him in 2013 (Hollanda and Alfonsi 2013), a year before his death. This interview aimed to better understand the career of one of the introducers of soccer studies into Brazilian universities in the 1980s. The interaction with Witter led us to learn about the existence of a series of recorded accounts from that same decade, thanks to the initiative of the so-called Oral History Program at MIS, as detailed in a guide to the Museum's collections.

The need for more information about this program encouraged us to conduct a new interview, now with professor, historian, and photographer Boris Kossoy (Hollanda and Alfonsi 2018), director of MIS at that time. His administration, from 1980 to 1983, was responsible for the museological initiatives to produce oral recordings relating to a plethora of areas and subjects, including "History of Brazilian Soccer," as the project was initially named. Although Kossoy had taken the role of general mentor of the Museum's oral recordings, he granted Witter the responsibility for selecting the athletes and other figures from the field, as well as preparing the lists of questions and conducting the interviews.

One of the first aspects to draw our attention upon engaging with the sound recordings of MIS was the discrepancy between the guiding principles for oral history recording at that time and those adopted by us, almost two decades later, in our own research. As an example, we may mention the implementation of the projects "Soccer, Memory, and Heritage" and "Territories of Cheering," respectively, dedicated to gathering oral testimonies from former players of the Brazilian National Team and founders of fan bases in the city of São Paulo (Hollanda 2017a, b). To structure the interviews, both projects were based on the methodology presented by the *Manual de história oral* [Oral History Manual] (2005), by Verena Alberti, first published in 1990.

The book is a landmark in Brazil, and its second part, "The Interview," delineates oral history's constitutive steps and general procedures, from research and preparing questions to ways to end an interview. The instrumental nature of the volume, which since its initial publication then has oriented many individual and collective activities in oral history in Brazil, aims to clarify some fundamental issues, such as the interviewer's role in conducting the interview. Among the principles she lists, that are central to oral history, Alberti stresses that "during the recording of an interview, one should dedicate their full attention towards the interviewee, not only for the importance of what they say, but also because this demonstration of interest encourages them to speak" (2005, 114–5).

The narrator's central role in an interview contrasts with the sharp, loud interference of interviewers that we identified in the practice of the MIS Oral History Program, at least as exercised under the leadership of Witter, who stood out in the recordings by frequently overlapping his speech over the guests'—which alerted us to traits of oral recordings produced before the wide dissemination of oral history methodologies. Thus, it is not a matter of requiring interviewers to carry values only subsequently brought to a consensus, risking an anachronism, but to understand how this posture affects the result of the project as a whole. In a recently published chapter, researchers Luciana Heymann and the already-mentioned Verena Alberti (2018) observe that using third-party oral history recordings is still minimal in historical research, disproportionate to the dissemination of programs and projects. Furthermore, when it happens, this use is often ambivalent in its understanding of oral recordings as sources—they are embedded rather than critically analyzed.

Heymann and Alberti point out important questions put to the investigator by examining a collection created by a third party:

> Creating these collections often serves to justify investments in oral history projects, using the argument that they represent public goods. This argument is based not only on the appreciation of records of life experiences, but on the premise that, once recorded, these experiences can be utilized to consider questions not actually raised at the moment of their creation. (2018, 13)

In order to reflect on the reuse of interviews and the possible unexpected aspects that may arise, we will attempt to put the subject into context, detail the circumstances involving the MIS oral history collection, and describe how the interferences detected in the interviews resulted from conflicts between Witter's personal goals as an interviewer and the purpose of the institutional project. If such intrusions somehow pushed him away from what has been established as best practices in oral history, they, on the other hand, enabled the unexpected digressions in his interactions with the interviewees to serve as clues to rebuild the professor's thinking on the history of Brazilian soccer.

Based on the initial survey from the data available on the Museum's website, we identified around 40 long interviews linked to the "Memory of Soccer" project. Facing the vast yet under-explored content, since no analytical publication resulted from the original project, we considered the possibility of dividing the collection into groups such as coaches, goalkeepers, and other sports experts, to facilitate the analysis of the dozens of interviews.

Considering our own experience producing oral history interviews, we expected to find accounts roughly structured around the interviewee's life or particular chosen topics. However, contrary to these expectations, the recordings seemed much looser and combined life story elements with debates specific to the "sports talk" (Hollanda 2013) often observed in radio and television discussions.

Consequently, the interviews recorded for the Museum would ask their subjects to revisit memories, but also to deliver diagnoses—or simply express an opinion—on the current status of Brazilian soccer, impacted by the circumstances relating to the World Cup of 1982 in Spain. As commonly witnessed in discussions on television or in group talks at bars, these debates would see interviewees and interviewers engage in long discussions, presenting their theories on that sport and its development in the country of Brazil and the city of São Paulo. Among the interviewers, Professor José Sebastião Witter was by far the most proactive, presenting data on the soccer situation and, more specifically, the battle for the world title—be it the preparations, the competition itself and its matches, or its feedback, following the national team's traumatic disqualification against Italy, in 1982, later nicknamed "The Sarrià Tragedy" by the press, after the name of the stadium in the city of Barcelona where the match took place.

Upon recognizing this unusual "voice" (of the interviewer) amid the "Memories of Soccer" recordings, we realized that this collection presented an opportunity to learn more about the mind of a scholar who played an important role in defining soccer as a research subject, especially in the field of history. It is worth noting the symbolism in the year of 1982 (not by chance the year a World Cup took place) for sports social studies and the professor's role. It was the year in which two compilations were published, both seen as milestones in the assimilation of the subject by Brazilian academia: *Universo do Futebol* [Universe of Soccer], organized by Roberto DaMatta (1982), with articles summarizing urban anthropology and sociology research, and *Futebol e Cultura* [*Soccer and Culture*], coordinated by José Sebastião Witter and José Carlos Sebe Bom Meihy (1982), with essays written by historians.

Despite his seminal role in organizing the compilation and leading the project "Memories of Soccer," Witter confined himself, in the broader context of his career, to producing short introductory articles on the subject. Thus, little is known about his reflections and analyses on the subject—some of which, incidentally, were never published. Even though the series of interviews conducted at MIS had long been known, given the lack of transcripts, we only came to notice the professor's strong presence as the original recordings were more thoroughly scrutinized. Even if fragmented, his free and apparently unimpeded interventions during the interviews carried important thoughts and theories about the history of the soccer. To prove this point, we will now enter the structure and dynamics of the interviews through a selection of four interviews conducted by him.

A Topsy-Turvy Interaction: The Interviewer's Speech

In a 1982 interview for another oral history project housed at MIS, named "Brazilian Studies," Professor José Sebastião Witter revealed his primary intellectual ambition at the time: "this project, everybody's tired of hearing me talk about it ... the greatest project in my life. A project to tell the history of Brazilian soccer." Not surprisingly, the scholar had initiated the aforementioned series of interviews, "Memories of Soccer," at the Museum in 1981, the year before, originally under the title "History of Brazilian Soccer." Just as the journalist Mario Rodrigues Filho had done in the 1940s with a series of interviews with pioneers of Rio de Janeiro soccer for *O Globo* newspaper to later write the classic *O negro no futebol brasileiro* [Blacks in Brazilian Soccer] (2003), Witter intended to collect oral testimonies from outstanding sports personalities to deliver later what he expected to be his greatest academic achievement.

Being involved with the supervision of preservation and research institutions both within and outside the University of São Paulo, as acting supervisor of the Public Archives of the State of São Paulo from 1977 to 1988, José Sebastião Witter would never come to complete his "great work." Still, from 1981 to 1984, he led this pioneering experiment so relevant to the history of soccer in Brazil. As the "Memories of Soccer" project coordinator, the researcher relied on many interview partners—both as interviewees and as co-interviewers.

Throughout two years, from late 1981 to the end of 1983, his interviewing became more intense, conducted once every other week. Witter, later, in an interview of 1993, recalled that those were busy times at MIS. At such times, he could not always gather all interviewers and would end up guiding some of the accounts alone or joined by less experienced interlocutors. The series of four recordings commented in this chapter refers to such cases, which took place between 1982 and 1984: the interviews with José Poy (1982), Luís Augusto Maltoni (1983), Rui Campos (1983), and Alberto Helena Junior (1984).

An unexpected procedure took place in them. With no other researchers to share the conduct of the conversation, the professor felt comfortable to test some of his theories—or opinions—on Brazilian soccer, which would likely guide how his great work would be organized. Unlike what would be expected from someone trained in oral history or focused on the institutional goal of generating a standard series for public consultation, the professor would hold true debates with his subjects, delivering his own long digressions, disregarding the guest's point of view.

He would present anecdotal episodes, such as when he went to the stadium to watch Brazilian national team star Leônidas da Silva play his first game for São Paulo Soccer Club, in 1942. Witter lived in a city in the interior of the state at that time and took a train to the capital with his father to watch the game. Far from the rectitude expected from an interviewer, his condition as a passionate club fan would be frequently pointed out, especially in the conversations with former athletes of the club he rooted for. Likewise, his experience coaching amateur teams in São Paulo and his engagement with the sport at the University of São Paulo would be brought up or even exalted.

The recordings carried out by Witter followed a certain structure, dominated by recurring themes that help understand his thinking about soccer. All interviews would begin with the interviewee being asked to present a brief "biography," listing remarkable events, and end with their "Brazilian dream team of all times." One could say that while the initial question related to oral history interview procedures, the latter involved a type of question more usual in sports talk. Incidentally, 1970s and 1980s São Paulo was greatly influenced by a weekly sports magazine named *Placar* and it is possible to note that the last question had links, deliberate or not, to the style of questions asked by journalists specialized in soccer interviews.

Depending on the guest's professional status, Witter would introduce topics representing his personal concerns or fundamental tenets. In this sense, his interventions enable us to draw a map of topics the professor considered to be central to understanding the development of soccer in Brazil, topics that would possibly shape his "great work," never written or published. These thoughts would mingle with then-current hot topics and with the researcher's formulations based on his experiences, idiosyncrasies, and research ambitions.

In an interview with José Poy, former goalkeeper and coach of São Paulo Soccer Club's minor league teams, Witter describes an episode that could strongly confirm his view of the dereliction of a national sports culture.

JSW: I lived this; you know? I've experienced this at the São Paulo [the team]. And I'll tell you why. When I went through this experience at the São Paulo [team], I experienced taking the boys [to tryouts] and seeing them being ruled out even though I knew they shouldn't be.

JP: But quite often, you know, boys will get emotional at tryouts and that's normal.

JSW: Sure.

JP: And we're the ones who have to watch these boys when we work at the minor leagues, we have to be patient, we have to watch them [going to tryouts] three, four, five times.

JSW: Yeah, I tell you this because it's nice to hear you say it. Because at the time, out there was [coach Rubens] Minelli, directing the professional team and on the other side—I can't recall the coach's name, I don't retain names—I think it was Cidinho, something like that ... And I took him to the São Paulo [team]. 'Cause I was always in the field. And there was a team that was a team of aces. They were kids—all aces. I took four of them [to tryouts].

JP: And none of them had any use ...

JSW: None! Now, when I went there and said: "Listen, I'm not here to promote anyone. But I want to know why you ruled them out after only five minutes." "There's a hundred of 'em, a hundred, two hundred ..." And I said: "But geez!" "And one more thing, you brought me four shorties. And I'd rather have a bad tall player than a short ace." Well, you know there's all a ...

JP: But this is ... I respect that view, but I think it's completely wrong.

JSW: Oh, good.

JP: Because talent has no size.

Long sections such as this may be found in the interviews conducted by José Sebastião Witter. In such a relaxed environment, he seemed to abandon institutional concerns with the assembly and preservation of a museum collection that future generations would access. Aside from recording the interviewee's memories, it seemed he was testing his own theories on Brazilian soccer. He does that as he points out the prevalence of a view favoring athletes with greater physiques rather than scrawny skilled players. Countless are the examples in which he repeats such procedures, as in his debate with former São Paulo Soccer Club and Brazilian National Team midfielder Rui Campos over how the early victory mood spread by the press would have been crucial to the national defeats in the 1950 and 1982 World Cups. At the time, he took advantage of the presence of an athlete who played in 1950 to share his research findings based on newspapers from that period (interview with Campos in 1983).

These and other passages indicate that upon revisiting interviews conducted almost 40 years ago for the MIS "Memories of Soccer" collection, among the entanglement of memories emerges the unlikely (according to current scholarly standards) loud presence of interviewer José Sebastião Witter. A researcher who, despite performing an important role in consolidating soccer as an academic topic, wrote only occasionally about the subject, with minor non-scholarly pieces in the 1980s and 1990s.

In the brief material he published, we come across the same periodization and spectrum of themes he would bring to the interviews he conducted (Witter 1996; Meihy and Witter 1982). His monumental academic project was never completed. But, as he points out, interviewed in 1982:

> I always have and I think this is what I'm searching for, and my friends draw my attention to this: my desire for a great work. I mean, the intention of creating a masterpiece. (...) I think this coexistence, this is something in my mind, this coexistence is such an important thing to me, I think it's the piece we should do and not that great work in six volumes that I wish to do about the history of Brazilian soccer.

Although he never came to write the six volumes of his ambitious "History of Brazilian Soccer," José Sebastião Witter was responsible for creating one of the most significant sports oral history collections in Brazil. In his own affectionate and gregarious way, he could gather enthusiastic researchers and dozens of interviewees, entrusting his true great work to posterity: the "Memories of Soccer" collection.

Four decades after the interviews conducted for the MIS Oral History program, the collection remains as an important source both for soccer scholars and people interested in the methodological issues raised by researchers who rely on oral testimonies for historical research. The search for evidence from the past in the reuse of interviews conducted by third parties shows us how certain aspects in methodology compete with the goals established by their makers. In the words of Boris Kossoy, director at the time the soccer project was implemented:

> As a whole, such a collection of records [the MIS Oral History Program] provides countless data to the process of recovering our memories on many areas of

knowledge. Achievements of invaluable importance to the preservation of Brazilian cultural heritage took place in this institution. An example are the recordings of interviews with personalities of unquestionable relevance in their areas of expertise (...). The capturing and systematic production of testimonies through the oral history program developed in the past two years has been one of its priorities. (Kossoy, 1982, 5)

Not quite as a ban (which would configure an impertinent anachronism), what we have sought to emphasize is how the repeated interference and interruptions in the interview dynamics turned out to reveal a different side of dialog and interaction between interview partners. This topsy-turvy interaction thus emerges as one of many unexpected aspects that may originate from the reuse of oral history collections and archives, bringing to light theoretical and methodological challenges that tend to grow deeper as the deployment of these document collections becomes more recurrent.

References

Alberti, Verena. 2005. *Manual de história oral*. Rio de Janeiro: Editora FGV.
DaMatta, Roberto, ed. 1982. *Universo do futebol: esporte e sociedade brasileira*. Rio de Janeiro: Edições Pinakoteke.
Heymann, Luciana, and Verena Alberti. 2018. Acervos de história oral: um patrimônio silencioso? In *História oral e patrimônio cultural: potencialidades e transformações*, ed. Leticia Bauer and Viviane Trindade Borges, 11–29. São Paulo: Letra e Voz.
Hollanda, Bernardo Borges Buarque de. 2013. Mesas-redondas: da falação esportiva ao futebol falado. In *Olho no lance: Ensaios sobre futebol e televisão*, ed. Bernardo Borges Buarque de Hollanda and Victor Andrade de Melo. Rio de Janeiro: 7Letras.
———. 2017a. Futebol, memória e relatos orais. *História Oral* 20 (1): 101–123.
———. 2017b. O uso da história oral no estudo do futebol: etapas metodológicas de uma experiência de pesquisa qualitativa com Torcidas Organizadas na cidade de São Paulo. *Publicatio UEPG* 25 (2): 187–201.
Hollanda, Bernardo Borges Buarque de, and Daniela Alfonsi. 2013. Entrevista com José Sebastião Witter. *Esporte e Sociedade* 21: 1–11.
———. 2018. Entrevista com Boris Kossoy. *Estudos Históricos* 31 (65): 495–520.
Kossoy, Boris, ed. 1982. *Cadernos n. 3—Catálogo de Depoimentos (1970–1982)*. São Paulo: Imprensa Oficial.
Meihy, José Carlos Sebe Bom, and José Sebastião Witter. 1982. *Futebol e cultura: Coletânea de estudos*. São Paulo: Imprensa Oficial/Arquivo do Estado.
Rodrigues Filho, Mario. 2003. *O negro no futebol brasileiro*. Rio de Janeiro: Mauad.
Witter, José Sebastião. 1990. *O que é futebol*. São Paulo: Editora Brasiliense.
———. 1996. *Breve história do futebol brasileiro*. São Paulo: FTD.

CHAPTER 18

Commentary: Revisiting Oral Sources: The Unexpected and the Anticipated in Oral History Praxis

Jorge Eduardo Aceves Lozano

THE UNEXPECTED AS A MEMORY-MAKER

This book invites us to reflect on an issue integral to oral history praxis: the emergence of the unexpected, the unpredictable, that which suddenly or surreptitiously appeared in communication, in oral interview situations. It is rare to conduct this type of revisitation of our oral sources, highlighting what a closer look reveals upon a second reading performed sometime later or by an analyst who is not the creator of the original interview. Nonetheless, undertaking such analyses and reflections of our own work, applying doses of self-criticism to our processes as well as to their results, is both a necessary and creative task if our field is to advance.

Oral history, as an intersubjective encounter between people, produces meaningful interactions and a body of accounts that flourish between those who narrate their life and those who, by talking and questioning, conduct the interviews. In a dialogue, the imponderable often emerges, despite planning and elaborating instruments and devices intended to guide and control the flow of information. Neither the *a priori* agreements nor the shared expectations prevent the emergence of the unexpected. What is not anticipated nor

---

J. E. Aceves Lozano (✉)
Centro de Investigações e Estudos Superiores em Antropologia Social, Guadalajara, México
e-mail: jaceves@ciesas.edu.mx

planned erupts and can strain communication, pushing us away from the ideal route we may have had in mind and paving the way for new themes, situations, conditions and especially, novel and additional goals brought to the conversation table by those who narrate their experience, their lives.

Usually, when the oral interview is produced, and later systematized, or when the interviews are analyzed, the researcher can perceive certain unanticipated elements. In other instances, only *a posteriori* readings bring the unforeseen to the fore, where it can no longer be ignored. As time passes, revisiting oral sources brings surprises that point us toward unknown issues. Because all these are considered desirable steps, oral history praxis does not use instruments such as surveys or highly structured and directive interviews. This is a matter of methodological strategy: favoring the routes the interview itself may suggest is preferable. This opening for communication to flow free from the impediments potentially created by overly rigid research agendas has, on the one hand, enabled comprehensive and socially shared memories to be articulated. But, on the other hand, it also facilitates the emergence of issues, scenes, and stories not anticipated on the horizon imagined by the researcher.

The texts included in this third section—the first by Luciana Heymann and Verena Alberti, the second by Daisy Perelmutter, and a third co-written by Bernardo Borges Buarque de Hollanda and Raphael Rajão—address the recognition and attribution of meaning to the unexpected events appearing in interview situations and the testimony they generate. This occurs when researchers re-read their own oral sources or examine a promising source created by a third party. They are reflective essays about oral history praxis and its by-products. Without summarizing their content, I will use them as a pretext to venture into a few ideas and reflections, because these essayists have enriched me with their experiences and critical self-reflection. Their texts provide suggestive contributions—methodological, theoretical, and epistemological—that improve the praxis of contemporary oral history.

All three essays deliver autoethnographic notes and provide an analytical look based on research intentions and questions that are different from those that created the original *corpus* of interviews. Their authors ask themselves how and why unexpected elements guided the interview in directions other than those planned, providing performances and testimonies that were meaningful also to those who narrated their lives. Such events raise questions about the decision-making intentions of narrators who seize control of the interview situation as well as about the role played by the interviewers. What does surprise and perplexity mean when these unexpected events take place? What answers may be offered?

The chapters reflect on methods and practices as well as the challenges faced when one ceases to see oral history as a mere technique, and instead comes to consider it as a method with strategies and systematic practices that forge new historical sources that in turn may generate substantiated new interpretations. They offer a contrast between the *amateur* style of producing oral interviews and the stricter and more professional current styles prevailing in the academy.

They question themselves about the ideal forms and attributes of "being an interviewer" and "being a narrator," as well as the lack of a single pattern for best performances. They reflect on apparently unsuccessful interview experiences and the symbols they produce in order to better understand both the situation and the narrator. Another issue raised in these chapters is the strategic value of collaborative practices for creating a successful oral source.

One chapter emphasizes the vital need for interviewers to be willing to perform an "absolute" listening to the dialogue, not conditioned only by the act of questioning. It is crucial to note that oral history interviews generate "leftovers," remains that must be recognized so they are preserved and have their relevance maximized, allowing for the subsequent development of multiple analyses. Theoretical and methodological challenges also arise regarding the use of oral archives by potential future researchers, which leads to debates about the purposes and motives of creators of collections, as well as the reasons and intentions that potential users may raise. The chapters point to a need to differentiate the times in which the source was created and the times of its reuse. They criticize the view of oral sources as untouchable and unquestionable "monuments," calling for an epistemological review of both their production and preservation, as well as the role they assume in public history and in the propagation of official versions of history.

These chapters will be of interest not only to oral history practitioners, while also providing support for other social-historical disciplines and setting examples for praxis, in a reflective effort to search for better research procedures and ways to communicate their findings.

PRAXIS AND CRITICAL ANALYSIS

Current oral history praxis is a path shaped by theoretical, methodological, technical, practical, and ethical decisions, which reflectively and systematically contribute to successfully guide and organize one's research. It is a long-term collective effort that must be acknowledged and harnessed. The discipline (as many consider it to be) of oral history has diversified over time and its praxis displays a greater complexity of assumptions, methods, and styles. But, let me first further clarify my conceptual perspective on what I regard as the most striking features of this field.

Oral history has established itself as a procedure to create new historical research sources by producing a new *corpus* of information comprising oral accounts systematically collected for particular projects, based on explicit theoretical and methodological issues and starting points. Its full practice implies considering the oral source for its own sake, and not only as factual or empirical support, nor as a mere illustration. It implies gathering and criticizing the source, analyzing, interpreting, and locating, in socio-historical terms, the accounts and evidence provided by oral interviews. The field complements its oral materials with any other necessary sources and makes strict use of traditional documents; it articulates them and allows for more complex analyses rather than being limited to interviews.

The triangulation of sources is essential and impels us to know and consider the various bodies of information relevant to the topic being studied. At the same time, it may also turn out to be a dispersing factor that makes it harder to keep focus. Doing the research in a planned, systematic and balanced way would provide the researcher with multiple clues to interpretation and enrich the potential of unexpected discoveries. The practice of oral history may, thus, adopt different styles: from the "archivist" and "source creator" to those who choose to navigate the maze of theoretical and interpretative work. Styles may complement each other if there is a critical and reflective attitude toward the work being done. The key point is to formulate—and respond to—whether the oral source is the point of arrival or departure.

Collections granting public access may be consulted by individuals who were not involved in the production of the source material, adding a series of complications and new adventures to the harnessing and interpretation of these collections. The analysis, in these "second-hand" readings, may differ from the one deployed by the source producers. Similarly, with the passage of time, new circumstances offer different interpretative keys and allow for a different look even by the researchers involved with the original interview.

One key element must be reinforced in our methodology: the objectivation of the process of creating the source, and the description of the implications of the researcher's presence. The roles played by the different participants involved must become visible. If what we colloquially call the "behind-the-scenes" elements are made visible to any future users, they will make re-readings of the source more interesting. Knowing how, when, why, and who enabled the creation of such a source allows us to skillfully carry on with the desired review and appreciation of the historical source.

Revisiting Oral Sources: Paths and Challenges

I have mentioned that one of the main goals of oral history praxis remains the creation of new historical sources—the oral ones. There is no reason to interrupt the production of oral archives, even under conditions limited by the pandemic. Bringing innovation to our practices is our way to respond to such a great challenge. Working with digital ethnography and digital history is as a promising possibility. Time and circumstance will tell.

As oral history practitioners, we now rely on our own private oral collections and perhaps on the access to institutional and public archives. A few online repositories guard documents, interviews, and audiovisual materials. There are also a few interview archives linked to research projects conducted by educational institutes, social organizations, or government agencies. Possibilities are many, and selecting oral sources for reinterpretation or revisitation depends on personal interests. Whether they are products of your own work or the result of third-party research, they present their own qualities, challenges, problems, and particular contributions:

Working with your own material. Reading or revisiting interviews conducted by us is an analytic exercise that allows us to handle the oral source, or the collection of oral interviews deposited in an archive, in many alternative ways. We may try a strategy of "oblique proximity," examining the source in the light of themes, concerns, and assumptions differing from those used at the time of its creation. Intentions are relevant. Another strategy may involve an "indicial view and sensitivity," or, in other words, identifying topics that were not present in the questions we asked. This requires close reading and intense listening, since you are targeting what is tangential to the explicit, manifest content of the interviews. You are avoiding the most evident entrance to the source. The process of revisiting an oral source does not require following the same list of questions that were asked, but consulting such a script may help you to identify which elements and categories emerged spontaneously. What makes a re-reading promising is a curiosity that must guide you, the surprise sought in the processing of the oral source.

Working with third-party content. Accessing oral sources created by other people is similar to working with other types of documents and archives. It is important to access the protocols and all descriptive and reflective texts accompanying the interview (such as notes, content lists, reflections, and situation descriptions). If the oral source is old, you must retrace the historical context of its creation and learn the essential information about who narrated, who interviewed, and other key actors. The historical procedure of internal and external criticism of the source can be applied to oral history and is actually required to understand the context involving its construction and preservation. The analyst will likely come up with interpretations different, even opposite, to those of the creators of the source. The systematic, creative analysis may catch less explicit aspects. It may identify unforeseen accounts offered in responses to questions that were formulated. It may make possible uses of the source that the protagonists of the source had not intentionally planned. This process may be guided by best practices in terms of the use of the oral source, but it is also open to undesired misuses of the oral source.

In a research process like oral history, the emergence of the unexpected is too common—what is rare is its absence. Just as in sociocultural anthropology or qualitative sociology, the experience lived in the field is full of surprises. When curiosity is well applied, it makes its apprehension easier. The imponderable is an integral part of the fieldwork; we can only hope to be able to recognize it and, if we are lucky, register and examine it, in order to avoid major breaches in the original work plan. The sociological imagination accompanying our research involves predictions we expect to be confirmed. But then the unexpected emerges—either during the investigation or *a posteriori*, during the analysis. And not less during the stages of distribution, reception, and use of the contents.

Reference

Aceves Lozano, Jorge. 2017. La historia oral y su praxis actual: recursos metodológicos, estrategia analítica y toma de decisiones. In *Entrevistar ¿Para qué? Múltiples escuchas desde diversos cuadrantes*, ed. Graciela de Garay Arellano and Jorge Eduardo Aceves Lozano, 64–90. México: Instituto Mora.

PART IV

The Answer Is Another Subject:
The Unexpected as a Generative Device

Introduction to Part IV

Miriam Hermeto and Ricardo Santhiago

"Do we learn from our interviewees' narratives? In what moments, or in which interviews, is our gain greater than simply knowing a 'version' of the past?" asks Verena Alberti (2007, 79), raising a question and bringing a possible answer: for her, one occasion on which it can happen is "when the narrative goes beyond that particular case and provides us with a key to understanding reality." In a way, her commentary confirms the potential that encounters with the unexpected have in unveiling new problems, new research routes, and new areas for the researcher to explore. An "unveiling" that is a form of creation and revelation: from the fine stories we hear, thick worlds open up.

Internationally known for his work in popular education, Paulo Freire knew it well. He elaborated in his writings the conviction that knowledge is not a solipsistic enterprise; it is situated within relationships that take place in an intersubjectively shared world, where our conscious bodies interact. This powerfully simple belief led Freire to a quest for what he called "dialogical rationality"—one capable of overcoming the epistemological dualism between subject and object, as well as the hyper-fragmentation of knowledge into disciplines, processes that, in his view, would only distance knowledge from the lived world. It was in this light that Freire defended notion that "generative themes" (Freire 1975) arise from the dynamic and constantly altering nature of reality—themes that life itself gives us as a gift, and that would be particularly

M. Hermeto
Universidade Federal de Minas Gerais (UFMG), Belo Horizonte, Brazil

R. Santhiago (✉)
Universidade Federal de São Paulo (Unifesp), São Paulo, Brazil
e-mail: ricardo.santhiago@unifesp.br

effective in creating an interdisciplinary, integrative, and truly humanistic kind of knowledge.

This impulse is not exogenous to the usual attitudes of oral historians in the field or while designing their research, if they remain open to chance, to intuition, to the sometimes-overwhelming force of personal experience. While we prepare for the encounters that are at the heart of our practice (encounters that we attend duly informed by theories and hypotheses, and by a torrent of expectations), we are aware that there is no guarantee all these encounters will follow the same path. And what is required, in the face of research contingencies, is not only a willingness to listen to what was not expected; at times, this must be accompanied by attention to elements that may necessitate a significant change in the direction of the work.

Reaffirming what Alberti wrote, in these situations the oral history interview offers us something very different from "versions" of facts. These changes in the course of our work often enable the construction of highly innovative interpretations of historical events, confronting established scholarship with the force of concrete life experiences. In such situations, we complete our projects while also welcoming unexpected eruptions, made possible by the strongly hermeneutic inclination of the type of analysis we do. We recognize the interpretive authority smoldering in our sources: they are, as Cléria Botelho da Costa wrote (2014, 63), the first incidence of "an ordering of events, woven by the voice of the narrators."

Furthermore, there are stories that not only dismantle the hypotheses guiding a project, but also show the inadequacy or insufficiency of theoretical frameworks and even of the thematic areas in which we were operating as we read the individual and social realities we had focused on. In these cases, a mere adjustment is not enough: what may be required is the courage to start over, accepting the generativeness of oral history as a method able to build other research objectives and reconstruct old ones. "Loving the process more than the product," as a song by the composer Jorge Drexler puts it, is at times required—that is, having a sincere appreciation for core changes that fieldwork can produce. That is the attitude expressed (in some cases, not without initial resistance) in the texts in this section, in which Camillo Robertini, Plínio Ferreira Guimarães, Dieter Reinisch, and Linda Shopes rekindle the sparks generated in interviews from different countries and continents.

Camillo Robertini, an Italian in South America, came looking for heroes who resisted the 1976–1983 dictatorship in Argentina. He ended up finding workers who valued their jobs at the Fiat Company and a culture that is more complex than the binaries often employed to reflect class distinctions. Trying to confirm his initial hypotheses, he was derailed by the views expressed by his interviewees. He found an unexpected consensus that is far from the country's hegemonic public memory, largely based on the conflation of the recent past with collective struggles for human rights.

Something similar happened to Plínio Ferreira Guimarães, between his two investigations in the Caparaó Sierra region in Brazil. Interviewing local residents allowed him to identify how the relations between the left-wing *guerrillas* and the Armed Forces during the early years of the Brazilian military dictatorship troubled the population—galvanizing mixed reactions of fear, ignorance, and anxiety in relation to subversive actions. A new subject and a new research project emerged in this tense mixture.

Investigating the daily lives of activist republican prisoners in Northern Ireland, Dieter Reinisch narrates his need to stop being afraid of surprises. Travelling through a network of interviewees who were constantly evaluating his reliability, he encountered the reluctance of one narrator: everything had already been said in a previous interview, printed in a newspaper and framed on his wall. Paying serious attention to the hints given by the reluctant narrator, Reinisch triggered his narrative flow by taking hold of a shared love of sports—and, from there, he was able to mine new raw material for his research.

Linda Shopes, when examining the three texts together, ventures into a jazz riff, improvising melodies on the issues raised by the others: what do the unexpected events generate? Is it another theme, another set of questions, other researchers? Luckily for us, what Shopes does is bring up further unexpected, penetrating questions—which include the interviewees' views on our processes, the relationships between individual lives and generalizing scholarship, and the social purpose of oral history—to our reflection on the unpredictable.

References

Alberti, Verena. 2007. *Ouvir contar: Textos em história oral*. Rio de Janeiro: Editora FGV.
Costa, Cléria Botelho da. 2014. A escuta do outro: os dilemas da interpretação. *História Oral* 17 (2): 47–67.
Freire, Paulo. 1975. *Pedagogia do Oprimido*. São Paulo: Paz e Terra.

CHAPTER 20

Looking for Heroes, I Found Conventional Workers: A Labor Community in the Argentine Dictatorship

Camillo Robertini

Historical studies classically ask historians to conduct their research from a rational point of view: identifying an issue; posing questions; raising hypotheses; establishing a dialogue with what other colleagues have written; and, above all, finding new sources to question, or proposing new questions, for sources that have already been analyzed. We have learned from the contributions of social history that the construction of knowledge of the past is not necessarily linear, and that although it uses a scientific method, it cannot be considered an exact science demonstrable through the repetition of an experiment. The historian's subjectivity—in opposition to what one could assume until relatively recent times—is a unique feature present in each and every research project. It is crucial to recognize, value, and not conceal this element, but, rather, to think about it critically: why do we spend time on a given research topic? What is our end considering that such a topic deserves so much dedication? It is difficult to locate the origin of such a desire and the particular traits that make each investigation unique. It is not surprising, then, that the father of microhistory, Carlo Ginzburg, reflected on "chance and cases" declaring the "decisive" value of both in what was his journey as a historian.

C. Robertini (✉)
Universidad de Chile, Santiago, Chile

In these pages, I propose to reflect on an unexpected interview that, as has often happened to those of us who use oral history, has caused me to rethink not only my research but also my interests, thus also determining the unexpected direction of my subsequent works. The starting point of this text resides in the need to consider the interview a performance, a unique and unrepeatable encounter in which, at the intersection of subjectivities and the gazes between interviewer and interviewee, the oral source arises. This, the result of a dialogic construction, is a source that, more than others, implies greater participation of the historian who cannot find it in an archival box but builds it together with the testimony (Portelli, 2010).

Looking for Heroes

The history of lower classes in Argentina has, since I first set foot there in 2012, been instinctively attractive and interesting for me. As a newcomer, a young student of history, a European and the son of left-wing activists, having heard so many stories of the workers' resistance to the dictatorship, I had crafted a romantic, and in a certain way idealized, portrait: a "working hero," a fearless, altruistic, and revolutionary man, morally superior to others, and who fought the power of the local oligarchy and military violence.

Such an imaginary was based on my knowledge of the events that occurred between 1969 and 1976, that is, from the Cordobazo, the famous worker and student outbreak in the city of Córdoba, which opened an unprecedented stage of struggle of the subordinate sectors of the country. The images of the barricades, the protest songs, and the commitment of the revolutionary activists met up with the exotic imaginary that a 25-year-old European had of Latin America: a continent full of revolutions and revolutionary people.

When I had the opportunity to return to Argentina, between 2013 and 2016, to start the fieldwork for my doctoral research, my plan was crystal clear: I would analyze how the workers remembered the resistance to the dictatorship and, at the same time, I would record their testimonies on that period. My hypothesis was almost obvious: since the workers had been the main victims of the Videla regime, their memoirs would surely convey their resistance to the regime. By that time, the existing scholarship almost unanimously represented the working class as the main victim of the army, since 30% of the disappeared persons had a working-class background, and the regime was a political system based on the use of terror and the dismantling of ties among workers.

To begin my investigation, I had to narrow down the subject, and I decided to focus on the workers of Fiat Argentina. On the one hand, this decision was based on the opportunity, which had come to me *by chance*, of being able to consult the company's archives in Turin (an opportunity that is almost unique when it comes to their archives) and, on the other, on the importance that the Fiat workers had had during the 1970s (Brennan 2009). Even though the workers of Fiat at Córdoba had not starred in the famous social outbreak, they were at the edges of the workers' vanguards that, in the 1970s, had promoted the struggles in the city through the SITRAC-SITRAM unions [Workers of Fiat Concord Union and Works of Materfer Union] (Laufer 2020).

That is how I arrived in Córdoba to start the fieldwork and to finally meet the workers that, until then, I knew only through labor history scholarship. The first encounters of that stage made me realize that what I knew about metalworkers was indeed insufficient. At that time, I was concerned about filling blank pages with questions about the labor organization, the repression, how the coup d'état had taken place, and, above all, the disappearance of workers. As I got to know them, however, I became aware of the lack of relevance of such questions and the assumptions from which they derived.

The first interview I conducted was, in this sense, revealing. I met Víctor Hugo thanks to my contact with his son through social networks. The interview with this former worker of the "Forja" sector at Fiat in Córdoba was my first contact with "reality." On that occasion, I wanted to record his life story by focusing on the dictatorship years. And, as in many other later cases, I found that the former Fiat workers were more willing to discuss the meaning and pride of *being* a Fiat worker than the dictatorship years. The more I sought their testimonies to speak on strikes and confrontations, the more memories focused on the benefits provided by the company emerged. In addition to their sense of companionship and gratitude towards the company, I clearly remember from that meeting a few blunt words about a relative joining Fiat: "He wanted to enter the factory, I'd been working there for a long time. The first and only thing I said to him was, 'I'll kill you if they tell me you behave bad! You cannot betray the family nor the factory.' But it happened and I stopped talking to him."

That initial contact with the material experience of the world of work made me realize that I had underestimated the gap between what I expected and what I had found, and I construed it as if it were a "problem" of the testimony, as a result of the persistent will of an individual determined to deny a universally known reality. Moving forward with interviews, I became aware that the "mistakes" in the interviewees' memories were replicated every time I met another former worker.

An interview with two families of workers from the Concord and Ferreyra plants was revealing and unexpected. At that moment, I opted to introduce the subject of dictatorship in a soft way, asking about their entry and initial years at the factory, and the years before the *coup d'état*. And I learned about the importance of those events in the self-representation of labor families.

Alfredo: It was wonderful to be at Fiat—you could make progress. I got my first house with the Fiat salary. Your first ambition was getting your own house. And we friends would help each other, making the china, the ceilings. And I made progress.

Francesco: We comrades were very close … We used to have roast feasts, meetings… most of us were united, we helped each other … even though *there's always somebody who* … we always helped each other to progress, to share … you had a Fiat badge, they'd trust you, you'd come to a business and they wouldn't ask for any guarantee.

	Sure, at that time not everyone joined the company. They made a good staff selection. Bad people would not join Fiat.
CR:	Who were the "bad guys?"
Francesco:	The harmful people ... those who hurt the company.

Much of the interview revealed a deep and peculiar pro-business sentiment that, in a partly de-industrialized Argentina, emphasized the positive aspects of Fordism: high wages and mass consumption. With today's eyes, they evoke a "smokestack nostalgia" common in areas that have lost the industrial potential they had reached in the 1970s (Garruccio 2016; Braga 2003). Beyond an identity based on an imaginary fabricated by the company, in the first minutes of the interview, a core duality that would accompany me throughout my research arose: the constant clash between "us" and "the others" had established a paradigm of otherness through which the subjects drew the emotional, behavioral, and social limits which their everyday lives could develop.

Such a dual view of reality, the idea of a world divided between "good guys" and "bad guys," did not seem to me an issue that deserved to be deepened but, nevertheless, it was later revealed as a trigger capable of evoking the symbolic elements that form this working community imaginary. The representation of a "we," as if it were a harmonious community consonant with the dominant social order and coinciding with the company's interests, was raised against "the others," a labile category comprising all the people who questioned the system, private property, and the company's right to exploit its workers.

Alfredo:	The others weren't liable; Argentina couldn't rely on them ... When the union gets out of hand, it becomes reckless, and it produces damage—it's not a union anymore, it's subversion ...
Francesco:	Yes!
CR:	So you think the SITRAC-SITRAM was a "subversive" union?
Francesco:	It ended up being so ... When they started the SITRAC-SITRAM, which was "combative" but in reality was destructive ... because they sabotaged the line, they broke gears and machines to harm Fiat ... That's when the disaster began ... Then that all happened in 1976.
CR:	In a certain sense you've raised a significant difference between those who wanted to work, and those who were in politics and "things like that."
Francesco:	It was a division, yes, between good and bad ... Our society has always been very divided. Between the military, who wanted to restore order, and another part, that pointed to disorder ... That's when the balance was broken and the military had to come in.

The interviews revealed conflicting imaginaries: one, around which class and revolutionary experiences orbited; the other one, for which social conformity and respect for the company, the state, and private property were a motto. In other words, these images condense the archetypes of "good guys" and "bad guys"—key categories in the imaginary of the interviewees. In the midst of statements highlighting the existence of antagonistic worlds that are rarely connected, a central element of the self-representations of the Fiat workers now appeared more clearly: the conversion of the duality between "good" and "bad" into a confrontation between revolutionaries and reactionaries.

Little by little, I realized that my preconception, the image of the "hero worker" that I was so tenaciously looking for, was morphing into something different and, in a way, disappointing. To describe those former workers who did not see themselves in the revolutionary epic, it was natural for me to resort to a native category that had appeared several times during the interviews. If "the others" were often branded as "the subversives," "those who did not want to work," our workers define themselves as "people who work," "ordinary workers," or, as Alfredo clearly expressed, "the real worker always liked to live quietly, doing his job, enjoying his time at work."

The unexpected turn of the interview was 180 degrees and, due to the insistence of my questions, it opened space for a subject I could not imagine that I would work on: social attitudes, daily life, and the social consensus of the popular sectors and workers during the last Argentine military dictatorship (Robertini 2019).

Since in this 2015 interview the importance of the subject was not clear to me, I persisted—making my narrators quite uncomfortable—and that, surprisingly, generated stories introducing this unexpected subject. But at the same time, when I had not yet fully understood the importance of the topic, my insistence in asking about the dictatorial times on several occasions bothered my interviewees:

CR:	How was the *coup* in Córdoba and in Fiat, how did you experience it?
Francesco:	At Fiat we didn't notice the *coup*. We were just working. We learned from the radio that there'd been a change of government … we kept going to the factory every day. Every morning the military stopped the bus for checking and then we got into the factory … but our life outside the factory was good!
CR:	But living under military control did not affect you?
Francesco:	No! For me, not at all. It didn't affect me or many of us at any time. Who was affected? Those who did, they were involved in things that … I don't mean they weren't right … but …
CR:	But did you talk about it at the factory? Did you talk about it among yourselves?
Francesco:	No… when you started a shift, you didn't talk … much less about politics.
CR:	Not even on such a transcendent event in Argentine history?

Francesco: But we, the newlyweds, the young guys ... I and my friends talked about things that interested us ... we wanted to know how to build our house, how to solve material problems...

CR: So you didn't see a relationship between politics and your lives.

Alfredo: That's right, because it [the dictatorship] did not affect our progress. It did not affect our progress at any time. There was stability, there was food, life went on.

While I insisted with my questions, hoping to get to any fragment of voice that would confirm my research hypothesis, any word supporting the idea that the popular classes had been victims of the dictatorship and that, above all, they were aware of this and had created some form of resistance, a crucial aspect that is always at stake during a military and/or authoritarian regime was revealed: the existence of a social basis and a consensus on which that political regime builds its own legitimacy (Passerini 1987).

An unexplored field of consensual memories of the dictatorship was opening up for me, but I kept returning to questions that, in a highly unfair way, held those workers responsible for the lack of resistance and rejection towards the regime. Listening to the recordings again, one can observe the typical temptation to become a judge, and to turn the interview into an interrogation.

However, the insistence of my questions exposed discursivities and memories that, in the Argentina of human rights, seemed to have disappeared. The justification of the *coup* as a "return to order" and the equating of guerrilla violence with military violence are stories that explain much of the way ordinary people process the big story.

CR: Well, but there were also missing persons in Fiat!

Francesco: Yes, well ... there were ... we found out later ... during the dictatorship we were calm, one knew nothing about it.

Alfredo: Now I'm going to tell you something: what happens is that in Europe you don't know what a "military coup" is and you say "oh, a coup, a coup!" When I talk to an Italian I say "Tell me about military coup!"... For us in America and Argentina it's usual, ancestral—since the Republic was formed there've been military coups. And people have always been extraneous to all that ... There were fights between them, between those who were in politics. The ordinary man was always distant from the military coup and we have arrived at the 1976 coup, that happened in silence. Before the military coups there were many attempts at revolution (...) but the ordinary man didn't take part in anything. We had no knowledge of the military coups. We found out by radio ...

CR: But the fact that [the coup] affected people so much, how does it fit with what you're telling me?

Alfredo:	Look, we live in such a benign country: there is meat, corn, wheat, it is a fabulous land. And the ordinary man looked at all that; he was more focused on his physical integrity, his progress, his stability, his well-being ... why would he care about politics?
CR:	However, I do not understand how you could keep on with your daily lives in the midst of state terrorism, 30,000 disappeared persons, the anti-worker dictatorship....
Alfredo:	In Fiat there weren't so many, but there was... There was not a military pronouncement against the working class like "you don't get to work anymore," no, no, no....

The last excerpt from the interview brings up some questions that are worth considering. In the first place, we can observe a binary conception of the dictatorial reality, in which the narrator consider that the only victims were political activists, while ordinary people could be considered safe. Second, we see how the "ordinary man" represents himself as extraneous to the country's social reality and substantially extraneous to politics and the exercise of power. And another dimension of this issue appears strongly: the adaptation to a military regime that, discursively, offered peace and work in exchange for the most ruthless use of terrorist violence. The contrast between the well-being of "the good," of the harmonious Community, as opposed to that of "the others," marks a discursive circuit, and it was thanks to it that part of the popular sectors survived the terror installed by the dictatorship and the extraordinary daily life.

Finally, it should be noted how the disagreement between the imaginary of the Italian researcher and that of the Argentine worker generates a blunt and harsh response: "You don't know what a 'military coup' is." This disagreement was followed by a long explanation about a supposed national idiosyncrasy through which the narrator normalizes the imposition of a military dictatorship and, at the same time, justifies his apolitical position, considering it the only possible one in a context of strong repression.

Conclusion

The goal of this journey through the beginnings of my fieldwork in Argentina was to unveil the historian's kitchen and to emphasize those elements capable of nurturing a research question and even radically mutating it. In the case illustrated here, the search for the "hero worker" was transformed into an investigation on the consensus the common worker offered towards the Argentine military regime.

The need to rethink my object of analysis matured as I progressed with the fieldwork and got to know the former Fiat Concord workers. Although from the beginning my questions were oriented towards "political" issues (the dictatorship, strikes, and moments of confrontation with the bosses), the workers I interviewed were much more interested in talking about other issues. That is how, in the open space of a life story interview, I let myself be carried away by the narrative thread of the narrators, "discovering" extremely interesting and unexpected elements: on the one hand, the forms of adaptation and strategies that ordinary workers put in place to defend themselves against the anti-worker policy of the dictatorship; on the other, the relevance that the philo-entrepreneurial identity continues to play in their self-representations.

The gap between what I expected to find and what I found, between an idealized and epic image of the working class and the flesh and blood workers, highlighted the relevance of the unexpected interviews I reanalyzed. The ability to modify the research agenda and to "divert" the search for unanticipated paths represents one of the great challenges posed by the use of oral sources in historiography. The "discovery" of labor groups that accepted the dictatorship and lived alongside the military power represents the main result of those interviews that so markedly influenced and guided my work.

Not only oral sources invite historians to rethink their research hypotheses, and yet, one of their peculiarities is the existence of happenstance and chance. The interview is an extremely creative and free moment, which in most cases leads to unexpected endings. Memory, desire, and intersubjectivity are combined in the narrative space of the interview, determining stories and memories not always expected.

References

Braga, Ruy. 2003. *A nostalgia do fordismo: modernização e crise na teoria da sociedade salarial*. São Paulo: Xamã Editora.

Brennan, James. 2009. *The Labor Wars in Cordoba, 1955–1976: Ideology, Work, and Labor Politics in an Argentine Industrial Society*. Cambridge, MA: Harvard University Press.

Garruccio, Roberta. 2016. Chiedi alla ruggine: Studi e storiografia della deindustrializzazione. *Meridiana* 85: 35–60.

Laufer, Rodolfo. 2020. Intervención de las izquierdas y politización obrera en SITRAC-SITRAM, la experiencia paradigmática del sindicalismo clasista de los 70. *Izquierdas* 49: 743–766.

Passerini, Luisa. 1987. *Fascism in Popular Memory: The Cultural Experience of the Turin Working Class*. Cambridge: Cambridge University Press.

Portelli, Alessandro. 2010. *Ensaios de história oral*. São Paulo: Letra e Voz.

Robertini, Camillo. 2019. *Quando la Fiat parlava argentino. Una fabbrica italiana e i suo operai nella Buenos Aires dei militari. 1964–1980*. Firenze: Le Monnier.

CHAPTER 21

The Devious Paths of Memory: Reflections on the Experience of Interviews with Residents of the Caparaó Sierra

Plínio Ferreira Guimarães

Every historical researcher has once started his investigations by following a path he had previously traced, guided by a thread that appears solid enough to justify his hypotheses—but then he came across clues that made him change his route and take a road unforeseen in his original plan. Or perhaps he even stuck to his original plan, but the discoveries nonetheless nourished that welcome discomfort that advances the historian's work, making him pursue another path and follow the signs left by evidence previously found. These vestiges, residues left by human groups from the most remote times to the most recent, are the substance that must guide our attempt to understand the marks and pitfalls that "the past drops along its road" (Bloch 2001, 77). A well-known example can be found in *The Cheese and the Worms*, a classic work by Carlo Ginzburg (1987). While researching the Inquisition's documents about a sect in the Italian region of Friuli, Ginzburg came across the trial of Menocchio, a miller sentenced to death for creating a very particular version of the origins of the Universe, that is, a cosmogony. Ginzburg persisted on his initial route and completed his project, but he returned to the story of Menocchio, which would later become his best-known work.

P. F. Guimarães (✉)
Instituto Federal de Educação, Ciência e Tecnologia do Espírito Santo (IFES) campus Ibatiba, Ibatiba, Brazil
e-mail: plinio.guimaraes@ifes.edu.br

© The Author(s), under exclusive license to Springer Nature Switzerland AG 2023
R. Santhiago, M. Hermeto (eds.), *The Unexpected in Oral History*, Palgrave Studies in Oral History,
https://doi.org/10.1007/978-3-031-17749-1_21

Such residues are perhaps more often found by researchers working with memory and oral history than by those who employ other types of sources. In fact, most of the time, recollections are not viewed as remnants or evidence—but rather as an unparalleled memory, full of images and information ready to rise to the surface. These memories, for which the researcher is eager, allow us to learn about experiences hitherto relegated either to the margins or to oblivion, opening gates for a broader understanding of particular periods and communities, as well as of elements of the imaginary that we could not usually access through a source other than interviews.

Assuming that narratives provide access to lived experiences, to ways of seeing and representing the world, and that they are signs of how individuals appropriate information and events, I will report on the research I undertook for my master's thesis between 2004 and 2006, drawing on the memories of residents in the Caparaó Sierra region, an area on the border between the states of Espírito Santo and Minas Gerais, in the Brazilian southeast. My project dealt with locals' recollections of the Caparaó guerrilla movement against the military dictatorship that followed the 1964 coup. This was a resistance organized by members of the Movimento Nacionalista Revolucionário [Nationalist Revolutionary Movement] (MNR) between 1966 and 1967. My research focused on the fear of guerrilla fighters, which is quite common in the memories shared by the residents. Indeed, what led me to investigate this theme were occasional narratives of uncertainty and anxiety that I has heard as someone born in the area.

In the preparatory work that preceded my interviews, I tried to build a framework with relevant data that could support the narratives. In addition to learning more about the attempts to establish a guerrilla *foco* there, I needed to know more about the people who lived around the Caparaó National Park and who had been close to all these events, from the arrival of the men who planned to organize an armed struggle against the dictatorship to the occupation of the area by military troops pursuing and arresting MNR members. Such aspects involved, on the one hand, the population's distrust of outsiders seen wandering high up in the Sierra or communities close to the park, which elicited alerts to the authorities about strangers prowling the surroundings, and, on the other, the subsequent military presence, leading to the fear of conflicts and violence.

Based on this background research, I chose the locations where I would contact potential interviewees. Priority was given to towns and communities closest to the events, especially those places where the guerrilla fighters were spotted or arrested, and also to places where the army had a stronger presence. I was led to a few interviewees through suggestions of people I already knew, as happened in the mining towns of Espera Feliz and Caparaó. Other locations I visited in advance, wandering around in search of people who had experienced close up all the agitation caused by the guerrillas—as in the town of Alto Caparaó and the village of Pedra Menina, which belongs to the municipality of Dores do Rio Preto, in Espírito Santo.

In the first contacts and conversations to prepare for the interviews, a few issues became clear. The first was that some interviewees had no knowledge of the events, even of those that had taken place in Caparaó Sierra. It was a sensitive point, something unforeseen in my initial planning: a few interviewees even asked me for information about what the guerrilla was before agreeing to the interviews. Providing them such information would interfere in the construction of their narratives, of course, but denying it would impact the relationship of trust established between narrator and listener. Their fear of saying something inaccurate or incorrect must be acknowledged and respected. The solution I found was to change the interview script and give them more space to elaborate on their life stories and the communities where they lived. By doing so, I was trying to make the guerrilla emerge in the interviews more naturally, without evoking anxiety about what was not fully known. It is important to highlight that when introducing myself to the people I intended to interview, I never failed to mention that I would discuss the guerrilla—and I have even received denials from residents willing to talk about their own lives but not about that specific event.

My perception of their fears should also be stressed. Initially, given our early contacts, I anticipated that the narrations would invariably be filled with moments of tension, but in some cases, memories came in a mocking tone, with strong laughter when recalling episodes involving the fear of the guerrilla warriors, the presence of the army, the curiosity about the equipment, such as the helicopter, that they used. But some narrators showed great apprehension and distrust. In one specific case, the interviewee refused to grant further testimony and was reluctant to sign the release form regarding his first and only interview.

The different ways of narrating memories of the movements created by the presence of guerrilla warriors highlight the need for special care with this type of source. Making fun of and laughing at the fear and apprehension that had been experienced exhibit an awareness different from those who narrated the same events in a tense, troubled way, still worried about whether they should speak of what they had witnessed. If both groups had the opportunity to record their memories shortly after the events, perhaps their perceptions would not have been as different as they were in interviews conducted early in the twenty-first century.

After All, Who Is the Guerrilla Warrior?

Another relevant aspect is how some interviewees understood the word "guerrilla." For many, the term did not refer to MNR members who climbed the Caparaó Sierra. On the contrary, the "guerrilla" in their eyes would be the military—the troops that occupied the region after the corralling and imprisonment of the warriors and the subsequent investigation and sweeping of the areas in and around the National Park. Therefore, contacting the narrators before the interviews was essential; it allowed me to shape the questions according to how each interviewee referred to the guerrillas and the military movements. And it was here that the experience of these interviews about the Caparaó Sierra guerrilla movement opened the way for another research project.

To my surprise, the moments of anxiety, tension, and fear of the guerrillas shared space, in the memory of my interviewees, with the social care initiatives carried out by military troops on behalf of the civilians. The interviews described medical and dental care, vaccination campaigns, distribution of medicines and food, and support to rural landowners by instructing them in agriculture and animal care. In addition, the military reportedly held picnics and played with children, visited schools, and held sports tournaments with local residents. Thus, the narratives that were initially full of tension and showed fear of both the guerrilla and the military troops took on lighter tones accompanied by smiles and sympathy toward the military when the interviewees recalled their helpful actions. These actions were part of a program developed by Brazil's army forces starting in the 1960s known as Ação Cívico-Social [Civic-Social Action] (Aciso). It was widely implemented during the dictatorship in isolated regions, where the state had been almost entirely absent until then and also where movements of resistance to the military government, as was the case of Caparaó Sierra, took place.

At that time, I did not fully understand the enormity of Aciso in terms of its military goals. Still, I realized that it was important in the interviewees' memory. I explored these reports in my master's thesis, which included a discussion of the recollections of the social care activities of the military forces involved in the repression of the guerrillas. My interest in the topic was reinforced by several pieces published in newspapers of the time, mentioning the assistance provided by the troops and, later, by papers about Aciso activities that I found in the archives of the Military Police of Minas Gerais (PMMG) about the guerrillas, kept at their museum in Belo Horizonte.

These documents clarified that the type of operation with the civilian population was more than an isolated action set in motion during the combat against implementing a guerrilla *foco* in the Caparaó Sierra. What the interviews brought to light was the result of military programs drawing on the post–World War II situation, on the disputes and conflicts derived from the Cold War, and directed above all on the revolutionary movements taking place in the Third World. The military doctrines underpinning the care provided to civilian populations aimed to erect a barrier against the advance of revolutions such as those arising from independence struggles in the French colonies in Asia and Africa, or the Cuban Revolution in America. The defeats brought attention to the organizational model and role played by the Armed Forces and police. Watching out for the internal enemy and erecting a barrier to prevent it from reaching the civilian population—especially those living in poor or isolated areas, where the state was less present—become an imperative.

In this context, the doctrine of revolutionary war and counterinsurgency stand out. The first appeared with the French Army and was developed during the war against Algeria in the 1950s, the latter was North American and resulted from alarm at the advance of revolutions such as the one that occurred in Cuba under the leadership of Fidel Castro.

In Brazil, discussions of such doctrines among the Armed Forces' high-ranking officers began in the late 1950s and reached the training of troops in the 1960s. Aciso was a program built on these endeavors as part of the effort to fight possible revolutions. That explains its employment, in 1967, in the Caparaó Sierra region, during actions designed to defeat the attempt to implement a guerrilla *foco*.

From the Recollections of Caparaó Sierra Residents to Military Documents

The narratives of the interviewees sought out for my master's degree (Guimarães 2006) opened a new path, a new research project. The narrators' words were not in harmony with my initial chosen topic: I expected to hear more about the guerrillas and the moments of anxiety experienced during the period than about the military who moved into the region. However, by allowing the interviewees to feel free to narrate their perceptions of the events, information, and feelings that were different from what I imagined could emerge. A population hitherto abandoned by the state found itself supported in several areas by the actions carried out through Aciso. The narratives expressed gratitude and sympathy for the soldiers who were in Caparaó Sierra.

That aroused a welcome discomfort in relation to what I had noted based on the interviewees with the local residents. When I was searching for more information about Aciso, I realized that until then there was no major work on the subject; at most, there were sparse mentions of its existence. The narratives on the social care initiatives, which at first might seem a deviation from my original topic, illuminated a broader dimension regarding not only the history of Brazil during the military dictatorship but also disputes in the time of the Cold War. It led me to a doctoral dissertation (Guimarães 2014), in which documents on military doctrines and internal news from the army on the achievements of Aciso throughout the national territory served as my main sources.

One might wonder whether the recollections of the military presence and their social work actions were merely a loose thread leading to something more important. What else could one extract from such recollections? In fact, even before understanding the mechanics of the military actions used in the repression of the Caparaó guerrilla, the narratives are, by themselves, a powerful document. They reveal aspects of the local residents' daily lives, their world perspective, and, above all, how they were neglected by the state, even though they were not far away from the country's large urban centers. For many residents of the more remote areas of Caparaó Sierra, Aciso was the first occasion they had to see a doctor or a dentist. They did not normally pay much attention to the state, and then the state appeared to them through its repressive arm. But it had a caressing policy designed to create a positive portrait of the government and military corporations, aiming to gain popular support so the revolutionary ideals would not find a fertile ground. That perception stands out in the stories: the assistance, the feeling of being seen and helped for the first time. In some narratives, you can notice the change from an initial fear of troops to an attitude of sympathy and support for the actions carried out there, even showing a clear admiration for the repressive forces.

Oral sources revealed elements of our recent history that had not yet been explored by historical scholarship on the subject. The narratives are filled with peculiar and important understandings that no other source can convey. Moreover, they allow us to assess the power of persuasion that social care actions carried out by specialized military forces had with isolated populations.

Those same recollections provoked a strong reflection on my own work as a researcher, touching on the ways to approach somebody you hope to listen to, on the mismatch that may exist between what you expect to hear and what is actually said, on the care and patience needed to let the words and memories flow. And I inevitably stumbled over the vestiges that the past dropped along its own road. Far beyond what I expected to hear from the interviewees—their fear of the guerrilla—other recollections emerged, making me embark on new research. Also, more than opening a portal for events related to the Cold War or the Brazilian military dictatorship, the narratives about the Caparaó guerrillas conveyed a little bit of the daily lives of the people who lived there: how they related to each other, how they understood their community, how their lives were impacted by the events they narrated, how there was, at that time, a lack of understanding about political issues, national and global. These are stories that only memory allows us to reach. They trace paths that are sometimes uncertain but always lead us to rewarding destinations.

References

Bloch, Marc. 2001. *Apologia da história, ou, O ofício do historiador*. Rio de Janeiro: Zahar.
Ginzburg, Carlo. 1987. *O queijo e os vermes: o cotidiano e as ideias de um moleiro perseguido pela Inquisição*. São Paulo: Companhia das Letras.
Guimarães, Plínio Ferreira. 2006. *Caparaó, a lembrança do medo: A memória dos moradores da região da Serra do Caparaó sobre o primeiro movimento de luta armada contra a ditadura militar—a Guerrilha de Caparaó. Juiz de Fora*. Master's Thesis. Universidade Federal de Juiz de Fora.
———. 2014. *Outras formas de enfrentar a ameaça comunista: os programas assistenciais do Exército brasileiro como estratégia de combate à guerra revolucionária (1964–1974)*. Doctoral Dissertation. Universidade Federal de Minas Gerais.

CHAPTER 22

"Everything Has Been Said": Surprising Encounters from Oral Histories in Ireland

Dieter Reinisch

Oral history is a fascinating adventure. I have used the method for over ten years since I started researching women in paramilitary organizations during the recent conflict in Northern Ireland. For the past 250 years, Ireland has seen several militant conflict waves, anti-colonial wars, and civil wars. While most of the island became independent from the British Empire in 1921/1922 as a result of these uprisings, the northeastern corner remained part of what became known as the United Kingdom of Great Britain and Northern Ireland. In Northern Ireland, a Protestant-led state emerged that was characterized by systematic discrimination of the Catholic minority. Against this discrimination, a civil rights movement emerged in the 1960s. However, the Northern Irish police force and radical Unionist opponents of this civil rights movement attacked the peaceful marches. From 1968 on, the province descended into full warfare, and the British Army was deployed. In the following three decades, almost 4000 people died due to what became known as the Northern Ireland Troubles.

In the past 15 years, I made this conflict on the most western corner of Europe my research topic. Back then, I came to oral history out of necessity. My research subjects since then have been convicted terrorists. From the very beginning, I was particularly interested in the biographical background and the motivations of the activists in Irish republican organizations, as well as the inner lives of those organizations. To understand these issues, I was initially

D. Reinisch (✉)
Webster Vienna Private University, Wien, Austria

© The Author(s), under exclusive license to Springer Nature Switzerland AG 2023
R. Santhiago, M. Hermeto (eds.), *The Unexpected in Oral History*, Palgrave Studies in Oral History,
https://doi.org/10.1007/978-3-031-17749-1_22

forced to conduct oral histories because proscribed organizations do not hold archives. Speaking to activists remained the primary source of data. This necessity to conduct interviews turned into a passion over the years.

For several research projects—starting with my MA thesis, then my PhD project, and my postdoctoral work—I have conducted over 80 interviews with Irish republicans. My fascination with oral history sprang from the fact that the research leads me to people and talking with them over a cup of tea about their lives. My former flatmate, an Ottoman historian, found the greatest joy in sitting throughout summer in a dark, tiny, and dusty archive somewhere in Istanbul, digging through diplomat correspondences in languages and dialects long gone. My greatest joy was renting a car and driving to all four corners of the island of Ireland, meeting Irish republicans of all generations. When we used to come back to our apartment in Florence in the autumn, two contrary worlds of historian fieldwork clashed.

Oral history is as much about the narrator as it is about the researcher. The whole interview process from selecting the interview partners, establishing contact, until you meet your narrators, conducting the interview, and turning off the audio recorder shapes the story narrated throughout these 90–120 minutes. For this reason, unlike archival sources that might only be interpreted differently, the data that is recorded—the interview—is influenced by outside factors, sometimes within the range of influence by the interviewers, sometimes outside my own control, for example, if the interviewer has a migraine. Hence, you never know what will happen in the subsequent interview when you enter the door of the interviewee's house. I usually aim to inform myself about the interview partner as much as possible in the preparations for the interview, though, since I work with gatekeepers in the Irish republican movement and through snowballing, all too often, I don't know anything at all about my interview partners other than that they are Irish republicans.

While oral history research provides exciting surprises and unexpected revelations in the process, such as interview partners providing me with previously unknown archival material hidden in their sheds, it also carries certain dangers. Most importantly, it is enormously time-consuming, compared to other historical methods. Moreover, for PhD students and early career researchers, the expenses of travelling to numerous interview partners is a financial burden, not always reimbursed by their academic institutions. For this reason, one aims to avoid what can be considered as a failure in the interview process. Unexpected events like the reluctance of interview partners to speak to you are the most significant danger. But this is what happened to me during my field research trips from Florence, where I did my PhD, to Ireland, where I conducted my oral histories.

My research focuses on the Northern Ireland conflict, also known as "The Troubles," the longest and deadliest armed conflict in Western Europe after World War II. Between 1968 and 1998, almost 4000 people died. There were three main actors involved in the conflict. First, Irish republicans, the minority population in Northern Ireland, who are overwhelmingly Catholic. They demand reunification with the southern Republic of Ireland. For, in 1922, after the War of Independence, Ireland had been partitioned between the independent South and the Northeast, which remained a province of the United Kingdom. The mostly Protestant majority supported the Union between Northern Ireland and the United Kingdom; hence, they are Unionists. Their more radical sections formed paramilitary organizations. They are called "Loyalists" which is a socio-cultural term of radical Unionists who are "loyal" to the British crown. The so-called Loyalist organizations were, inter alia, the Ulster Volunteer Force (UVF) and the Ulster Defence Association (UDA). The republican side also had paramilitary organizations; their most prominent was the Irish Republican Army (IRA), which was initially formed in 1913. At the outbreak of the conflict in Northern Ireland, it split into two opposing factions, the Provisionals and the Officials, in 1970. It was the first that became the mainstream IRA and the military wing of the Irish republican party *Sinn Féin*. The third actor is the British state and its intelligence organizations operating in Northern Ireland, such as MI5. In the summer of 1969, the British army was deployed to the region to assist the Royal Ulster Constabulary (RUC) police force. An attempt to end the conflict with the signing of a peace agreement on Good Friday 1998 was only partially successful.

Internees and prisoners performed a significant role in the conflict. In the context of this research, internees are held in internment camp usually without or before their conviction, while prisoners are inmates of prisons who are either on remand awaiting their trial or after their conviction. In 1971, the Northern Ireland regional government introduced internment. Until 1976, 3000 men and a few dozen women were interned. In that year, the internment policy was phased out and, from March on, convicted prisoners were held in high-security prisons on both sides of the Irish border. The central high-security prison in Northern Ireland was HMP Maze, the H-Blocks, while Portlaoise Prison was the high-security prison in the Republic of Ireland. Although the IRA fought for the reunification of the island, it was considered a subversive organization not only in Northern Ireland but also in the Republic of Ireland. Following the Good Friday Agreement's signing in 1998, most of the prisoners were released, and HMP Maze ultimately closed in the summer of 2000.

The Field Research Experience

Between 2014 and 2017, I interviewed 34 former IRA prisoners for my PhD thesis. My primary interests were memories of life in prison and the informal self-education by republicans in the internment camps and prisons. Interview partners were selected through my own contacts in Ireland, snowballing, and gatekeepers from ex-prisoners' organizations and other republican groups. Most of the interviews were held in the narrators' homes; the life story interviews lasted between two and three hours each.

In the spring of 2015, I spent several days in the remote, rural area of County Kerry—the very deep southwest and picturesque part of the island. In this rural area, people earn their income from tourism, some are fishers, and few can live from herding cattle. Support for republicanism is traditionally strong there. The area saw some of the worst atrocities by the British army and its allied Black and Tans, a paramilitary militia made up of British World War I veterans during the War of Independence. These atrocities fill the narratives of the local population. Children are raised with the stories of the heroic fight for Irish freedom of their grand- and great-grandparents in the area.

My gatekeeper expected me at the railway station in the small town of Tralee, which marks the entrance of the Dingle Peninsula. On this peninsula, some people still use the Gaelic language in their daily routine—the rest of the island speaks English. I had just arrived by train from Dublin, Ireland's capital. My gatekeeper's name was Maurice, a farmer from outside Tralee. I had met him before at a political meeting in Dublin. This time, contact was established by the general secretary of Republican Sinn Féin, a fringe party with an office in Dublin; it split from the larger Sinn Féin in 1986. Maurice trusted me, not because he knew much about me, but because of the Dublin people who asked him to help me. In a violent field, research depends on who you know as much as who you are. Maurice had organized me "a couple of republicans." I didn't know how many or who they were. Yet, I also trusted him because I was promised in Dublin that he would do it for me.

The following four days, I stayed on his farm just outside Tralee. He woke up early, left me breakfast on the kitchen table, and worked on the cattle farm until day's work was done. That was usually just before noon when he collected me from the house and drove me to interview partners in the area. The first two interview partners used to live in the same town. They were elderly men, way over 80. Both had spent their whole lives in the Irish republican movement, playing an active part in the IRA since they were old enough to join as teenagers. Both had several spells in various prisons in Ireland. They were friendly and happy to talk to me on record. We met other interview partners in remote areas west of the town along the Atlantic coast. Again, these men were in their seventies or eighties and happily spoke to me because Maurice had established the contacts. They didn't know me, but they trusted Maurice.

One of these men asked me who my other interview partners were. I told him that I could not reveal the names of other people without their consent, which I didn't have. During the interview, Maurice was there, and he gave him the names of the other republicans he had organized for interviews. They all knew each other for decades. But this man was interested in the people that spoke to me from outside their area. Again, he asked me, and I told him I couldn't tell. This man was a seasoned IRA member who fully knew that IRA members' names could not be revealed. He didn't know at the time that, in the end, all interview partners gave me consent to reveal their names because they all had previous convictions and served time in prison. Hence, their IRA membership was no secret. Did this man test me if I was trustworthy? If I can keep secrets? How talky am I? In the end, I told him that before coming to County Kerry for this round of interviews, I was in a small town on the Atlantic coast but much further north in County Mayo. I had interviewed a high-profile republican there. This interview partner would have been well-known to the men I was about to interview—so I guessed. I was right, the man remained silent for a few second, looked at me, and after this moment that felt like an eternity because I was unsure about his reaction, he said to me calmly: "If that man in Mayo speaks to you, I will speak to you as well." Most interviews started with episodes like that. Although I didn't know what would expect me at each interview, I trusted Maurice that it would go well, and the republicans would talk to me.

One of the last interview partners was Matt. He was in his sixties and lived with his wife in Tralee. Matt was a former republican prisoner who had served several years in the high-security prison Portlaoise in the late 1970s and 1980s. I was familiar with his name because Matt remained active in the Republican Sinn Féin party's local branch. However, I could not prepare for the interview because Maurice had only told me on the way to Matt's house.

When Maurice parked the car and opened the gate to the fore garden, Matt had already opened the door. He was expecting us. However, from the beginning, I had the stark impression that the mood was not as welcoming as in other interview settings before. He offered me tea, and we set down in the living room. "So, what do you want from me," he asked. What followed was my usual introduction to the research that I give to every interview partner. I give them all the information they need to understand why I want to talk to them and what I plan to do with the stories they tell me, but I don't give them too much information. I don't want to influence their following answers by providing them with too much detailed information about my research questions and hypothesis. I explained the interview procedure, asked for consent to record the conversation, and explained the interview consent form. He listened and then pointed to a framed newspaper article on the wall: "It's all there." Some years earlier, he had given an interview to a small republican monthly paper called *Saoirse* (Freedom). They had printed an excerpt of the conversation on a full page, accompanied by Matt's photograph. This interview had primarily focused on his republican activism before and after the prison with only summative references to the years he had spent in Portlaoise.

In contrast, my research focus was on prison life and, particularly, prisoners' reading habits and self-education. So, I explained that my interview had another focus, which was to no avail. Yet, after several more attempts to convince him to speak to me, he finally agreed that we start the interview.

I turned on the recorder and started with the usual biographical question that serves to generate a narrative answer: "Can you tell me how you became a republican activist?" Most of my interview partners answer this question with a lengthy recollection of the memories of their upbringing, family, childhood, youth, friends, and social and political issues in Ireland that brought them to their republican involvement and eventually imprisonment. Not with Matt, he just snapped: "You can read it all there" and pointed to the article on the wall again. This reaction was most surprising to me since Matt was an active and known political party member. For several years, he held the local branch's position of chairperson, and I knew him as a speaker at republican events. From a political activist like him, I didn't expect such reluctance. While I explained to him that I would like to hear his story again and I would like to record it in his own words, I rephrased my initial question to get him to talk to me. He finally said a few words. But his answers were concise, merely one or two sentences. He was unwilling to give me a narrative. Most of my questions were initially greeted with the same reaction: "I have already talked about it in that paper [on the wall]."

The interview proceeded rapidly from one topic to another due to the mere snippets he gave me. His body language proved that the whole situation annoyed him. I was disappointed and asked myself: What did I do wrong? Was it me? Was it my initial appearance? Were there any reasons beyond my own knowledge that made him reluctant to speak to me? Was there an issue with his political organization? Or the gatekeeper Maurice? Did Matt just have a bad day? Was it busy and had no time to give this interview? I still don't know the answers.

Dealing with the Unexpected

In another situation, I could have wrapped up the interview, stand up and mark it as a failure, and not use it for further research. Yet this was one of my main field research trips, one year into my PhD thesis research project. It was also the only possibility to meet these republicans who lived in such a remote corner of Ireland. Besides, I wanted to collect as much interview data as possible because Portlaoise prison, where Matt was incarcerated for several years, is still a vastly under-researched topic. I didn't want to give up and let the chance to interview him fade away.

Matt was not particularly keen on discussing the issues related to my research focus—reading habits and self-education. But when I asked him a follow-up question about the daily routine in prison, he mentioned that he was a good football player and he liked playing team sports in jail. I immediately recognized that this was the first moment Matt used a positive connotation to refer to activities throughout the whole previous interview process. He had used the word "like." So, I continued speaking to him about sport. Initially still reserved, he quickly opened up. His body language and tone changed when he remembered sports, organizing teams, playing Irish sports like Gaelic football, and other related issues. Moreover, he could not refer to the newspaper article on the wall because the sport was not a topic of the newspaper interview. It was something new that he had not told before. We talked about sports in prison, team selections, competitions, and how outside supporters facilitated the prisoners with the necessary equipment for the next 30 minutes or so. That was much longer than the previous 15 minutes that provided me with hardly anything useful in terms of my research question—despite exciting observations from an oral historian's point of view, yet that was not the purpose of my trip to him.

After a bit more than 30 minutes, I had the feeling that he had said everything he wanted to tell me about sports in prison. I asked him if there was anything else he wanted to tell me or if there were any other areas he considered relevant that were not yet covered in the interview. His tone and body language immediately turned back to the annoyed interview partner of the pre-sport's conversation: "Everything has been said. I think we are done with this thing now," were the words that ended the conversation. Nonetheless, I was happy that I had collected new insight into the daily routine of prisoners. I didn't collect anything that I used to answer my PhD thesis' research question, but I had data for future use in different projects. I was satisfied with the day, although the interview didn't go as expected.

Over the following years, I continued including questions about sports in prison in my interview guide. If I stumbled over archival material, photos, and other data related to sport in prisons, I collected it, for Matt had ignited a new interest in me. In 2018 and 2019, I eventually published a book chapter and a journal article on sports and Irish republican prisoners. Matt's initial surprising refusal to talk to me generated a new research interest during the interview process.

As these memories, collected from my field notes demonstrate, oral history interviews—mainly if they are biographical, narrative interviews—not always go as expected. As a young PhD researcher, as I was at that time, I tried to be well prepared, taking with me a clearly outlined interview guide that reflected both my narrative methodology, as well as my research interest. Such research trips are a difficult task for PhD researchers. On the one hand, you are still relatively inexperienced; on the other hand, you feel the pressure to collect as much data as possible since oral history is a costly—travel tickets, car rentals, and so on—and time-consuming—organizing interviews, transcriptions, and so on—historical research method. In the intense weeks of field research in a foreign country, failures are not allowed. In the worst case, you might be faced with too little data to finish your research. These concerns are not the same for all projects. Such dangers are mitigated in life story history projects when biographical, open-ended interviews are deployed, than in oral history projects with more clearly defined research interests. The latter was the case in my research project. While I adopted the method of narrative interviews, starting with biographical sections, I was primarily interested in the self-education process and the reading habits of the Irish republicans in the camps and prisons.

In the last decade working as an oral historian, I learned not to be afraid of surprises in the interview setting. Unexpected developments in interviews, such as silence, reluctance, and negative emotions, are a chance to develop your own research project and understanding of the field you are researching. As much as silence gave rise to an understanding of what had not been said in the interview, Matt's reluctance to speak about anything else but sports gave rise to my newly found research interest. As a result of this unexpected interview experience, I became, unknowingly, an oral historian of sports in internment camps and prisons.

CHAPTER 23

Commentary: The Answer Is Not Only Another Subject: It Is Also Another Set of Questions

Linda Shopes

The three articles in this section, focusing on the way interviews can unexpectedly generate new areas of inquiry, have for me generated some questions, not especially new questions perhaps, but still pertinent ones. I raise them in the following paragraphs and suggest some possible responses that I hope stimulate further questioning. I hope too that the sequence of questions suggests a certain progression of ideas, from method to interpretation to practice, not simply the perambulations of my own mind. I don't know much about jazz, but maybe it's appropriate to say I'm riffing off the articles and drawing on other work too, while trying to keep a theme in play. Also, my comments obviously reflect my own position as a US-based oral historian.

* * *

Given how easily an interview can go awry, I wonder, what do narrators think of the experience? Of course, not all interviews go wrong—archives are filled with many good enough interviews, some outstanding ones that cumulatively have mattered in one way or other. And some interviewers and narrators have over the years developed mutually interrogating relationships. But other interviews (and relationships), more perhaps than we are willing to admit, do miss the mark, or at least the mark as "we" have defined it. Daniel James (2000) has reflected thoughtfully on one such encounter in his "Listening in the Cold"; and Alessandro Portelli (1997)—or more accurately Mrs. Julia Cowans, whom

L. Shopes (✉)
Carlisle, PA, USA

he interviewed—reminds us that we always talk across lines of difference, a structural condition of our work that creates plenty of opportunities for misunderstanding. So, I wonder: what we might learn if we asked narrators, after the interview is over, why they consented to speak with us? And if the experience of being interviewed was what they expected or something else altogether?

I wonder how often we fail to learn about something significant to a person because we don't, unlike the authors in this section, inadvertently stumble onto it—or, as Tom Strohl said to historian Thomas Dublin about a topic that came up long after their interview was over, "Well, you never asked" (Dublin and Harvan 1998, 21). Some interviewers do ask, towards the end of an interview, a version of "what haven't I asked you about that you'd to tell me?" Or maybe open an interview with something like "we're here to talk about ____, but let's start with you telling me something about yourself," and then see what unexpected might come up. Or frame questions pertinent to our—and not necessarily a narrator's—area of interest within a more expansive life history. These seem like good ideas. Good too is to approach an interview not as a fact-finding mission for our project but as an exercise in relationship building; it can shift the dynamic. Which of course raises a troubling imbalance: we get to know them, but how much do they get to know us? Should they? One and done seems like the wrong approach, but what's a realistic alternative? Longer interviews? Multiple sessions? Moving towards an ethnographic model? I am reminded here of something Walter S. Carr, Sr., a Black man, said in 1979 to interviewer Lucy Peebles in response to her question: "Is there anything else you'd like to say about the whole thing [the community history project for which he was being interviewed]":

> Well, it might sound one-sided because I've only heard your side, but I didn't have to hear your side once I learned that a white man was at the head of this project. Because there is no way in the world that he could present this thing in the light that it is supposed to be presented—unless you bring him down here to live with me for a week and go with me for a week, then I might qualify him for heading this project because he doesn't know what it's all about. That's how I feel about it. Ain't no way he could sit up there in that ivory tower and tell me what's going on down here, or even make you or anybody else who's going to understand these people realize what it's all about.[1]

Mr. Carr may have been way ahead of us oral historians.

* * *

---

[1] Walter S. Carr, interviewed by Lucy Peebles, November 7, 1979, interview tape 4: 027:00–029:00, Baltimore Neighborhood Heritage Project collection, University of Baltimore, Baltimore, Maryland. Quoted in Jessica Douglas, "Charming City: The Amplification of Baltimore's White Ethnic Community Narratives and the Baltimore Neighborhood Heritage Project" (paper presented at the virtual Oral History Association Annual Meeting, October 18, 2020), 8. I am grateful to Ms. Douglas for bringing this quote to my attention. In the interest of full disclosure, I was employed as an oral historian for the Baltimore Neighborhood Heritage Project, under whose auspices Mr. Carr was interviewed.

I wonder too how much we don't get of what narrators do say to us, if not always in so many words. Camillo Robertini and Plínio Ferreira Guimarães realized they were hearing something quite different than what they had expected or even wanted from narrators because these narrators—or some of them—were willing to go against the grain of their questions. But how many others go along and respond politely to our questions (or brusquely, like Matt, interviewed by Dieter Reinisch)? Or wonder why don't we ask them about *this*? Or tell us what they presume we want to hear? Or misdirect? Or refuse to be interviewed? And how many of us don't hear what a narrator says or is trying to say underneath the words—and silences? Here I think it is important to listen and relisten to interviews in their entirety to catch the context of a given statement and nuances of speech—not, in other words, to rely solely on transcripts for our work, for these can all too easily obscure meaning. And to be wary of the short excerpt.

But still: what arrogance. We go in for one, two, five, fifteen, whatever number of hours, inviting, coaxing, sometimes, in current parlance, extracting knowledge from a narrator, knowledge that we then expect to make something of. If we are lucky, as the three authors here have been, we learn something unexpected, not just about the topic at hand, but about the research endeavor we are engaged with. For these articles lead me to ask why people's behavior often doesn't conform to theory or what scholarship tells us is important. Why should we expect workers to be revolutionary heroes, to not regard a measure of material stability as "good"? Why would local people not be apprehensive—or mocking or ignorant—of guerilla warriors or not appreciative of the much-needed material aid provided by the military, even if it was under the control of a dictator? Or to even want to talk about years as a political prisoner? What do our expectations tell us about us?

Of course, part of the problem is that oral history is intrinsically about individual lives, whereas social-historical scholarship aims beyond the specific, the particular. And individual lives spill over the lines of scholarly generalizations. So, I wonder how scholarship, what we use to inform our work, what "prior research" we seek to "build upon," however much it may focus our attention, may also narrow our inquiry, leading us to either hear what we want to hear or not hear what we are being told. I think this is what Portelli was getting at, albeit from a different angle, when, in a devastating takedown of historian Louise Tilly's equally devastating critique of oral history as "unrepresentative," he compares oral history to literature. He wrote:

> What we learn from literary scholarship is that an exceptional work is not representative of the average, run-of-the-mill book production of a given time and place. But it represents a possibility; it opens a road, it points a direction; it sets a yardstick against which everything else will be measured. The same applies—with necessary adaptations—to oral testimony. More and more, I have grown to view oral history as providing us not so much a pattern of common experience as one

of shared possibilities, real or imaginary. That they are hard to unify under any precise, rigorous pattern, suggests the different shapes of destiny that are at any given time held before people's eyes and that find a place in their minds. It also helps us visualize the pattern of society not so much as a grid of geometric squares (as it is often—for many respectable and useful reasons—represented), but rather as a mosaic in which every piece, though it may resemble the others, yet differs slightly from all of them. I am convinced, incidentally, that this image is much closer to objective reality. (Thompson et al. 1985, 38)

It is indeed sometimes difficult to fit the evidence of oral history into the grid of existing scholarship. Portelli suggests one way of addressing this—as a mosaic of voices. My preference is via lengthy, individual biographical narratives, in print, in podcasts, on websites. Surely there are other ways of capturing this pluralist individuality without reducing every story to some sort of anodyne "equality."

* * *

But don't get me wrong. I am not valorizing the holy folk. I may have long abandoned the convenient notion of "false consciousness" as a way of explaining popular wariness and worse of progressive politics, but the disastrous 2016 presidential election in the United States and the aftermath of the contested 2020 election—and so many hate-filled events between these two—have disabused me of any lingering romanticization of the masses. Nor, I hope, have I fallen into what Michael Frisch years ago dubbed the "anti-history" approach to oral history, that is, the tendency "to view oral historical evidence, because of its immediacy and emotional resonance, as something almost beyond interpretation or accountability, as a direct window on the feelings and, in some sense, on the meaning of past experiences." To "confer unquestioned authority on direct experience," he continued, "is usually to mystify, rather than bypass, the process of drawing meaning from the stream of history" (Frisch 1990, 160).

So I am glad that Robertini learned something about the identity formations and mental constructs that workers develop to distance themselves from the brutalities of a dictatorship. I am glad that Guimarães came to ask deeper questions about Cold War politics in the face of Third World revolutionary movements. And I am glad that Reinish was able to publish about sport and Irish republican prisoners. But if oral history can lead us to questions about the conceptual framing of our work, I wonder if it might also raise questions about the conditions of its production and perhaps the social niche we oral historians, producers of knowledge, cultural workers—whatever we call ourselves—occupy.

A few years ago, Steven High, reflecting on his own work with the Montreal Life Stories project, stated that "community-university collaboration need not begin and end with the recorded interview" (High 2014, 7). Ours indeed has been a practice that frequently has ended with the recorded interview, specifically with its placement in an archive, an institution intimately connected to the discipline[ing] of history. I have no quarrel with archives in and of themselves—I worked at the Pennsylvania State Archives for more than a decade and fully support the imperative to preserve completed interviews and make them publicly available in appropriate repositories. But at least since the 1970s, there has been a popular, sometimes activist strain in oral history, some of it codified in what is now termed public history, much of it taking place outside of traditional academic structures, in places like local libraries and historical societies, community organizations and churches. Recently we have seen work in oral history linked directly to issues of social justice. Two examples that come immediately to mind are the Densho Project, which records interviews related to the incarceration of Japanese Americans during World War "to promote equity and justice today"; and the Texas after Violence project, which interviews individuals impacted by state-sanctioned violence in order to "shift narrative power to marginalized and oppressed communities and promote restorative and transformative justice."[2] Both build upon the work of those, often people of color, who are pressing the urgency of profound, often racialized inequalities on public consciousness, including mine; both not incidentally are community-based organizations. Recently too, we are seeing work that situates a social change-oriented oral history historically, placing it in the mainstream of our practice. Daniel Kerr (2016), for example, has begun to define a new narrative of oral history's origin, finding it not in the creation of archives but in the work of popular educators such as Paulo Freire, Myles Horton, and Septima Clark, who used first-person oral narratives as a way to stimulate reflections that link personal troubles to a broader critique, which, in turn, could generate collective, political action.[3]

This work—and perhaps too the digital revolution, which increasingly demands that our work be public facing in some way—has led me to think lately about oral history as a civic—or public—resource, in addition to, or even instead of a scholarly one. I am imagining a flip in emphasis, so that we don't do a documentation project with an ancillary public outcome but rather a public project, driven by public concerns, that also has an archival outcome. What, you might ask, does this have to do with the three articles in this section? Something like this: I wonder how the authors' thoughtful conclusions as they confronted the unexpected in their interviews—about the memory of a dictatorship, about personal need, desire, and ignorance in the face of want, about prison and the everyday life of political prisoners—might be directed outward. These authors are thinking about matters of enormous public—civic—significance, so how might the insights gleaned from their oral history interviews become useful for not only a thesis, a dissertation, or a journal article, but also

---

[2] Densho, densho.org, accessed April 13, 2021; Texas after Violence Project, texasafterviolence.org, accessed April 13, 2021.
[3] See also Denise D. Meringolo, ed., *Radical Roots: Public History and Social Justice* (2021), which includes several articles focused on the radical roots of oral history.

a tool for popular education, a spark for change? How, if we are being imaginative here, can work like theirs—deeply scholarly, part of an academic project—be reimagined as a public inquiry, even help us reimagine public life? How can oral history, so deeply embedded in the world, serve the world? How might we oral historians become public servants?

Paul Thompson began his 1978 study of oral history with the sentence, "All history depends ultimately upon its social purpose" (Thompson 1978, 1). The three later editions of this work, most recently that of 2017 coauthored by Joanna Bornat (Thompson and Bornat 2017), also begin with this sentence. It bears repeating.[4]

References

Dublin, Thomas, and George Harvan. 1998. *When the Mines Closed: Stories of Struggles in Hard Times*. Ithaca: Cornell University Press.

Frisch, Michael. 1990. Oral History, Documentary, and the Mystification of Power: A Critique of Vietnam: A Television History. In *A Shared Authority: Essays on the Craft and Meaning of Oral and Public History*. Albany: State University of New York Press.

High, Steven. 2014. Introduction. In *Oral History at the Crossroads: Sharing Life Stories of Survival and Displacement*. Vancouver: UBC Press.

James, Daniel. 2000. Listening in the Cold: The Practice of Oral History in an Argentine Meatpacking Community. In *Life History, Memory, and Political Identity*, 119–156. Durham: Duke University Press.

Kerr, Daniel R. 2016. Allan Nevins Is Not My Grandfather: The Roots of Radical Oral History Practice in the United States. *Oral History Review* 43 (2): 367–391.

Meringolo, Denise D., ed. 2021. *Radical Roots: Public History and Social Justice*. Amherst, MA: Amherst College Press.

Portelli, Alessandro. 1997. There's Gonna Always Be a Line: History-Telling as a Multivocal Art. In *The Battle of Valle Giulia: Oral History and the Art of Dialogue*, 24–39. Madison: The University of Wisconsin Press.

Thompson, Paul. 1978. *The Voice of the Past: Oral History*. Oxford: Oxford University Press.

Thompson, Paul, and Joanna Bornat. 2017. *The Voice of the Past: Oral History*. 4th ed. Oxford: Oxford University Press.

Thompson, Paul, Luisa Passerini, Isabelle Bertaux-Wiame, and Alessandro Portelli. 1985. Between Social Scientists: Responses to Louise A. Tilly. *International Journal of Oral History* 6 (1): 19–39.

---

[4] The second edition was published in 1988, the third in 2000, both also by Oxford University Press.

PART V

Nothing but Surprises:
The Unexpected as a Given

CHAPTER 24

Introduction to Part V

Miriam Hermeto and Ricardo Santhiago

We return in this section to one of the core ideas on which this book was conceived: the understanding of the unexpected in oral history not as a "new topic" nor, alternatively, as an episodic occurrence in our practice—but rather as an almost inescapable element, inherent to this method and the field activities it involves. Thus, the following chapters propose less an epistemological excavation than a narrative refocus, which, however, has a strong generative potential for new methodological reflections.

In view of the case studies already presented, we can ask ourselves: do the field experiences these cases communicate hold something extraordinary, demarcating a discontinuity in relation to the usual oral historian's attitudes toward narrators, sources, and techniques? In our view, no. Above all, they sharpen our perception of the pervasiveness of astonishments, shocks, collisions, consternations, and even collapses in our research efforts. They reveal an attitudinal trace that, congenitally or forcibly acquired, must be considered a part of the oral historian's toolkit: flexibility. Or as said by the best-selling physicist and science disseminator Leonard Mlodinow (2018): an "elastic thinking," inevitably sustained by the ability to analyze the situation in which the researcher is found, to restructure one's guiding issues, to combine imagination and logic, to experiment and learn how to deal with mistakes—conditions that are fundamental to promote change and solve problems.

M. Hermeto
Universidade Federal de Minas Gerais (UFMG), Belo Horizonte, Brazil

R. Santhiago (✉)
Universidade Federal de São Paulo (Unifesp), São Paulo, Brazil
e-mail: ricardo.santhiago@unifesp.br

The contributors to this book have learned the virtue of making mistakes, of revising one's own convictions, of reshaping anticipated research designs, rather than stalling in stupefaction when encountering unusual events. The solutions they propose in the face of the unexpected are unique, it is true, but at the same time, they rely on a specific intellectual culture—ours and on a sensitivity that seems to be the very same that leads a researcher to oral history, to this narrative and participatory practice that is undeniably dependent on the other and is vulnerable to the multiple circumstances that inform an encounter. Oral history is, in itself, a way of proposing a relationship between research participants that assumes, from the outset, the unforeseen as a given. Therefore, those researchers who are easily scared away by uncertainty, frustration, and adversity perhaps have little chance of being bewitched by a method already defined as an art—and a multivocal art at that. Those who embrace it, however, have a significant chance of finding "exuberance in the smallest things"—as the poet Manoel de Barros once wrote—including in the unexpected as a *given*, as *data*. Suggestively, *given* and *data* in Portuguese share the same word, *dado*.

"The initial question prompts responses which may be taken up in unpredictable ways, unpredictable to both sides," Joanna Bornat writes of the initial moments of a dialogic encounter in her appreciation of the "interrogative character" of both oral history and reminiscence (Bornat 2001, 225). "The possibilities of human memory are inexhaustible," writes Lucilia de Almeida Neves Delgado, warning that "dealing with them is walking on fertile but also slippery ground, which requires sensitivity, creativity, ethics, and consistent historical knowledge" (Neves Delgado 2006, 64). In a recent collection on queer oral history, a notion underpinning the chapters is that this focus is ripe for the emergence of trauma and vulnerability (Murphy et al. 2022). We would amend this observation by noting that such a danger inheres in oral history interviews as a whole. And, using oral history as an educational tool, with Greek students invited to interview Albanian migrants, Riki Van Boeschoten states that he deliberately sought to produce a "culture shock" (Van Boeschoten 2008, 216). Those who resort to oral history after reading such cautionary words are doing so at their own peril, having been fully alerted to what they may encounter.

This distinctive sensitivity, which involves acceptance of (perhaps even an inclination toward) the unstable and unfamiliar, may well be related to the very genesis of oral history. As an (in an epistemological sense) anti-establishment method, exposed to challenges coming from the most diverse disciplinary traditions, oral history scholarship has needed to develop and express an enormous awareness of its own limits, openly responding to theoretical writings and reports from the field. This awareness includes knowing that research expectations contain in themselves the possibility of being thwarted—from multiple directions. Interviewees, as we know well, also have expectations, and are often baffled. Daphne Patai writes that "there is also, in the interview situation, a problem of raised expectations: a hope (…) that the interviewer might solve a problem or know what to do" (1988, 6), pointing to one of the sources of what she herself later considered a fulcrum to researchers' incessant dissatisfaction: the incapacity to respond to narrators' expectations. Indeed, these may cover the most diverse range of desires: that the interviewer becomes a good friend, or mediate family conflicts, or produce a glorious and laudatory public portrait, or even improve your living conditions, as with Marella Hoffman, who received gifts from interviewees who wished her to intercede with powerful people and arrange jobs in public service (Hoffman 2017). Idealization, in short, runs in all directions.

In view of the unexpected *data* that is also a *given*, do researchers develop a friendly relationship with surprises or they do insist on keeping them at a distance? Indira Chowdhury, Leylianne Alves Vieira and Regina Helena Alves da Silva, Iara Souto Ribeiro Silva, and Gabriel Amato bring to the table their experiences with surprising data, leading to findings that eventually (and serendipitously) were integrated into their discussions and helped to solve anticipated research questions while raising a number of others.

Indira Chowdhury, when conducting interviews to assess the impact of the work of an Indian NGO, found in a "baffling bandit"—who is now a kind of a teacher—the depiction of characters such as Robin Hood who are familiar from children's literature. The narrator's ease, in contrast to the researcher's estrangement, leads her to a deeper understanding of the dynamics of social violence and gender hierarchies in that geographic area, an understanding that was only possible once she accepted that she would not emerge with the heroic narrative the NGO may have wanted to see. Instead of what third parties expected (and actually commissioned), Chowdhury's sensible oral history allows a complex and fascinating story to emerge.

When interviewing three generations of women involved in one of the greatest recent tragedies in mining areas in Brazil, Leylianne Alves Vieira and Regina Helena Alves da Silva found an unexpected structure: geographical and cultural references, traversed by trauma, revealed a transition from hope to mourning. The oral histories they conducted showed how an enormous disruptive event that saddened and shocked the world and collapsed the natural environment also transformed the dynamics of transmitting memories.

Iara Souto Ribeiro Silva analyzes a specific situation: the erasure of Mr. Irany's case from the archives and from the official corporate memory that a university produced about its own history during the Brazilian dictatorship—a university in which Irany worked, and where Silva now works. Leaving behind tense memories of the dictatorial past, the narrator brings out the moment when the staff union was created and transforms the interview into a situation in which he praises and encourages the "new generation" of public servants, represented by Silva, to act. By recounting his story not as a victim of the dictatorship but as a victorious person who succeeded in labor activism, he gives his interview partner a glimpse of a different approach to her research questions.

Finally, Gabriel Amato names the link among the particularities of these three cases—and of two others that he experienced—in a conceptual commentary that sees oral history as a "culture of research ." This is his anthropological explanation for the oral historian's keen desire to incorporate the unforeseen into the research, without denying that the oral historians' research instruments themselves (such as the apparently innocent lists of questions) constitute embodiments of expectations.

These are five researchers who share the experience of being surprised. They have embraced this experience just as they had embraced a common research method and its sensibility, without ever losing sight of the oral historians' professional responsibilities.

References

Bornat, Joanna. 2001. Reminiscence and Oral History: Parallel Universes or Shared Endeavour? *Ageing and Society* 21 (2): 219–241.

Hoffman, Marella. 2017. *Practicing Oral History to Improve Public Policies and Programs*. New York: Routledge.

Mlodinow, Leonard. 2018. *Elastic: Flexible Thinking in a Constantly Changing World*. New York: Pantheon.

Murphy, Amy Tooth, Clare Summerskill, and Emma Vickers, eds. 2022. *New Directions in Queer Oral History: Archives of Disruption*. New York: Routledge.

Neves Delgado, Lucilia de Almeida. 2006. *História oral: Memória, tempo, identidades*. Belo Horizonte: Autêntica.

Patai, Daphne. 1988. *Brazilian Women Speak: Contemporary Life Stories*. New Brunswick: Rutgers University Press.

Van Boeschoten, Riki. 2008. Public Memory as Arena of Contested Meanings. A Student Project on Migration. In *Oral History and Public Memories*, ed. Paula Hamilton and Linda Shopes, 211–229. Philadelphia: Temple University Press.

CHAPTER 25

The Case of the Baffling Bandit

Indira Chowdhury

SHAPING AN INTERVIEW

I grew up in Bengal in eastern India, which has a strong tradition of writing for children. The stories I grew up with ranged from mythological stories, folk tales, detective stories, and stories about dacoits, thugs, or bandits. Dacoits who were infamous for armed robberies have been around since medieval times; the Mughal records as well as early records of European travelers in India talk about the dangers of being attacked by armed robbers while traveling in India (Kaur and Kour 1983). The British rulers encountered this prevalent practice for the first time, and administrators like Colonel Sleeman wrote books documenting what came to be known as *thugee* in the nineteenth century—the practice of strangling and robbing travelers by secret criminal groups. By contrast, Bengali children's literature often characterized the dacoits differently—Rabindranath Tagore's Raghu Dakat was a Robin Hood-like figure. But the bandits of the Chambal region, mainly comprising the Baghi caste, were perceived as criminals who aroused fear in most. The Chambal region remained inaccessible for several decades after Indian independence. In 1967, the journalist Tarun Bhaduri wrote *Abhisapta Chambal* ("The Cursed Chambal") (Bhaduri 2012) in Bengali which was made into a film the same year. But the best-known film set in the Chambal region in which bandits played a major role was G.P. Sippy's *Sholay*, which became a popular hit in 1976, playing in theaters for over a year (Ghosh 2013). The Chambal remained in the news through the 1960s as several dacoits surrendered before the

I. Chowdhury (✉)
Centre for Public History, Srishti-Manipal Institute of Art, Design, and Technology, Bengaluru, India

© The Author(s), under exclusive license to Springer Nature Switzerland AG 2023
R. Santhiago, M. Hermeto (eds.), *The Unexpected in Oral History*, Palgrave Studies in Oral History,
https://doi.org/10.1007/978-3-031-17749-1_25

Gandhian Vinoba Bhave and later in the 1970s to the socialist political visionary Jayaprakash Narayan. The feared Phoolan Devi, known as "Bandit Queen," surrendered in 1983 and, after serving her jail term of 11 years, stood for election and became a Member of Parliament from that region.

All these stories echo through my head when I prepare for my visit to the Chambal region in November 2008. I was commissioned by an NGO to do a few interviews with people who had experienced change in their lives because of the NGO's strategic interventions in health, education, drinking water, and livelihood generation. Most community-based NGOs tend to collect quantifiable data and want short approbatory interviews about the work they do. While I did use the term "oral history" when I met with the NGO which was at that point celebrating a decade of existence, they were keen that I enabled them to collect "stories of change" that they could effectively use in their reports, grant proposals, or commemorative collaterals. But the oral historian in me could not be satisfied with a straightforward story of "progress." Rather, I was interested in finding out what drove people to change themselves. And what sorts of larger repercussions did such changes have on the family and on the community? My training as a historian alerted me to the historical dimensions of residual colonialism that often revealed itself in the collective memory of a community (Arnold 1984; Banerjee 1984; Guha 1999). My experience as an oral historian had also honed my instinct for the life story approach that so often opened windows into people's life choices and the formation of their identities. All this worked on my mind as I prepared. Unlike the preparation for interviews I did in urban and highly erudite contexts, where I was usually handed a profile or a curriculum vitae of my interviewee in advance, I had very basic information available about my interviewee—all I knew was that he an erstwhile bandit who now worked in a school. I concluded that he was literate. But what kind of education had he had? I am curious.

My journey begins in the south of India, in Bangalore, where I live. The distance from Bangalore to Sheopur in the northern part of Madhya Pradesh is nearly 2000 kilometers involving first a flight to the capital, New Delhi, then a train to Sawai Madhopur in Rajasthan, and a jeep ride through the forests for the final 62 kilometers to Sheopur. Sheopur is one of the westernmost towns of Madhya Pradesh and became a district town only in 1998. This area has an agrarian economy and grows wheat, mustard, and *bajra* (millet). It is also known for its artisanal work, especially wood-carved furniture.

It is nearly 11 pm when I arrive at Sawai Madhopur—a city built by Maharaja Madho Singh I of Jaipur in the eighteenth century. On the way to Sheopur we cross the Chambal River over the Pali bridge. It is past midnight and pitch dark; I am not lucky enough to spot the animals of the Ranthambore forest through which we drive. I joke that I would never tell my mother that I crossed the Chambal around midnight; after all, the place is notorious in her imagination as an area where if the tigers didn't get you, the bandits would. We arrive at Sheopur around 2 am. My interview with Gyan Singh Meena is scheduled for 10 am that day. I know that all the stories I had heard about bandits and about the Chambal will play a role in configuring this interaction.

Meeting the Bandit

In the morning, accompanied by one of the NGO workers, I make my way to the village of Chhota Kheda to interview Gyan Singh, who works at the school there. When we arrive, he is busy teaching the children the alphabet. I assume he is a schoolteacher, but I am told that he is actually a *Bal Mitra*—literally, "friend of children," a post that has been created to help children, most of whom are first-generation learners, to do their homework. In addition, the *Bal Mitra* keeps an eye on the children and makes sure that they come to school instead of being sent off by their parents to graze the goats or take care of the buffaloes. A *Bal Mitra* is paid extraordinarily little—Rs 1500 a month in 2008 (about 20.45 dollars). The work is not meant to be full-time. But Gyan Singh could well be their teacher as he spends most of his day with the children at school. Inquisitive about this extraordinary devotion to work, I begin my interview in Hindi.

He tells me about the home in the village where he was born—Bijarpur—just two kilometers away from the school. His family did agricultural work, and he still farms on a small plot of land. He also does some amount of seasonal sharecropping, but he enjoys teaching the children. He tells me he is about 42 years old but does not know the year of his birth. Where was he educated, I ask, not at all prepared for what he tells me. He had started going to school in Nanavad, a village in Sheopur, but had later studied in the town of Itawa, in the state of Rajasthan. He tells me that he had gone by himself to Itawa and adds broodingly, "Sometimes circumstances overtake your life. I also did some wrong things." Although the NGO worker wants Gyan Singh to elaborate on the second part of his statement, I am drawn to his introspection about how events overtake one's life. Gyan Singh does not explain right away; instead, he starts talking about his school education in Itawa—he studied there till Class 8 (the last year before high school), paying for it with his earnings. It is at this point that he explains the nature of his work: "I earned my own money by carrying out *chanda-wasuli* [extortion]—you know, forcing people to pay money. I would go into the marketplace and threaten and harass people for money."

He elaborates what he considered "work" at that point—he would raid stalls in markets and hold up buses forcing innocent passengers to part with their money.

The Bandit's "Work" and His Self-Image

I am a little stunned not just by his frank and matter-of-fact admission of the kind of "work" he used to do but also by the realization that he was not a dacoit at all but an extortionist. He chose this way of life because of what he describes as "circumstances"—he did not get along with his family and had run away from home. I realized later how deeply embroiled in family politics his life choices had been. He elaborates that he left after his mother "expired" (he uses the English word). He left home, crossing over to the neighboring state of

Rajasthan where he began to put himself through school with the money he earned through extortion. I wanted to know if he liked this "work." His answer is thoughtful:

GSM:	At first, I liked this work but later, I told myself I am doing something wrong and what am I doing all this for? I am completely ruining my own image. This is wrong.
IC:	Your what?
NGO *worker*:	He is using the English word—image.
GSM:	My image.
IC:	Okay. So you didn't like that image of yourself.
GSM:	No.
IC:	That was when you felt that you should not be doing this kind work? [Sound of tractor passing.]
GSM:	After this realization, I came back to Sheopur and passed Class X.

The English word catches me off guard. Gyan Singh, I notice as I go through the interview afterward, uses quite a few unexpected English words—"expired," which is common in those parts of India for dying—in fact, it is sometimes shortened to "pired" as I find out when interviewing Gyan Singh's wife. He also uses the word "tackle" when talking about what issues teachers do or do not teach in middle school. For Gyan Singh, it is important to maintain a respectable self-image—especially for the sake of his children. He tells me, "I wanted to change the way children looked at me. So, I decided that I had ruined my life, but my children should not follow the same path."

Gyan Singh's efforts to earn the respect of his children was treated with some skepticism by some villagers but most accepted him in his new role as a "teacher of children." He says, "They feel it is a good thing that he is different now, or he would have terrorized people here. But a few are still scared of me." He adds after a pause, "But it is not the same situation as earlier." At another point in his interview with me, Gyan Singh returns to the distrust many members of the community had. His reputation often came in the way even as he sought to reform his ways; when he went to attend the training of *Bal Mitras* at Sheopur Fort (a historic site and museum) and the Hindu Dharmashala (a hotel) at Sheopur, he tells me that some villagers thought "we had gathered there for gambling. But I told them what I did there."

Gyan Singh reiterated the story of his new self-image several times—at different points in his interview, always placing emphasis on his great determination to change himself. Although it appeared in some ways to reaffirm the discourse of reform that the NGO wanted to record, the narrative perhaps concealed deeper layers that were possibly part of the community's collective memory.

Colonial Identities and Collective Memory

The area of the Chambal as I have noted earlier is notorious for the dacoits that roam its ravines. During the colonial period, the British were unable to contain the violence that was rampant in this region. Historically, the colonial administration often mistook rebellions for criminal activities. Many of the tribes and castes that were engaged in armed robbery and "dacoity" came to be identified along with others as belonging to the "Criminal Tribes" of India (Brown 2003). The Criminal Tribe Act of 1871 was repealed only in 1949, two years after Indian independence. Three years later, the Indian Government enacted the Habitual Offender's Act in 1952, which once again branded many of the tribes that were identified as "criminal" in the past. Gyan Singh Meena belonged to the Meena tribe that was earlier a "criminal tribe." It was the burden of this identity that his search for an "image" signaled. In choosing the new identity of a "schoolteacher," this *Bal Mitra*—from a tribe that was viewed as "criminal" in the not-too-distant past—was perhaps attempting a break with that past. But the "bandit's" return to the community and the community's acceptance of him in his new role as a "teacher" of children also fostered the discourse of reform that shaped so much of our understanding of "development" in India. Indeed, Gyan Singh's self-reflection too indicated that in choosing his new identity he was discarding, what he called in Hindi, the "*galat kaam*"—those numerous "unlawful actions." But as he reflected further, this act of metamorphosis was not triggered by a single desire to become good. In fact, he tells me that he had left his village after his mother died and returned when three members of his gang died—two in a motorcycle accident and the third killed by villagers. Obviously, extortion "work" is impossible in the absence of a gang. Alone, he faced the threat of being attacked or killed by those he had relentlessly tortured earlier. In choosing to work in the school, he had chosen life over death.

Moreover, life came with uncertainties. "Normal" peasant life was unfamiliar to him. Besides, as he said with some resentment—"My father is still living, and he has land. I have no land. And I don't have any relationship with my father." He set himself up by becoming a tenant farmer. Not really used to plowing the land, he worked with hired help. This arrangement also freed him from spending all his time on farming and allowed him to spend his entire working day at the school, even though his position as a *Bal Mitra* was not a full-time one. His hard-earned identity as the "schoolteacher" thus remained intact.

Discovering Another Perspective

I wondered how Gyan Singh's recently acquired identity was perceived by others in his family. Did the story of the bandit's transformation resonate in the same way with his wife? I had earlier, in the course of this project, spoken to successful coffee farmers and their families. In the case of Gyan Singh, the NGO did not expect me to interview his wife, but I sought out a short interview with her, Rukmini. Shy at first, Rukmini opened up as she began to show me her stitching and the handcrafted items she made. She had a sewing machine and stitched *salwar kameez*, *sari* blouses, and petticoats for women; she also made large bedspreads that people around bought from her. She also made patchwork cloth fans and beautiful carrying rings on which village women could balance the pots of water they carried. This brought in earnings for the family which struggled to hold their lives together, but it also contributed to making Rukmini an active member of the village community.

It is Rukmini who throws light on the reason behind Gyan Singh's wrath—on why he left the village in the first place. In Gyan Singh's interview, he had mentioned to me that he left the village after his mother died. Rukmini's elaboration sheds further light: not only had his mother died, but his father had married again. A furious Gyan Singh had stopped eating the food cooked by his father's new wife; he made his own *rotis*. Soon afterward, he left the village and in the course of his wanderings found his gang. Gyan Singh was vague about what happened to his wife during his absence. Rukmini tells me that theirs was a child marriage, and as was customary, she had lived with her parents until she had children. She claimed that was not really affected by what he did as she lived at her parents' home. After his return, Gyan Singh never kept in touch with his father or his half-brothers, but Rukmini did. To her the larger village community and her husband's extended family mattered. Gyan Singh, she tells me, was as angry as he was proud. He was, she tells me, a *badmash* (she uses the Hindi word that means hooligan) and says that he never gave her any money, even when he had money. But his work with the NGO had reformed him. Now he leaves for school at 8 am every morning and sits with his books in the evening. Rukmini laughs as she tells me, "I say to myself, in his old age, he has started studying!" But the fact that they remain landless still rankles, and she adds, "People say, 'His father gave him nothing, but he became a Master'. But this Master has nothing!" However, he has no patience to teach her, and she laughs light-heartedly about his temper: "He has such a temper that I cannot even sit and talk to him for five minutes." I wonder what then had changed. She laughs and tells me that everyone says he has transformed. But then when the NGO was conducting a training program at Motikunj for 10 days, he went away. "I was extremely sick and weak and there was nobody to look after me. But he just went. He is so fond of this NGO! That is when my in-laws had said, "What kind of magic has the NGO worked on him? Here you are ill, and he is gone!"".

Gyan Singh's efforts at restoring his tarnished self-image came at a cost. Rukmini suffered and was rescued by the community she had built a relationship with. This fact strikes me when I return to this interview while teaching oral history. The purpose of my interview was to seek out a story of transformation. But only by moving beyond the individual can we understand the interconnected nature of change and the ripples it creates as it disposes of the past and embraces and creates a new present. I realize that I would not have understood this process had I not spoken to Gyan Singh's wife.

My interview with Rukmini takes place in their home, in Bijarpur—about two kilometers away from the school where I had interviewed Gyan Singh that same morning. As we are winding up, Gyan Singh comes home and makes me a cup of tea. I am struck by the fact that Rukmini speaks her mind about her husband's neglect and his temper quite openly, ignoring his presence. My interview with her demonstrates how decisions taken by Gyan Singh, as head of the household, had shaped Rukmini's life and instilled in her the ability to accept what would remain unchanged in her marriage and pushed her towards the one thing she could change—herself. From that perception began her journey to self-reliance. She had come to recognize that despite the cracks, she could survive. Fearlessly.

My interview with the erstwhile bandit was supposed to yield a narrative of heroic metamorphosis aided by the work of development. Instead, I returned with a fresh understanding about what enables people to change and how stories of extraordinary and heroic transformations have domestic counterparts that can redefine the contours of the extraordinary and challenge the notion of heroism itself.

References

Arnold, David. 1984. *Criminal Tribes and Martial Races: Crime and Social Control in Colonial India*. Paper presented at the Institute of Commonwealth Studies, University of London.

Banerjee, Sumanta. 1984. Peasant Consciousness. *Economic and Political Weekly* 19 (24/25): 942–945.

Bhaduri, Tarun Coomar. 2012. *Abhishapta Chambal [1967]*. Kolkata: New Age.

Brown, Mark. 2003. Ethnology and Colonial Administration in Nineteenth-Century British India: The Question of Native Crime and Criminality. *The British Journal for the History of Science* 36 (2): 201–219.

Ghosh, Bishnupriya. 2013. Sensate Outlaws: The Recursive Social Bandit in Indian Popular Cultures. In *Figurations in Indian Film*, ed. Meheli Sen and Anustup Bose, 21–43. London: Palgrave Macmillan.

Guha, Ranajit. 1999. *Elementary Aspects of Peasant Insurgency in Colonial India*. Durham, NC: Duke University Press.

Kaur, Madanjit, and Madanjit Kour. 1983. A Note on the Practice of Dacoity in 19th century BENGAL: A Contemporary Account. *Proceedings of the Indian History Congress* 44: 538–543.

CHAPTER 26

Tragedy, Trauma, and the Transformations of Local Memory

Regina Helena Alves da Silva and Leylianne Alves Vieira

The act of remembering is culturally marked, leading to variations informed by the time and by the cultural background of the individuals who remember. Moments of trauma often create cracks in the memory structure of the survivors. Such moments cause the past to be rewritten from the point of view of the present. In fact, we never fully remember how things happened; memories are built according to the impressions we have today about what happened. Furthermore, narratives related to earlier moments in life also help to shape how individuals come to understand their place in mnemonical terms. According to Jörn Seeman,

> although memory is essentially an internal process, its projection does not happen in a vacuum: memory needs place to be activated and stimulated. In this sense, concrete places, where events, historical landmarks, or everyday practices occur, as well as visual (maps or photos) and non-visual (literature, music) representations, can serve as spatial references for memory. (2002/2003, 44)

In January 2019, the second-largest industrial disaster to occur in Brazil in the past 100 years occurred. A dam burst in the village of Córrego do Feijão [Bean Stream] village, in the town of Brumadinho, state of Minas Gerais,

R. H. A. da Silva (✉)
Universidade Federal de Minas Gerais (UFMG), Belo Horizonte, Brazil

L. A. Vieira
INCT, Políticas Públicas e Desenvolvimento Territorial (INPuT), Belo Horizonte, Brazil

© The Author(s), under exclusive license to Springer Nature Switzerland AG 2023
R. Santhiago, M. Hermeto (eds.), *The Unexpected in Oral History*, Palgrave Studies in Oral History,
https://doi.org/10.1007/978-3-031-17749-1_26

causing the death of 270 persons and enormous environmental damage due to the release of 12 million cubic meters of tailings. This event also significantly impacted the villages of Pires and Parque da Cachoeira.

We approached these communities after the dam rupture, in the context of a research project intended to draw a social cartography of the communities and the event's impacts on the families living there. The research design initially included semi-structured interviews with residents, especially those who had been there since the early establishment of the villages and who experienced local life in differing ways. Our initial observations and interviews highlighted the complexity of the event and the trauma that affected the villagers, leading to our first encounter with the unexpected: the need to make changes in the methodological design. The interviews showed us the way to opt for a "cartography of controversies," a methodology associated with the actor-network theory that makes it possible to map polemics and divergences that constitute a given context. With this methodology, the diverse views expressed by the interviewees, as well as the relevance of non-human elements pertaining to the tragedy, could be better analyzed.

The construction of social bonds in countryside communities located far from urban centers, whose origin relates to agricultural or extractive villages, is marked by proximity and acquaintance between the individuals and the families that compose them. When we were still in the exploratory stage, that is, before the fieldwork, one option we had in mind was to form groups with the older members of the communities. We aimed to talk to some of the elderly to grasp the event's impact on those who had lived in the area for a long time and built their lives around the local mining activities. And so we did. What surprised us in the fieldwork was that, even in small communities with very close ties, the interviews reveal how social bonds are reconfigured the further you are from the founders' generations.

Since the traumatic event had reconfigured spaces and relationships—in addition to local opinions about mining, community, and life—it made access to residents and the formation of interviewee groups more difficult than we had anticipated, leading to yet another methodological change and our second encounter with the unexpected, which was the need to incorporate generation as a category. Our initial first field trips made us realize that a traditional social cartography would not be sufficient to express the nuances of the relationship between individuals and the ways of cohabiting with mining. Our approaches had to unfold slowly and individually, identifying and contacting persons who felt comfortable talking about the event, its past, and future. Through these research paths we found individuals who were part of the same family but who experienced the event and community life differently. Specifically, we were put in contact with women and their perceptions about everyday life and mining operations.

When having contact with the different generations that inhabit Córrego do Feijão, we realized that spatial references such as those mentioned by Seeman take the form of a mosaic composed of both the subjects' own experiences and their family narratives. Because of this confluence, we started to build "generational sensobiographies" (Aula and da Silva 2019). This method has allowed us, for example, to present how the memories of a grandmother, a daughter, and a granddaughter transect each other, revealing recollections crisscrossed by the traumatic event that gave new meanings to the places that mark the family history. According to Aula and da Silva, in a "sensobiography"

> any experience of living in a city is mediated by unique life trajectories and sensory perceptions. These, in turn, are mediated by local sensory regimes, routines, and bodily and socio-cultural habits, and by various material transformations such as buildings, new architectural designs, and the development of technological devices that surround us on a daily basis. At the same time, the increase in the mobility of goods and people has affected environments, experiences of the place, and ways of sharing stories. (Aula and da Silva 2019, 20)

It was the reconfiguration of the research design required by the field interviews that made us arrive at results that turned out to be quite different than what we thought we would have at the end of our journey. The memories of the residents with whom we spoke turned out to be thoroughly permeated by geographical and temporal references that involve mining and its history in the region, in addition to explaining territorial conflicts over land and even over the population's ways of life. Mining, once a dream, came to be narrated as the highest point in the destruction of the dreams of those who survived the mud but have to live, directly or indirectly, with death.

The women's narratives that we bring to this article tell the story of the place and their family; they deal with work relationships linked to family mining and farming and show how different generations relate to place and trauma. They are individual narratives that, at the same time, complement and rub against one another, revealing ways of looking to the future that are distinct and particular. Let us now deal with their experience of the unexpected: what happened to and between these three women and their place after the dam ruptured.

First Generation: Places

The grandmother, whose parents were among the earliest community members, keeps memories of the place that are marked by the presence of the dam, which is, at the same time, a spatial reference and a kind of character in family narratives:

> I'm from here, I was born here. But, however, I was from over there, from the dam. I was born on the edge of the dam. Then my father sold a piece [of that land] to the Ferteco [mining] company. (...) And we were left with a [smaller] piece. Then my brother-in-law from [the state of] Goiás built a house up here. I was single when we were living over there. After I got married, and my other sister got married, then [my father] sold the other half to Ferteco, right on the

edge of the dam. But even so we stayed close to the dam. They stayed. I was already married. So, that's in this piece [of land] where my brother-in-law built a house (...). That house, the one the dam took away. (...) But we had already abandoned it, 'cause we wanted to sell the land to Vale.

The house, the land, and the dam permeate her life story: these elements offer clues to learning more about personal relationships, births, and contact with mining companies (Ferteco, one of these companies, was in charge of the mine decades before it was taken over by Vale, the current company responsible for it). The grandmother's answer ends precisely with the image of the dam carrying the house away. A similar movement, filled with spatial references, happens with the name of the place:

There was a stream there, where—at the back of our house, where I was raised—they say an ox cart filled with a bag of beans overturned, then they say that's why the place was named Córrego do Feijão [Bean Stream] (...) They said it turned from an ox cart—it was an ox cart, right? With the bags of beans. And they, 'Oh, a stream of beans.' It fell into the stream, that stream was big, that stream is still there. Oh, it's not... the dam took it away.

In this account, her memory about an unexpected accident, with the ox cart, is interrupted once again by a still greater unexpected: the traumatic dam rupture. She refers to the stream—which would still exist, were it not for the dam's rupture—in the present, only to subsequently reformulate and update her childhood memory. We face a rearrangement of memories, in which recollections that seemed to be well established now have their meanings relocated and changed by the dam rupture, with its breaking and destruction. The dam rupture buried the first foundations of the village (the stream) and took away the building built by the interviewee's family (her house), both spatial references in her life story. The mining industry, however, is still there. It makes up her family's past, present, and future environment.

Against common sense expectations of the recollections of an elderly woman, we found a grandmother who did not cultivate a nostalgic memory, one that navigated the past by yearning for whatever had long ceased to exist. What is stronger in her narrative is the memory of the drastic, quick disappearance of her spatial references, which until very recently were right in front of her eyes.

Second and Third Generations: Paths

In Córrego do Feijão, each image from the autobiographical memory of the interviewees carries information that is significant from a collective perspective, expressing meanings that pertain to the entire local community. Details are important. While the grandmother makes references to the dam, the house, and the stream, her daughter intertwines the new spatial configurations of the place with her older relatives, with the paths that connect the village with the town center: "The Antônio Santana Hill, [the name of] my grandfather—exactly where the mud passed—now it doesn't exist anymore, it's in the middle of the mud, it was the road for us to go to Brumadinho [the town center], the road I've always used."

The subtle change of inflection in the daughter's narrative reflects the value that family relationships assume and, at the same time, a generation that had to distance itself, to some extent, from the local place. When her parents lived there, they used to cultivate the lands "that had been my great-grandfather's, my mother's grandfather," whom she names "the founder of Córrego do Feijão." The daughter puts more emphasis on the role of the family in the foundation of the place than her mother does. The family used to grow peanuts, corn, beans, sweet potatoes, and yams. But again, her childhood memories, linked to agriculture, are interrupted by the marks of the dam rupture:

> I used to go there too, I liked it a lot, a lot. When I was little, seven, eight years old, up to ten years old, I would stay all day, I took lunch, we helped them—I'm not kidding! It was so good to be with daddy! Daddy would plant, teach, we'd take the seeds ready to plant, [as for the peanuts we'd] throw about five grains in the land—the land Dad had worked—and [then later] we'd pull it all out and take the peanuts out. (...) It was good. There was a creek—creek Casa Branca, which comes from [the district of] Casa Branca, passes at the bottom of my great-grandfather's land and goes to Brumadinho [the center of the town], meets Paraopeba [river], right there where that bridge is now built.

The bridge: a reference to the present, and post-disruption. It was built after the disaster to re-allow access between local communities and the town center. The roads (connecting Córrego do Feijão and the center of Brumadinho) are generously mentioned by the interviewee: when she describes her pregnancy, the birth of her daughter, the child's schooling, and the child's moving out for college. Her daughter (the granddaughter, in this story) is now about 30 years old. She is an architect and lives in Belo Horizonte, the capital of Minas Gerais. Born in Brumadinho, she nurtures a strong feeling of belonging to Córrego do Feijão, even having had to leave the place to study and work. She was also interviewed and said: "I never really left, I never managed to really stay away. I'd stay away from Monday to Friday and came here on the weekends (...). We're sentimentally dragged here."

Feelings towards the place intersect the stories of these three generations. Aleida Assmann (2011) writes about family places, or generational places. She notes that "what endows certain places with a special memory force is, above all, their fixed and lasting connection with family histories." "Cradle and grave," she adds, create a link that permeates the remembrance of the birth and death of all those related to a place.

DISRUPTIONS: UNEXPECTED EVENT, UNEXPECTED MEMORIES

In Córrego do Feijão, we observe that memories transmitted from mother to daughter, from old age to youth, adapt to the situations and practices of each generation. The recollections draw a cartography of affective memory locations that collides with the new spatial configurations resulting from the traumatic dam rupture. The memories of the event mix intimate and collective aspects, contents activated by different triggers. The daughter recounts:

> most people who do not dream of working in mining want to leave [Córrego do Feijão], they dream of going to Brumadinho, to have a house in Brumadinho. That was already a dream of many people, and today [after the dam rupture] I notice it's increased. I, for example, who have always lived here, and I like it—look at my story here!—I don't want to stay here anymore, I'm too distressed by everything that's going on.

A "violent event," writes Reguillo (2005), impacts several levels of social life, from everyday life to relations with authorities. In this case, violence persists. Despite the so-called "reparation" actions the mining company carries, nothing can be taken for granted: there is no social consensus, no local peace, and no guarantees. The company's actions are continuously re-signified from the residents' experience in the territory. The grandmother, for example, re-signifies the removal of mud: "It all became that most horrible thing in the world! (…) That dam released so much ore, so much ore, they don't even know where that much came from. The ore was like chewy, like chewy."

The pleasant place of her memories is now an open pit mine. In Córrego do Feijão, the interviewees reveal their dreams; they imagine, remember, and forget what gives meaning to their realities in the present. Our interviewees are in a space-time that they share with those who make up the community, not just with the family. The dam rupture—an unexpected, disruptive event—has changed not only the lives of local inhabitants but the very history of the place, transforming memories and narratives that seemed well-sedimented. A transformation that indicates how much individual and social memory is influenced by trauma and violence.

While we began our approach to this reality hoping to draw a social cartography that would express the relationships with mining, our plan was gradually modified by the responses collected in the fieldwork, by the findings that new interviews and interviewees brought us by the very impact that oral testimonies had on the project. Family and land relationships, as told by the unique interviews we gathered, were the key to understanding the varying relationships of residents with the world of dreams arising from generations of mining, a world that was destroyed in a few seconds.

REFERENCES

Assmann, Aleida. 2011. *Espaços da Recordação: formas e transformações da memória cultural*. Campinas, SP: Editora da Unicamp.

Aula, Inkeri, and Regina Helena Alves da Silva. 2019. Metodologia sensobiográfica: Novos conhecimentos sobre o sensório urbano. In *História oral e direito à cidade: Paisagens urbanas, narrativas e memória social*, ed. Andrea Casa Nova Maia, 15–36.

Reguillo, Rossana. 2005. La mara: contingencia y afiliación con el exceso. *América Latina Hoy* 40: 70–84.

Seeman, Jörn. 2002/2003. O espaço da memória e a memória do espaço: Algumas reflexões sobre a visão espacial nas pesquisas sociais e históricas. *Revista da Casa da Geografia de Sobral* 4/5: 43–53.

CHAPTER 27

Uncomfortable Stories and Tensions in the Official Memory of an Institution

Iara Souto Ribeiro Silva

My first contact with oral history was at the Federal University of Minas Gerais (UFMG), where I did a history major. During that time, I also worked as an undergraduate research assistant on a project to commemorate the 80th anniversary of the university's founding, celebrated in 2007. The project's goal was to create a collection of interviews that dealt with the development of some of the fields established at the university. Thirty-two professors from different areas and generations were interviewed. Although the project's central theme did not involve the Brazilian military dictatorship (1964 to 1985), its repercussions on the academic environment were topics present in most interviews (Dulci 2014).

In 2011, having just graduated, I returned to the university as a staff member. Thereafter, I often encountered professors, other staff members, and administrators evoking the university's tradition of democracy and resistance during and toward the dictatorship. These two themes influenced my choice of a research subject when I went on for a Master's degree in history: I sought to understand the impact of the military dictatorship on UFMG, as well as on the public memory of the university's role during that period (Silva 2017).

Brazilian institutions of higher education were among the favorite targets of the authoritarian regime's repression and surveillance, mainly because of fierce student activism, which demanded basic reforms during the volatile political

I. S. R. Silva (✉)
Universidade Federal de Minas Gerais (UFMG), Belo Horizonte, Brazil
e-mail: iarasouto@ufmg.br

© The Author(s), under exclusive license to Springer Nature Switzerland AG 2023
R. Santhiago, M. Hermeto (eds.), *The Unexpected in Oral History*, Palgrave Studies in Oral History,
https://doi.org/10.1007/978-3-031-17749-1_27

moment that preceded the 1964 coup and that, later, served as a center of criticism and opposition (Motta 2014). However, universities were not seen only as an incubator of subversive figures. They were also central to the national-developmental policies adopted by most military presidents. Reforming higher education, whose institutions were then seen as archaic and outdated, was on the agenda. Modernizing them would dampen the impetus of the student movements and meet the needs of preparing a qualified workforce and advancing national technologies.

One of the central hypotheses of my work is that the leaders of UFMG built, around these ideas, an official memory that has been reproduced, narrated, and reaffirmed in the most diverse ways and occasions until the present day. In this official memory, UFMG, unlike other large Brazilian universities, would have managed to resist repression and preserve its autonomy amid an adverse reality.

In commemorative books published by the university itself, filled with various ephemeral accounts, there is no reference to a single staff member who had suffered persecution or been fired for political reasons (Salomon et al. 1979; Resende and Neves 1988). But they devote much attention to memories that involve the forced retirement of seventeen professors—including four college directors, a former dean, and an acting dean—as requested by the military regime. These forced retirements were usually motivated by the individuals' involvement with leftist movements before the 1964 coup, as well as by their refusal to persecute colleagues and students after the coup (Fernandes 2016).

With the political opening as of the late 1970s, these professors were honored; some became professors emeriti; a book on the subject was published; theaters in their colleges were named in their honor. Thus, their names, always remembered, are part of a narrative of resistance. Indeed, in the case of these professors, their persecution and the order for termination came from outside: announcements of their forced retirement were published in the official federal gazette, and there are no records of any procedure or "cleansing" process that came from inside the university. According to the documents created by the UFMG, the expelled professors and the students withdrawn from the institution due to the infamous Decree n° 477, and even murdered, would have been the only individuals belonging to the university community directly affected by the repression.

An Unexpected Finding: From the Analysis of Termination Documents to the Narrative of Union Struggle

As I have stated, the existence of an official memory and narrative created by the UFMG about its own past, affirming its resistance and the existence of a democratic spirit within the institution, was the starting point of my research. From there, I sought to understand how this memory was constituted and its internal logic.

We should remember that a plural and diverse institution, such as a university, is composed of individuals with widely varied political stances. Although the UFMG presidency did not have a position of alliance or collaboration at any time during the military dictatorship, there were leaders within the institution and the governing board who were enthusiastic about the military regime. Suffice it to mention that the School of Physical Education, incorporated into UFMG in 1969, had as one of its directors and as a prominent leader, in the 1970s, a Military Police Colonel, Ellos Pires de Carvalho, later identified as a torturer by the project *Brazil, Never Again* and ranked in the list of public servants denounced as torturers in the report of the Minas Gerais Truth Commission (2017, 250).

Instances of violation of the university's autonomy can also be pointed out. They include harsh control over professors' career paths. Appointments to leadership positions, authorization to leave the country for research, and even hirings had to be "approved" by surveillance bodies. When the interested party's political background was not problematic, a document called a "Qualification Sheet" was issued, stating that "nothing was found to discredit the above-named." How, then, can one sustain the notion that UFMG preserved its autonomy? A specific case allowed me to reflect further on this issue.

Born in 1932, Mr. Irany Campos joined the UFMG Hospital (at the time, connected to the Medical School) as a laboratory technician in 1958. He began his political activism there, influenced by left-wing Catholicism. He participated in the creation of the Medical School's union in 1961 and became its president in 1964. In contact with medical students, he joined the left group Ação Popular [Popular Action] and later the Política Operária [Workers' Politics], until he opted for armed struggle with the creation of the Comando de Libertação Nacional [National Liberation Command], known as COLINA.

To fulfill his tasks of organizing the guerrilla movement in the town of Uberlândia, and intending to create an alibi for his absence, Campos took a leave from work at the Hospital for seven months, utilizing his premium vacations.[1] In the meantime, COLINA was brought down with the arrest of key members in a police operation in the São Geraldo neighborhood in Belo Horizonte (Leite 2009). With no contacts and wanted by the police, Campos went underground and moved between several cities, hiding until he could reestablish a connection with members of his organization. On a trip from Rio de Janeiro to Belo Horizonte, his bus had a serious accident, driving off a bridge and killing thirty people. Only three survived the accident, including Campos, who was hospitalized and underwent surgery to contain internal bleeding. Then, a week later, while still convalescing in the hospital, in August 1969, he was arrested and taken to the Department of Political and Social Order (DOPS), the most significant federal repressive body.

---

[1] Premium vacations are the benefit granted to public employees after a predetermined period of uninterrupted work (generally several years). It consists of a three-month paid leave. Since the 1990s, premium vacations are no longer a right for public employees in Education.

Subjected to torture to force him to divulge the whereabouts of his comrades, Campos was later taken to another prison, in the town of Juiz de Fora. There he learned that an inquest against him had been opened at UFMG, ultimately resulting in his dismissal for "scandalous public displays of intemperance." Banished from the country in 1971,[2] he went into exile, first in Chile, then in Mexico, West Germany, and Angola. In his words, returning to the university was always on his mind:

> Then we went to Angola. Then the returns to Brazil started and I'd always have it on my mind. I'd say to them ... to the people, like: "Look, I'm going back to university one way or another. Even if I go to the university one day and leave the next—but I'll be back. They're gonna have to admit that I got kicked out of the university not because I had any scandalous public behavior, but because of my political activism. They'll have to swallow it", as [the soccer coach Mário Jorge Lobo] Zagallo says, right? And I got fixated on that, and it really came about. And that brings up the case of the professors, you know?

Campos' name does not turn up in any product of UFMG's official memory. As far as I could gauge by my survey, his is the only case of an employee fired because of his political activities and also the only one that was not granted amnesty nor acknowledged by the university. His return to UFMG, where he remained until retirement, took place in July 1980, due only to a review of the administrative procedure that led to his firing.

A succession of accidents allowed me to learn about Campos' history and to become interested in interviewing him. In 2013, at a conference where UFMG's employees presented their academic work, I discussed my exploratory research that would be submitted as a master's pre-proposal. At the end of my presentation, someone from the audience asked if I knew of any employee who had been persecuted in some way by the military dictatorship. Then, the Union of Workers in Federal Education Institutions (Sindifes) president mentioned the name of Irany Campos. At that moment, I experienced the first unexpected event related to the research: the very existence of a staff member expelled from the institution during the military dictatorship—a situation that, until that instant, was thought to apply only to professors. From then on, I started to investigate this relic.

The uniqueness of Campos' case—also due to the erasure of his dismissal from the university's history—added to my conviction that, to understand such events, it is necessary to listen to people and attempt to understand their subjectivities. That led me to interview him—a conversation I had neither planned nor foreseen.

---

[2] Irany Campos was among the 70 Brazilians who were released from prison (and subsequently banished by the military dictatorship) in exchange for the release of the Swiss ambassador, Giovanni Enrico Bucher, kidnapped by the left-wing guerilla group Vanguarda Popular Revolucionária (VPR) in December 1970.

From our first contact, Campos established the dynamics of our relationship. He called me a "comrade;" he was willing to talk to me but stated that he would only agree to the interview because I was a "colleague," adding that he no longer talked to journalists because of experiences in which his statements were distorted. In our dialogues, the use of pronouns in the first-person plural was constant: "our" university, "our" employment category," and "our union."

The fact that I am a staff member at UFMG defined the tone and path that our interview followed, as well as the impact that our dialogue had on me and my research. Every in-person oral history interview is always about two people looking at each other, and the positivist illusion that there is an observer here and an observed there must be avoided: the interviewee also observes our gestures and our appearance and attributes meaning to that dialogue (Portelli 2010, 2016). And the relationship in this specific interview was permeated by the interviewee's reading of me at a deeper level than in other experiences. This is because Campos and I share something very dear to him: as much as we are from different generations, and decades separate our activities, he sees a continuity in terms of our belonging to the same employment "category" and institution and being engaged in the same struggle.

Campos directed the interview more than I did, and he did not answer some of my questions. At times it felt like what I asked did not matter to him. Sitting in front of the interviewee was a young researcher, in his eyes, practically a novice, since I had been at UFMG for only five years. When he was talking about projects in which he participated and developed as a union leader, the roles of interviewer and interviewee had a slight inversion, indicating Campos' curiosity in knowing more about me and my trajectory inside the university:

IC: You heard about April Roses [a cultural and sporting event organized by the union], right?
IS: I did.
IC: But you no longer ... how long have you been at the university?
IS: Five [years].
IC: You're still a newbie! [laughs] New to the university still. Oh, I miss my first five years at university ...

From the perception that I was his "comrade,' added to the clear generational and age difference between us, Campos placed himself in a position of an authority who had lessons to teach me. And the second—and biggest—unexpected event in this interview is related to this point: he was much more interested in talking about his union activism in the 1980s and 1990s, in evaluating the current situation of our category and the political conjuncture of UFMG, than in talking about his experience and his memories of the dictatorship. When we, researchers, set out in search of a particular interviewee, we believe that he will tell us something that can contribute to our research agenda.

But, as Portelli reminds us, "what the historian wants to know may not necessarily coincide with what the narrator wants to tell" (2016, 10).

Campos knew I was interviewing him because of his unique situation as an employee who was fired for political reasons and who was erased from the official memory of UFMG. Still, his memory functioned so as to lead him to highlight not this silencing, not his political resistance to the military dictatorship, and not the impossibility of acting against arbitrariness—but rather his actions after the political opening to democracy. What gained prominence in his narrative were the newer forms of action and the successful articulation of a type of unionism that openly fought for the expansion of workers' rights.

Campos' interview has a largely triumphant tone, despite the not-so-optimistic scenario for left-wing social movements when it was recorded. The meaning he attributes to his militant trajectory is that, despite the defeats suffered and experienced with prison, torture, and years of exile, his "fight" is filled with conquests. He situates himself as one of the main agents who led the politicization of the employees' union, which had been recreationally oriented until then. In his words, the scene he encountered in the early 1980s was that "at the university, in terms of struggle, like … there was nothing! There was nothing." And he goes on:

> When in 1981, it hadn't even been a year since I had returned... since I had joined the union, and we had our first strike. A lot of people find that folkloric. A day of strike! [laughs] "What is a day of strike worth?" Another year we took seven [days] (…), and another time we did twenty-one. The fourth lasted for a hundred days.

At the time of drafting my thesis, these topics about the university in the 1980s did not interest me and went unnoticed in my analyses. Nevertheless, I have realized with this re-reading that, at the moment of the conversation, I was drawn to his unexpected narrative and wanted to know a little more about the history of union activism among employees. That is why I did not interrupt Campos' narrative and did not insist on questions related to my main topic.

Strikes, union congresses, and internal disputes at the unions were prominent in Campos' narrative. This is full of meaning, even if it was not exactly what I wanted to hear. The interview can be read as an affirmation, for me and my generation of staff members, that many of the rights we now have and enjoy were achievements of the generation and the trade union movement in which Campos fought after his return from exile. At the time of the interview, in which he praised the first 100-day strike held nationally, in the 1980s, I commented on the most recent strike of this category of employees, in 2015, which lasted 133 days—the biggest strike of our category in the country. I called the strike "enormous," and Campos stated:

Yeah, but it wasn't actually... it wasn't really a strike. I was attending all the time and... when I got there... At that time, we used to... we had meetings of a thousand people. And we didn't have half the employees you have today. A thousand people! [Having] six hundred people [in our meetings] was normal [during a strike]. We would hold an assembly with six hundred people.

The interview became, unpredictably, a space for trade union training, a narrative by the interviewee about the transformations in the spaces of workers' political struggles. What Campos does is consider the unionism of the 1980s as a "golden age," in which his generation, unlike mine, led the unions to a concern with broader struggles. Campos' main criticisms toward the current unionism are twofold: the first involves the absence of a strong political training of union members; the second, even though Campos does not use the term, is identitarianism:

> I've got to fight for human beings to have rights. It doesn't matter if he's... if he's gay, if he's... whatever he is, it doesn't matter. He's got to be [treated] like a human being, you have to treat the person like a human being. I won't give up on that. I mind my own business because it's not worth getting into an unnecessary fight. But when I have the opportunity ... depending on the debate, I don't refrain from speaking out. Because that ... no ... it doesn't help in freeing people, quite the opposite. Quite the opposite. [If] I'm here fighting for the rights of homosexuals, you're over there fighting for the rights of Black people, the other one, for this, that, and the other, and we end up not really getting together to do what we actually should do.

In a testimony for the Minas Gerais Truth Commission in 2015, Irany Campos highlighted reports about his political militancy in the 1960s, his experiences in the dictatorship's repressive prisons, and his time in exile. I only read the transcript and cannot know what might have been said when the recorder was turned off—but, even so, that interview was quite different from the one he offered me, despite the facts narrated about the dictatorship being similar. This is a point that the experience of this interview made crystal clear: an oral history interview is not just about content and facts. When he bore witness before the Truth Commission, the context was distinct from the interview we did just over a year later. Established in 2013, the Commission was collecting *testimonies* from people affected by the military dictatorship—that is very different from dialoguing with a young researcher, a "comrade" at UFMG, at home, in less formal and less intimidating circumstances.

Concluding Comments

Irany Campos' narrative spreads tension over the UFMG's official narrative about its own past and points to the silencing of uncomfortable memories. As much as the university represents itself as a democratic place, there is little room for problematizing conflicts and disputes. Campos, in his interview, said that at an event to celebrate the 50th anniversary of the 1964 coup, he would have stated in front of the then president, Jaime Ramirez:

> I, as a technical-administrative employee, was exiled, expelled from the university and returned, I've never been amnestied by the management. The teachers were amnestied, and I was not. So you can see that the people who rule this university the way they wish are the professors.

Campos' story shows that there must be more room for history in the ethical-political debate about the university's past. In addition to not being remembered in the institution's official narrative, he was not amnestied, much less honored. Yet his was the only dismissal case carried out by the institution itself, from inside. His name was listed along with that of students who were to be judged by a specific decree and then expelled. The process conducted at the Medical School used as documentation testimonies offered by Campos himself to an external police investigation, in which he supposedly confessed to "the practice of so many crimes." It was found, though, that the acts attributed to Campos (his involvement with guerrillas, more specifically bank robbery actions) took place before the date of publication of the aforementioned decree. Therefore, the punishment could not have been legal. It turns out that the arbitrator suggested that a common administrative process against Campos could be opened instead, fitting him under the Statute of Public Employees. That could be one reason for UFMG's official memory fails to embrace his case. Furthermore, we should not ignore Campos' conclusion that there is a distinction in the treatment offered by the administration to professors and staff members.

The experience and analysis of Campos' interview raised several questions that concern not only my role as a historian but also my role as a staff member working in that same institution. Among them is the clear perception that achievements related to social and labor rights are not gifts: they result from social struggles carried out by organized workers. Equally important is realizing that these achievements are not definitive and can be lost—as administrative reforms in recent years have shown. Other questions, too, arose. Which version represents the institution I believe in and want to see as our public university? How do institutions build their official memories and how can we make them less monolithic/univocal and more plural/diverse?

I understand recounting the past is not historians' monopoly, but I believe that the discipline of history can mediate and qualify disputes over memory (Pereira 2015). Research experiences with oral history rebuild us, modify us, and—why not say it?—shape us as researchers, and I dare to say that they also form us as citizens and individuals open to listening and bringing to that listening the sensitivity of perceiving and analyzing subjectivities.

REFERENCES

Comissão da Verdade em Minas Gerais. 2017. *Relatório*. Belo Horizonte: COVEMG.
Dulci, Otavio Soares. 2014. A universidade, os cientistas e os governos militares. In *50 anos do golpe civil-militar: a Igreja e a Universidade*, ed. Robson Sávio Reis Souza, 69–85. Belo Horizonte: FUMARC.
Fernandes, Luan Aiuá Vasconcelos. 2016. *Professores universitários na mira das ditaduras: a repressão contra os docentes da UFMG (Brasil, 1964–1969) e da UTE (Chile, 1973–1981)*. Master's Thesis, Universidade Federal de Minas Gerais.
Leite, Isabel Cristina. 2009. *Comandos de Libertação Nacional: oposição armada à ditadura em Minas Gerais (1967–1969)*. Master's Thesis, Universidade Federal de Minas Gerais.
Motta, Rodrigo Patto Sá. 2014. *As universidades e o regime militar: cultura política brasileira e modernização autoritária*. Rio de Janeiro: Zahar.
Pereira, Mateus Henrique de Faria. 2015. Nova direita? Guerras de memória em tempos de Comissão da Verdade (2012–2014). *Varia Historia* 31 (57): 863–902.
Portelli, Alessandro. 2010. *Ensaios de história oral*. São Paulo: Letra e Voz.
———. 2016. *História oral como arte da escuta*. São Paulo: Letra e Voz.
Resende, Maria Efigênia Lage de, and Lucilia de Almeida Neves, eds. 1988. *Universidade Federal de Minas Gerais: memória de reitores (1961–1990)*. Belo Horizonte: Editora UFMG.
Salomon, Délcio Vieira, et al. 1979. *UFMG: Resistência e protesto*. Belo Horizonte: Vega.
Silva, Iara Souto Ribeiro. 2017. *Memórias sobre a UFMG: modernização e repressão durante a ditadura militar*. Master's Thesis, Universidade Federal de Minas Gerais.

CHAPTER 28

Commentary: Oral History as a Culture of Research

Gabriel Amato

After exchanging messages via apps and a couple of phone calls—facilitated by the recommendation of a former interviewee, thus using the famous snowball method—the interview is scheduled. The interviewee prefers to talk at home (while others could choose to come to the university or do the interview at a café). The researcher arrives on schedule and is welcomed with a mixture of eagerness and hesitation. The interviewee and the interviewer seem to test each other, searching for affinities that might somehow bring them closer. Both seem to constantly reassess their expectations regarding the interview. Perceptions involving race, class, and gender also enter the process. The interviewer must arrange the paraphernalia: a digital recorder, a video camera, the microphone, and, at times, a list of questions prepared in light of a broader research project (regarding this last instrument, there is much debate among the initiated: some claim the list may induce the interviewee's narrative, which should be as "free" as possible; others argue that it assists the interview, by all means limited by particular conditions of enunciation). The devices are turned on, and the interview unfolds for some time, with exchanges of gazes as well as moments marked by more or less emotion. The interview's duration is variable. Some last less than one hour, while others extend to the point of exhaustion. And the work does not end when devices are switched off. In the case of life stories, a new session may be scheduled. Then what comes is the verbatim transcription, the reviewing, the different forms of return and acknowledgment, in

G. Amato (✉)
Instituto Federal do Sul de Minas Gerais (IFSULDEMINAS), Três Corações, Brazil

some cases the literary treatment of the transcription, and finally, in most situations, the start of a scholarly reflection that brings the interview (or a collection of interviews) to other text genres, such as articles, books, or a thesis.

Briefly described, an oral historian's work reveals attitudes, procedure, and know-how specific to this methodology. To some extent, this set of codes and conducts form the *culture* of the oral history researcher. There are variations between interviewers, moments in the history of oral history, and different research groups. But isn't *culture*, in an anthropological sense, precisely a repertoire that is both diverse and specific of practices, significations, and habits deployed with a certain amount of both creativity and predictability in a given context?

Understanding oral history work as *culture* may sound like a novelty, but it entertains a dialogue with a similar argument developed by US anthropologist Roy Wagner (1981). In the book *The Invention of Culture*, published in 1975, Wagner advocates for a self-analytical anthropology that accepts its condition of "relative objectivity." The author comes to this conclusion while understanding the anthropologist's work as an "invention" of the social groups' culture, based on concepts and procedures specific to the researcher's culture. In other words, Roy Wagner argues that anthropology—with its unique repertoire of methods, concepts, and authors—is the anthropologist's culture. In their complex work, researchers perceive difference based on what is familiar; they establish what *culture* is by assuming it is an existing attribute among those with whom they dialogue in the field. Anthropologists, Wagner warns, base their work on an assumption of culture; they substantiate it by drawing on an exercise of dialogue with their "informant" and "can only communicate this understanding [about the "natives'" culture] if his account makes sense in terms of his culture" (Wagner 1981, 11).

Something similar happens in the work of the researcher who resorts to oral history. If anthropologists assume the presence (or lack) of culture among the "natives" they encounter in their fieldwork, we, oral historians, often assume the existence of social memory, as well as certain forms of narrative or performances—and also, depending on the disciplinary focus, culture. Anthropologists do not speak from a disciplinary or methodological non-place, nor do oral historians. We have criteria to build a list of potential interviewees, specific ways to formulate research questions, ways to behave during an interview (currently caring to guarantee the narrative autonomy of our interviewees—an ethical position that is more recent than we tend to imagine), and needs in terms of technological requirements (recorders, microphones, video cameras). Such aspects account for oral history as a culture of research, one that mediates the construction of our research problems and creates conditions for the visibility of narratives, silences, unspoken things, and recollections. This culture is also marked by a maze-like dynamic between the expected and the unexpected, the given and the invented.

If we accept the premise that oral history may be conceived as a culture of research, we can also question ourselves as to what extent predictability, surprise, and creativity haunt our dialogues with the people we choose to interview. We can consider to what extent the knowledge produced in, by, and from interviews is a result of dialogues established not only between two people with distinct experiences, but also between our *methodological culture* (oral history) and the multiple standards, values, and modes of perception of our interviewees. How the unexpected is inscribed in this dynamic is the issue on which I wish to reflect, although briefly, in this text. In the context of a methodological culture such as that of oral history, I ask, how does the *unexpected* reveal itself as a *given* that can be treated creatively if the researcher, as Roy Wagner urges, assumes a self-reflective stand—in this case, about the numerous aspects that form the enunciation conditions in an oral history interview.

Let me proceed by drawing on the account of two interviews I was involved in. The first took place in 2014. At the time, I was researching the Rondon Project, a program led by the Brazilian military dictatorship, from the 1960s to the 1980s, with the alleged goal of promoting national integration. It was focused on college students, who were invited to carry out outreach activities within needy and isolated communities in the recesses of the country. Many considered that the program was a strategy of the military dictatorship to co-opt young students, moving them away from the left. Therefore, a strong polarization existed between the program and the leftist student movement of the time.

Oral history was not in the project's core methodology. I was mainly dealing with press sources and official documentation from that period, produced by the project participants themselves. However, as a trained historian interested in how the experiences under the dictatorship were given new meanings through memory operations, I conducted interviews with former program participants. To some extent, that impulse toward oral history was also facilitated by my personal interest in the debates on this methodology. To yet another extent, it was due also to the fact that whenever I would speak about my project, a former Rondon participant would mention another former Rondon participant willing to narrate their experience. The latter factor raised an additional thought-provoking aspect: while there were no significant studies on the initiative and little was debated about the Rondon Project, providing conditions for these memories to be told was enough for them to appear in the public space, as if it were one of the "underground memories'" that Michael Pollak writes about (1989).

My interview with Marina Nogueira took place in this context. I have already discussed her case in a previous essay (Amato 2017), and I return to it here to discuss the relationship between predictability and surprise in oral history methodological culture. I met Marina when I was offering an outreach course at the oral history center of the Federal University of Minas Gerais (UFMG). On the first day of the course, I spoke briefly about the subject of my research. At this occasion, Marina reported that she had applied to the Rondon Project when she was a pedagogy student in the 1970s. She had served in the town of Barreiras, in the interior of the northeastern state of

Bahia. She immediately made herself available for an interview. We arranged it, and on the scheduled day, I went over to her workplace, a memorial to the history of education in the state of Minas Gerais. Before I switched on the recorder, Marina insisted on introducing me to all her coworkers as the "researcher coming from the university" interested in her story. She also took me to visit the exhibition spaces and the memorial's collection, which included several interviews. When we finally sat down to talk about her participation in the Rondon Project, the unexpected appeared. Whenever I asked questions about the subject that had led me to interview her, Marina was emphatic: she claimed she did not have much to say about the Rondon Project because she had not engaged in left-wing student movements during college. But at the same time, and quite paradoxically, she would provide interesting recollections both about the Rondon Project's *campus* in the town of Barreiras and about the experience of traveling in unprecedented conditions for a young middle-class girl in the 1970s.

At this point, oral history emerged as *my* culture. I expected to listen to my interviewee's recollections about what it meant to be a young college student during the dictatorship, about her experience as a Rondon Project member, within a federal program aimed at undermining the left-wing student movement. I carried with me my expectations and planning, which materialized in my list of questions. However, the dialogue brought the unexpected. While recounting her recollections, she proved to be more prone to reassert socially accepted perceptions of what it meant to be a student than to describe other forms of living a college life during the years of dictatorship. The memory culture that ties students to resistance and rebellion was so strong that Marina did not even feel legitimized to share her experiences. She would instead indicate that I should talk to one of her peers from the Rondon times—because that colleague, yes, could have better recollections since she had been active in the student movement.

The reflections following my initial surprise guided me to this question: wouldn't this reaction provide a clue about the silence around the Rondon Project within the broader picture of memories about the military dictatorship? Reflecting on my own expectations about that interview and on how they were transformed by the dialogue with Marina impacted the very structure of my historiographical analysis. I could conclude that, in today's Brazil, the memory around the so-called youth power (Saldanha 2005)—that is, the construction of Brazilian students as committed, rebellious and libertarian—is so widely accepted that it overrides other recollections about the students living in the 1970s. It also marginalizes memories about the times of the dictatorship that do not adhere to the rhetoric of resistance. Facing the unexpected as a given that led me to self-reflection—Marina's narrative, after all, was a significant incident to me more than to her—allowed me not only to realign my expectations for dialogues with other former Rondon members. It also allowed me to ponder to what extent the unexpected and the discomfort are indeed constitutive of the active recollecting of one's participation in a program promoted by the dictatorship in the interior of the country—in contrast to the more common recollections about urban street demonstrations against repression, boycotts against state policies, and the elections in student unions.

Another interview in which the unexpected in dialogue developed into data for reflection took place in 2018. It was the seventh public interview conducted as part of a collective project on the memories around the year of 1968 in Belo Horizonte, the capital of the state of Minas Gerais, and its metropolitan area. We were 11 researchers sharing an interest in today's recollections about a year mythologized in public memory, working in the context of its 50th anniversary. We shared multiple tasks of oral history work: selecting interviewees, preparing questions, recording interviews, and analyzing narratives. One of the interviews was conducted by my coworker Marina Camisasca with Carlos Melgaço, who had been involved in left-wing organizations both in urban and rural areas in the 1960s. As we prepared for the interview, we expected to listen to Carlos' recollections on his role in illegally organizing the Congress of the National Union of Students in 1966 (held clandestinely in a church basement), as well as his support for the labor strike of 1968 in the town of Contagem, close to Belo Horizonte. Once again, our expectations were materialized in our list of questions that also expressed our expectations on learning of his activism with the urban working class and peasants in the 1960s. And again, the dialogue led to the unexpected.

I was in charge of recording the interview on the evening it took place. However, as Carlos communicated his experiences, the unexpected aspects of his story evoked ambiguous reactions in me. He was keener to discuss the mechanisms of transitional justice in Brazil (explained by his political party affiliation at that moment) than to recollect the times of the dictatorship. At times, his narrative would even become professorial. He would explain the institutional intricacies of reparations to former persecuted politicians and analyze the conjuncture that led the far-right to power in 2018—but his activities in 1968 would remain on a secondary plane, even with the interviewer's intervention. Again, the expectations nurtured by the oral historians' culture of research were confronted with the dialogue's specificities—but, in this case, this small unexpected aspect was to some extent anticipated, since the interviewer had met Melgaço precisely during the institutional work at the state Truth Commission. These dynamics also had to do with the time in which the interview was being carried out: a time when self-declared "inheritors" of the military regime were coming to power, which presented risks of a possible dismantling of the transitional justice mechanisms.

It was not by chance that the set of reflections presented in this section led me to think of oral history as dependent upon the researcher's culture while also questioning my own expectations as an oral historian. Dealing with differing themes, the chapters by Indira Chowdhury, Regina Helena Alves Silva and Leylianne Alves Vieira, and Iara Souto Ribeiro Silva have led me to reflect on the place the *unexpected* occupies in the repertoire of practices and codes shared by oral history researchers. As a whole, these chapters demonstrate the heterogeneity of contexts and expectations in which this methodological culture presents itself: in data collection commissioned by non-governmental organizations, in academic research, and in fieldwork triggered by disruptive events. The self-analysis done by the researchers drawing on their data also reveals complex dynamics between the individual and the collective, the biographical and the social, and the predicted and the unpredicted.

Faced with life stories of resilience facilitated by the access to formal education, Indira Chowdhury came across the unexpected aspects of gender relations and household dynamics between husband and wife in the Chambal River area, in India. That led her to not only problematize the specific conditions in which oral history culture conforms to a commissioned work, but also to question herself about the practices that sustain heroic narratives. Driven by the urgency of a traumatic event (the collapse of a tailing dam in 2019 in the city of Brumadinho, Minas Gerais), Regina Helena Alves da Silva and Leylianne Alves Vieira found themselves facing controversies involving the mining industry, and they were led to the reflection on household and intergenerational issues which long preceded the 2019 environmental disaster.

For her part, searching for memories of political persecution on campus during the Brazilian dictatorship in the university where she works, Iara Souto Ribeiro Silva stumbled upon the collision between different temporalities. Through the analysis and questioning of her own expectations, Souto presents us with a provocative reflection on the overlapping layers of memory in what became, simultaneously, an oral history interview and a practice of political/labor pedagogy.

These three reports allow us to think and problematize oral history as a culture of research, as well as the increments that unexpected events bring to this same methodological culture, confirming that estrangement makes room for returning to what is familiar to us: problematizing instead of naturalizing the contexts in which stories are enunciated. That is fertile terrain for an inventive renovation of oral history as a methodological culture of research—a culture hopefully open to the sometimes-unexpected perspectives brought by those with whom we dialogue.

References

Amato, Gabriel. 2017. Memórias de rondonista: lembrando outras maneiras de ser estudante durante a ditadura militar. In *A ditadura aconteceu aqui: A história oral e as memórias do regime militar brasileiro*, ed. Caroline Dellamore, Gabriel Amato, and Natália Batista, 151–169. São Paulo: Letra e Voz.

Pollak, Michael. 1989. Memória, esquecimento, silêncio. *Estudos Históricos* 2 (3): 3–15.

Saldanha, Alberto. 2005. *A UNE e o mito do poder jovem*. Maceió: EDUFAL.

Wagner, Roy. 1981. *The Invention of Culture*. Chicago: The University of Chicago Press.

PART VI

Avenues and Openings: The Unexpected as a Method

CHAPTER 29

Introduction to Part VI

Miriam Hermeto and Ricardo Santhiago

"Method," one of the words we employ to describe oral history, may be too weighty a term to be used innocently. It refers, after all, to a long-established key concept that the very emergence and legitimization of modern science relied on. In the context of the cultural renaissance of the sixteenth century, "method" was a decisive factor that allowed scientific knowledge to be distinguished from myth, faith, the arts, and common sense (Chauí 2019). Since then, "method" has been central to the continuous collective enterprise of creating knowledge based on reason. Indeed, that is why it is on occasion the object of a sort of worship or fetishization that alienates it from the social world and its turmoil. It is for no other reason that some critics of methodological adoration speak of "methodologism" or "methodolatry" (Emke 1996).

While historians and philosophers of science have for decades discussed research methods as a social construction, a credo persists, according to which the sound adherence to a set of rules leads to the success of a research endeavor, assuring the fulfillment of previously defined goals. In our case, an unavoidable central question is: What is likely to count as success in oral history? This question in itself requires elaboration. Is success an outspoken but lukewarm thematic interview, a fascinating but equally fanciful life story, an exhaustive but also exhausting report of a past event? How does the contingent notion of success apply to our participatory research practices, so prone to the

M. Hermeto
Universidade Federal de Minas Gerais (UFMG), Belo Horizonte, Brazil

R. Santhiago (✉)
Universidade Federal de São Paulo (Unifesp), São Paulo, Brazil
e-mail: ricardo.santhiago@unifesp.br

© The Author(s), under exclusive license to Springer Nature Switzerland AG 2023
R. Santhiago, M. Hermeto (eds.), *The Unexpected in Oral History*, Palgrave Studies in Oral History, https://doi.org/10.1007/978-3-031-17749-1_29

unexpected? Is it possible to speak of a common methodological ordering that would allow all of us to fly high? A little reflection suggests that this is hardly the case.

Oral history, throughout its trajectory, has navigated within a broad scope that ranges from its conceptualization as a simple technique to be applied with no further implications all the way to the proposition that it constitutes an entirely new disciplinary field with its own object. Even in the latter case, however, its methodological dimension remains, one that has supported nurturing an entire pedagogical branch within the field. Workshops, courses, and, above all, books—our ubiquitous "manuals," "guides," "introductions," and "how-tos"—are founded on the idea that there is something precious to be learned and transmitted when it comes to oral history. This is a pedagogy of great value, which has facilitated the training of new generations of oral historians and the maturing of the field. At the same time, it is a pedagogy very much aware of its own limits, which—at least in the best cases—deals with the challenge of preparing for a practice whose actual demands persistently surpass what a set of methodological instructions can predict and contemplate.

"Hard and fast rules (…) are not always appropriate in approaching the in-depth interview," Valerie Raleigh Yow (1994, x) writes in the preface to her well-known guide to oral history, published in the United States. "Oral history is a more complex enterprise than we usually think, and the chances of successfully carrying it out are more fragile than we would like to admit," write the Argentinean researchers Liliana Barela, Mercedes Miguez, and Luis García Conde (2012, 10). Observations of this nature are not rare in our field, where the unforeseen is a constitutive reality. Indeed, when it comes to a research practice based on the relationship between human subjects, the method is above all a compound of reference points—perpetually incapable of offering any guarantees.

The last part of this book brings together case studies in which the relationship of researchers with the established and consolidated methodology undergoes considerable strain. It comprises four texts, four researchers, and four situations in which parts of the methodological traditions of oral history—well known by the authors—had to be put on hold as a condition for the research itself to be carried out. In other words, the *success* of these research projects (for the production of data or, at least, for the maturation of researchers) depended on a significant measure of pliability. Some deviations from accepted practice, which in other cases could be construed as a kind of mortal sin by oral historians, had to be tolerated and accepted.

Unrecorded interviews, non-interviews, conversations in noisy places, excessive proximity between interviewers and interviewees, and others—these are some of the issues that Mônica Rebecca Ferrari Nunes, Joana Barros, Juliana de Souza Ventura Fernandes, and Philippe Denis bring to the scene, followed by an astute commentary by María Laura Ortiz. They discuss the experiences of researchers who are far from navigating in a methodological vacuum, who, in fact, have fully recognized the uniqueness of their research situations and of their narrators and assumed their unexpected traits as a spark to fuel distinct forms (also unexpected, in the light of established methodological tenets) of listening. As they recount how their methodological paths came to reconfigure their very research focuses and strategies, they thus help us to reflect on the extent to which the unexpected itself can be considered to lie at the heart of the oral history method.

In the first chapter of the section, Nunes mingles with young geeks at a cosplay fair, in an equally mingled method that combines oral history, *flânerie*, and urban ethnography. Accustomed to dialogue with such groups in São Paulo, the city where she lives and works, Nunes (unexpectedly) had to reinvent herself in another town to make the conversations possible. Was there noise? Yes. Was there lack of time for preparing questions and better introducing her research to her participants? Yes. But that did not prevent Nunes from persevering in the hope of a weekend of fruitful research. And, in doing so, she managed to observe and to listen in a changed way: she noticed, for example, that the absence of young geeks in full costumes, in the city of Belo Horizonte, does not necessarily mean she found herself in a depleted cosplay scene compared to her hometown's. On the contrary, the dearth of costume items becomes a sort of metonym for forms of social inclusion developed by these young people.

Dona Margarida and Eduardo, two homeless people in the city of São Paulo, are the individuals who mobilized Joana Barros to reflect on the unexpected events scattered in her research practices with this community. Faced with the absence of causality and chronology in the narratives she heard, Barros fears she is making mistakes as a researcher. But then she starts to listen to the convolutions, the disruptions, the violence, the void, and the inexorable in her interviewees' speech. She lets herself be captured by how life on the streets is narrated—in dialogues that often catch her off guard, since they also mimic the spatial and temporal instability of her interviewees' lives.

Still in Brazil, but far from urban centers, Juliana Ventura de Souza Fernandes's chapter recounts more than one unforeseen event. Her text is based on the dialogue with Seu Valdemar, a Xakriabá indigenous leader, one of the many she interacted with in a large research project. Her first experience of the unexpected is the impossibility—not so unexpected, as she soon recognizes—of carrying out structured and well-organized interviews with members of these communities, in which orality is, par excellence, the noble vehicle for the transmission of knowledge and experience. The second involves her perplexity at realizing that this flow of orality does not cease, not even amid mourning: indigenous speech pours out generously and presents itself as a form of struggle.

In a very different context—his research on the Rwandan genocide and its consequences—Philippe Denis interviewed the Presbyterian pastor Malachie at his home in England after an initial contact in Rwanda. He meets him now to hear about the rebuilding of the pastor's church after the genocide. However, his interlocutor wants to narrate his own view of that historical event. By investigating Malachie's narrative decisions, which Denis accepts, the researcher is able to construct the notion of the "fallacy of ethnic classification," finding himself confronting the pain and compassion of a survivor who refuses to embrace any ethnic classification.

In the light of these four compelling field reports, and the embracing of the unexpected by the researchers, Ortiz defines facing the unexpected as a constituent aspect of the very method of oral history—not to question its legitimacy, but to explore its nature. More than *what* to do, Ortiz values the *how* in oral history: the importance of decision-making by researchers in view of the multiple options that the interview experience presents. We thus move from the familiar ritualized sequence of steps and techniques to a more unscripted methodology, refractory to orthodoxies. Surpassing a comprehension of oral history as a method, it becomes an open method, in the sense that Umberto Eco attributes to literary and, more broadly, artistic work: open to the infinity of possibilities, to valuing the creative and interpretive agency of those who mobilize it. Such a view can restructure the results of the research itself, but also the structures of thought that support it.

To return to a topic already mentioned above, success in oral history can be reconceived as something more than the familiar objective of discovering new contents. It also embodies the possibility and very experience of finding new avenues for intellectual discovery. Success can reside in the intellectual and aesthetic experience itself—the one that puts the method under fire and instigates methodological renewal—just as can happen when we face the unexpected in our interviews. Should we not, then, welcome and reinforce the unexpected as part of our method, instead of as its contrary?

References

Barela, Liliana, Mercedes Miguez, and Luis García Conde. 2012. *Algunos apuntes sobre historia oral y cómo abordarla*. Buenos Aires: Dirección General Patrimonio e Instituto Histórico.

Chauí, Marilena. 2019. *Convite à filosofia*. 14th ed. São Paulo: Ática.

Emke, Ivan. 1996. Methodology and Methodolatry: Creativity and the Impoverishment of the Imagination in Sociology. *The Canadian Journal of Sociology* 21 (1): 77–90.

Yow, Valerie Raleigh. 1994. *Recording oral history: A practical guide for social scientists*. Thousand Oaks. CA: SAGE Publications.

CHAPTER 30

Listening to Young Geeks in a Different City's Cosplay Scene

Monica Rebecca Ferrari Nunes

My trip to the city of Belo Horizonte (or Beagá, as it is called by many) was the first of a series of visits to capitals of the Brazilian southeast, planned as a follow-up to my prior research, *Communication, consumption, and memory: cosplay and youth cultures*, undertaken between 2012 and 2014. When I wrote the proposal for the sequence and submitted it to the National Council for Scientific and Technological Development (CNPq), I wanted to present a reasonable sample for the study of what I called "the cosplay scene, " and planning field work in the southeast region seemed coherent and feasible, since that is where I am based—more specifically, in São Paulo. The proposal was approved, and the substantial funding received covered travel costs and assisted in the publication of a book (Nunes 2015). The research issues revolved around how young people inhabit and consume memories of anime, manga, games, or other cultural texts that generate a desire for cosplay (a word that derives from "costume play"). It also reflected on how the very cosplay scene secures both its memory and permanence in youth cultures.

My encounter with these young people, the cosplayers, dressed up and acting as characters, put me in contact with a form of inquiry that I had not practiced before: the *flânerie*, the act of wondering, discovering the streets, their charm, and contradictions, all at random. I borrowed the concept from Edgar Allan Poe's story, "The Man of the Crowd," addressed by Charles Baudelaire

---

M. R. F. Nunes (✉)
Escola Superior de Propaganda e Marketing (EPSM), São Paulo, Brazil
e-mail: monicarfnunes@espm.br

and further developed by Walter Benjamin, and I started to employ it as a research method. But it was not that simple to speak, write, and publish that I was in the field in the guise of a *flâneuse*. One day, talking to a colleague about my research, I explained that this was how I behaved in the cosplay events, moved by the esthesia of the environment, by the erotic energy emanating from bodies that were costumed, made up, and immersed in games and media narratives, to the tune of old cartoons and sci-fi movies' musical themes. In the midst of a multitude of verbal-vocal-visual and gastronomic stimuli—the events where cosplayers gather also host numerous stalls and food courts—I participated in pop culture festivals such as Anime Friends and Anime Dreams, among many others spread throughout the city of São Paulo. These events bring together fans of Japanese and Korean pop culture. I remember that at that time, the largest of these fairs, Comic Con Experience (CCXP), had not yet arrived in the city. My colleague, who was listening carefully to my stories, interjected: "But, Monica, this is not *flânerie*, because you have a research intention."

He was right: there was a research intention. But how does this intention affect the fact that I literally got lost in the events, approaching young people randomly, following an abductive and intuitive approach to initiating conversations? Can I call them "interviews," or were they just approaches, not always started with me introducing myself and the research—approaches based on the question, "How did you start cosplaying"? From there, the forces of memory and narrative wove our dialogues, even when I asked permission to record or when I occasionally took notes or used video. These were warm encounters, characterized by meandering. I came to understand that, regardless of whether there was a research intention or not, the capturing of speech, the wanderings through the events, and the punctured lists of questions—all were marked by *flânerie*, guided by unforeseen events: the meetings and accounts I listened to.

It did not take long for me to come across the writings of Peter McLaren (2000), a professor, educational theorist, and cultural critic at Chapman University, and to find the theoretical basis for my methodological proposal. The *flâneur* or *flâneuse*, as McLaren proposes, is an urban ethnographer of postmodernity, "someone willing to wander through academic life and everyday life in a constant reflection about their own subject position in both environments" (McLaren 2000, 77). Being a *flâneuse* is a subject position that also deals with street life and the mysteries of narratives buried in metropolises. After all, the cosplayers' costumed bodies are products of the entertainment industry and consumer cultures, but they are also subjects of social, mediatic, and autobiographical memory at the same time.

In my more than 20 years as a researcher and professor, it was the first time I conducted a project based primarily on fieldwork, in which observations and approaches combined aesthetic communication with the strangeness of a practice unknown to me. In any case, the interviews (let us call them that) were key parts of my process, and even though I used documentary and bibliographic research, I really needed the testimonies.

The project was designed to be developed with the research group I direct on Memory, Communication, and Consumption, connected to the Graduate Program on Communication and Consumption Practices of the Escola Superior de Propaganda e Marketing (ESPM), in São Paulo. We began field research at events in the capital of São Paulo and prepared a schedule for visits to the other capitals of the southeast region, following the calendar of the events. *Anime Fest Winter*, in Belo Horizonte, was the first stop outside our city—but no one in the group could travel with me. I went alone.

An Unforeseen Saturday

I had been to Belo Horizonte as a child. Little or nothing reminded me of its verdant streets or its large downtown squares. Like the landscape itself, the cosplay scene in Minas Gerais was a novelty. With my backpack prepared, my tape recorder ready, and my notepad, pens, badge, and release forms in hand, I took a cab to cross the 14 kilometers between the Savassi neighborhood, where I was staying, and Buritis, where the festival took place.

When does fieldwork begin? At the restaurant doors where I have lunch, before starting the *flânerie* that integrates me into the cosplay scene? From there, I spy young people getting off the buses in front of the Paragem mall, carrying cardboard guns, and using wigs of several distinct colors, in the middle of a Saturday at Mário Werneck Street. If the cosplay scene expands through the city thanks to the circulation of artifacts, affections, and memories—so does field research expand. That is why, before even getting to the event, I photograph and record panoramic videos that register a group of teenagers dressed in all black, holding beer cans while they hang out at a sidewalk in front of the steep avenues where the entrance for the event's venue is located—a small university campus.

Anime Fest takes place in Belo Horizonte four times a year. The program, organized by the company AnimeCom, follows the rhythms of São Paulo events: concerts by cover bands that play genres such as J- and K-pop, respectively, Japanese and Korean pop music; *anime songs*, the anime soundtracks; parades and cosplay presentations; booths with pop culture, especially Japanese, products; places for video games and Pokémon card games; and quizzes about the anime universe. And what makes the scene experienced in Belo Horizonte different from the others researched in São Paulo? Its setting, the cosplayers, the forms of sociability around cosplay, and the circulation of artifacts. The setting is a university's sports stadium. Big, noisy, dark. Signs of *Japop*, a term associated with Japanese pop culture, are visible: numerous Japanese comic book sales booths, with posters of anime and manga characters covering part of the walls. The loudspeakers' echo deafens the scene, surrounded by numerous sonorities in addition to the J-pop being played on the stage mounted at the back of the gymnasium. At some point, music and dance make bodies move fast with Los Del Rio 1995's *Macarena* and the viral **2012** *Harlem Shake*, transforming the cosplay scene into a carnival party without masks, since in

Beagá there are few complete cosplays—that is, few who fully dress just like the character they represent. During the events, cosplayers can participate in the cosplay runways or move around the space, usually in groups, with friends and/or family members.

After having followed nine events in São Paulo to do interviews, I thought I was experienced enough to repeat the same procedures anywhere. That meant walking, feeling, losing myself, resting, and contemplating the young groups in their games, whether dancing, dueling, playing cards, and watching the runway shows. That meant approaching young people at random, without a previously selected sample, in no rush to chat, to explain the research, to talk a little more, to ask for the signing of the release forms, with no specific time duration for each interview. Not necessarily in this order. And so it was in Belo Horizonte as well. I would start the conversation by explaining that I was coming from São Paulo, researching the cosplay scene, and would like them to tell me how they had started with it. I will not go back case by case, but the unforeseen fact can be summed up: young people massively refused to talk to me, or to give interviews, or get into the vibe of my so charming *flânerie*. I stayed almost until the end of the event. And I left with no interviews.

This calls to mind Lévi-Strauss' "The Writing Lesson," narrated in *Tristes Tropiques* (1981), when the anthropologist spent the night uncomfortable with the episode he had witnessed among the Nambikwara native people, who were surprised when the tribal chief pretended he could read in order to forge complicity with the white man. For the author, the unexpected circumstance taught him how writing connects to power structures. Then, what lesson would the failed *flânerie* teach me? What would have gone wrong? Why did the young geeks of Belo Horizonte not indulge in the pleasure of narrating their lives, since they were usually eager to tell their stories? And what about me, who had already participated in several festivals and was conducting research in full swing ... What would the next day be like? I would only have Sunday to collect the interviews ... I would have to prepare a report for my funding source ... These concerns invaded the dawn and breakfast.

Sunday's Findings

Though discouraged, I went on. I thought of many clichés about identity, insisting on blaming my failure on the shyness or distrust stereotypically attributed to the people of Minas Gerais. But, among so many questions to myself, I stumbled across the simplest answer: my own arrogance. Using a daring method, taking the risks of going through a research path that depended on mere chance, I did not know how to deal with it. Intoxicated by the success of previous ventures, it took me a while to realize that my being from São Paulo, researching the cosplay scene with federal funding, and having left São Paulo specifically to meet those young people—none of that mattered to them. My initial rhetoric could be the trigger for the silence of the Minas Gerais cosplayers. I then changed my strategy: I started by saying only that I was researching cosplays. Surprisingly, that was enough to get me closer. I was a foreigner there: I did not need to flaunt the obvious.

I stepped into the scene gradually, sparing much explanation about what I was doing there—just making myself available to listen. Interviewing cosplayers in the midst of their party takes patience. That is not an ideal environment. There is noise, laughter, and gibberish. Sometimes you need to ask them to repeat what they have said because you cannot fully comprehend it; you often need to move around, in search of a less noisy corner. The scene's beauty depends on the very youthful, colorful grouping. If a young person stops and offers his or her story to the researcher, it is quite possible that other passersby will pause, curiously watching. It is worth picking up stories from those unusual individuals. Then, you must words, gazes, silences, and hesitations. And, in the case of cosplayers, listening definitely involves paying attention to their material realities.

The event I am commenting on took place in 2013. On that occasion, I found in Belo Horizonte a more impoverished scene than in the other cities where I had done field work. I interviewed cosplayers and/or lovers of Japanese pop culture who were unemployed or had menial jobs: as supermarket delivery assistants, grocery store clerks, metallurgy assistants, and security guards, coming from areas far distant from the place where the event took place: Venda Nova, Sete Lagoas, Boa Vista, and Santa Luzia, just to name a few areas mentioned in the reports. Many of these young people were not in school. Novaes (2012, 106) acknowledges that "being poor, female and black, or poor, male and white, makes a difference in terms of the possibilities of 'living your youth.'" In the same way, the area in which they reside "allows or prevents, expands or restricts their access."

Paula Cristina is a shy young black telemarketer. She did not want to be filmed. She chose to cosplay as a McDonald's server because "it's more like us. I could make [the costume] because it [the character] doesn't actually exist— let's say it's a clown. And people [at the party] will respect you because you're dressed like a character," she says. Her narration has an impact because it unveils the possibility of interpreting the ways of belonging and social recognition that the consumption of material and symbolic, mediatic, and simultaneously affective artifacts provides. The young participants in the cosplay scene are eager for inclusion, belonging, and recognition, thanks to their access to leisure, playfulness, and aesthetic forms—to the act of recreating the characters they perform. For cosplayers, a "well done" cosplay and its public acknowledgement is measured by requests for photographs by other site visitors.

In cases such as Paula Cristina's, the meaning of social recognition via cosplay goes beyond these photo requests. This young woman is able to play a clown, whose face is all covered, "cause it's more like us"—that is, it does not require her to be white and physically similar to the character. She feels respected by her peers by embodying a celebrity—one who has no face and therefore can represent her or be represented by her. There is a clear need for social inclusion, voice, and visibility, often denied to poor black men and women. And this inclusion is achieved thanks to her participation in the scene, to the status achieved through fantasy, which allows these kids to feel "just like the character," enjoying the significance and the symbolic value that the imaginary beings they incarnate possess within the culture of entertainment and consumption.

When I noticed the significant lack of full cosplays, I resolved to interview young people without costumes, but who had iconical artifacts that indicated their belonging to the scene: ornaments associated with characters, such as Naruto's buttons, coat, or bandana; Super Mario's hat; and Pikachu's and other mascots' gown—characters quite common in the cosplay scene. I also found many black and white kids walking around with black T-shirts.

The transference of cultural meaning within a consumer society (McCracken 2012)—a society in which meaning begins in culture, shifts to consumer goods, and then reaches the lives of consumers thanks to the instruments that allow such transference—helps us to understand why black T-shirts and/or ornaments serve both those kids who don't have financial means to cosplay and those who are shy, who lack the boldness to assemble and wear garments. Thiago, an unemployed 22-year-old black boy, states, "Everyone here wants to cosplay—you don't do it 'cause you don't have money or you're shy."

The black T-shirt—either plain or printed with movie scenes, names of games or bands, with characters, and others—ensures that once cultural meanings have been transferred to market goods, consumers seize those meanings to construct their "notions of oneself and the world (…) consumers always find meanings of gender, class, age, lifestyle, time, and space in their possessions, and they use them to shape aspects of their being" (McCracken 2012, 117).

Consuming those T-shirts not only responds to a practical need of these subjects but contributes with cultural meanings to the identity representations they build for themselves: being young, rocker, nerd, *otaku*, and *geek*, in their many belongings, regardless of what they are actually able to consume through their purchases. Yuri, a 20-year-old boy wearing a plain black T-shirt and no other ornaments, laments, "I don't cosplay 'cause there are other things to pay for. Playing is not for free."

Such artifacts, consumer goods, attain the same symbolic meaning of a full cosplay, even though that is done metonymically. And they are not exclusive to the Belo Horizonte scene. Even among those kids who do not narrate lack of possessions, the T-shirts are a sign of aesthetic belonging. They become "minimal cosplays" and somehow configure themselves as signs of inclusion and recognition: for, covered by these clothes and/or ornaments, kids are acknowledged as experts in Japanese pop culture. They can meet their peers, share their preferences, and make new friends—the latter, one of the achievements of these events, which are spaces of intense sociability.

On Sunday night, I went straight to the airport after the event was over. I was happy, because I had gotten important and revealing narrations for continuing my work.

Anyway …

My fear of flying always drives me to frugal conversations with other passengers. Just to relax. One word leading to another, talking to the girl in the next seat, I mention my experience with individuals refusing to be interviewed. "People from Minas Gerais always distrust you," she peremptorily states. I sit there thinking about the communicative power of stereotypes—about how they narrow the reflections that are needed to be in the world and to create, out of a research project, a way of life that is open to chance and unexpected shifts in direction.

References

Lévi-Strauss, Claude. 1981. Tristes Trópicos. *Lisboa: Edições* 70.
McCracken, Grant. 2012. *Cultura e consumo II: Mercados, significados e gerenciamento de marcas*. Rio de Janeiro: Mauad.
McLaren, Peter. 2000. *Multiculturalismo revolucionário*. Porto Alegre: Artmed.
Novaes, Regina. 2012. Os jovens de hoje: contextos, diferenças e trajetórias. In *Culturas Jovens: Novos mapas de afeto*, ed. Maria Isabel de Almeida and Fernanda Eugênio, 105–120. Rio de Janeiro: Zahar.
Nunes, Mônica Rebecca Ferrari, ed. 2015. *Cena cosplay: Comunicação, consumo e memória nas culturas juvenis*. Porto Alegre: Sulina.

CHAPTER 31

"Ain't You Afraid to Be around a Drifter Like Me?": Beyond the Nothingness and the Fragments of the Life on the Streets

Joana Barros

The invitation to write this text made me think about interviews I conducted and many unrecorded conversations during my fieldwork. I was struck by a mixture of surprise and discomfort, as the image I had of myself was one of a careful interviewer, compliant with the protocols recommended for open interviews in the field of oral history. Prompted to look anew at my collections of interviews, field notes, photographs, and sketches, not to discuss their themes but their very production, I confirmed that the nature of these elements is, in many ways, closely related to the circumstances in which I collected them.

Two interviews and two people immediately came to my mind: Dona Margarida and Eduardo. They lived on the streets of São Paulo and I interviewed them for my master's thesis in Social Sciences, defended in 2004. These interviews unsettled me because of the conditions under which they were done. I felt a discomfort in the face of their rhythm, the interruptions, the inaudible sections in the recordings, the noises that leaked in and permeated the audio recording, and, above all, because all these features were deeply mingled with what they narrated.

When I met Dona Margarida, she was a homeless woman. She had been through shelters, slum tenements, and sidewalks. By the time our paths crossed, she was assisted by the homeless social service. Dona Margarida used to go to

J. Barros (✉)
Universidade Federal de São Paulo (Unifesp), São Paulo, Brazil
e-mail: jsbarros@unifesp.br

Recanto do Novo Dia, a community house maintained by the Gaspar Garcia Center for Human Rights. These community houses were part of a network of homelessness assistance programs that aimed to create spaces of cohabitation and sociability. Services and space for bathing, food, and storage of belongings were provided—but not social work. In a house that offers only a few services, I managed merely to get flashes, small fragments of stories that usually reproduced well-known events: job loss, alcoholism, family breakdowns, and criminal episodes: in short, a litany of misfortunes that bring concreteness to the "disarticulation" that is abstractly mentioned in scholarship on the homeless.

I frequented the Recanto for months and only did one proper interview. All other attempts at structured conversations failed—and that caused me to deal with my frustrated expectations. Several interviews were arranged and scheduled; then, the date and time would arrive, and the dynamics of life on the streets would impose itself: the individuals would not show up; or they would show up but did not remember the interviews; or they were too busy with washing their clothes or sorting, tidying, and storing their belongings; or they were simply tired and wanted to "not talk." They just wanted to spend the afternoon resting at Recanto.

During one of these visits, I met Dona Margarida, and trying to arrange an interview for my next visit, I asked, "Would you talk to me about your life?" She replied abruptly, "Yes, now?" Taken aback, and without having prepared myself with a list of questions or a copy of a release form, I agreed: yes, we could do the interview right then. I asked permission from the managers to go upstairs to the administration room—a space quieter than the courtyard—and we talked for almost two hours.

The narrative Dona Margarida presented was circular. Several times during the interview I asked about the chain of events she was reporting. But the facts, narrated without much sequence, gradually formed a labyrinth of memories driven by one common thread only: loss, as we will later see. Much of what she narrated merged different times, places, and people. There was no beginning, no middle, and no end. The chronological line that I was looking for—so I could establish a timeline of her life story—either was not there at all or was precariously constituted. It was as if all the events she was narrating shared the same moment, an overriding present.

How, then, can one admit as research data a story whose temporal foundations are barely visible? In my first listening to the recording, I tried (as I had done at the moment of the conversation) to restore at least a little organization, a little causality, aiming to redeem a timeline that could clarify which moments marked her rupture from her previous life and led to her exit to the life on the streets.

The problem was that my research questions and my attention to established research procedures collided with the concrete life of this woman. A life story like that of Dona Margarida would never lead me in a straight line, but towards and through a labyrinth. Punctuated by successive losses and by wandering in the "world," her life resembles, at many moments, the life of a *trecheiro*—a roaming, almost nomadic individual—and unveils as a narrative thread the everyday violence she suffers. At the same time, the *trecheiros*—wanderers who go from one city to the other, chasing temporary jobs—end up having an experience that is similar to life on the streets: they sleep in shelters or boarding houses and use the social services in their travels in search of work. The *trecheiros*, however, distinguish themselves from homeless people, whom they call *sparrows*, on the basis of work. According to them, their roaming lives have meaning; their displacements and the narratives they offer have meaning and purpose: the search for work. This is a narrative thread that creates meaning but also constitutes itself as a boundary.

Notwithstanding this reality, Dona Margarida restored legibility to her own life by the very act of shuffling facts, names, and events in her comings and goings to and from the street. The fantastic became ordinary, covering loss and life on the streets with a coating of brutality. Her way of narrating ling was, in this case, amalgamated with the very life being told.

On the Edge of Reason

Ever since she was a little girl, Margarida had suffered violence at home. Her female condition deprived her of the possibility of going to school, since, according to her mother's moral code, that was no place for girls:

> Mom didn't let me, no, she would only let the males, the boys go to school, 'cause she said that all a woman, a girl, should write was a note for her boyfriend. It's ignorance, you know? Oh, the time … I went to school hiding it from her. Mrs. Jacira, the teacher, would pick me up early in the morning when my mother went to work picking coffee, and she would take me. And what the school taught was very poor, but I know something. To read, I read divinely well, but writing … (…) I can't write at all. My mother wouldn't let me, you see?

The same condition exposed her to harassment by a man, a nurse at the city's hospital, and a family friend, as well as to being raped, which led to the birth, at the age of 12, of her twin daughters, delivered in a distant relative's house, hidden by her own mother, so as not to embarrass her family. Dona Margarida never had contact with these first two daughters: one died shortly after birth and the other was given up for adoption. To this loss, two others were added: the death of her third daughter, Paula, and the supposed, non-confirmed death of her son, Emerson. These two losses show how the forfeit of family bonds can impact the future of people who live on the streets.

Dona Margarida anchors her narrative flow in such moments of rupture. The death of her son—announced by her daughter-in-law, who did not see his body—is remembered as a lament: "When I heard that they killed Emerson, my son, then I started [drinking]. He was my only boy!" Her story of successive losses and exits "into the world" (i.e., to the streets) after each of them made it impossible to consider a good life as plausible. She was left with astonishment, on the edge of reason:

Margarida: Sometimes I even lose sleep thinking about this mess in my life since I was born, damn it! Look, I've got a very good head, 'cause I was supposed to [have gone crazy] … (…) 'Cause I see young girls on the streets talking to themselves all the time, you know? I do. Beautiful girls!
JB: And why do you think you resisted this whole time?
Margarida: Look, I came to the street, and I got used to the street, and I am still on the streets today. I liked the streets 'cause I don't mess with anyone, no fights, nothing. Thank God *nothing* ever happened.

It turns out that this "nothing" is accompanied, in her actual life, by a series of situations of sexual violence, illnesses, and accidents on the streets, in addition to a type of work experience that is solely focused on basic survival day to day. What seems to make Dona Margarida construe this chain of events as something natural (after all, "nothing" bad happened to her) and tolerable is the sociability and solidarity in the street, thanks to a network of protection and to a way of life that begins with the strangeness of the first contacts and, over time, is transformed into a sense of belonging to a group. The street becomes a place of sharing—one that makes it possible to bear and even accept this succession of losses and violence in life.

My initial attempt to organize Dona Margarida's story and to establish a chronology failed to capture the meaning ingrained in her form of narration. Naming as "nothing" her unspeakable experiences of pain, she may be opening the possibility of envisaging another history and another story for herself. By narratively resisting the inexorability of a path of losses, her future remains open—it is, at least, imaginable. In this interview, which seems to call into question the lived reality itself, Dona Margarida's memory and narrative operate so as to establish a world that can be shared. In this sense, the "errors," interruptions, and chronological imprecisions of lived experience—materials that a researcher is not eager to find in fieldwork—seem to be a way to translate, to express, and to put into words the complexity of Dona Margarida's experience on the streets.

Order, Disorder, and Liminality

The same labyrinthic tension is present in the interview with Eduardo, whom I met again a few times after our initial interview. In these prolongations of our conversation, a tension was revealed—he insisted on raising repeatedly a question that always comes to my mind because of the strangeness it contains: "Ain't you afraid to be around a drifter like me?"

Eduardo was one of my first interviewees. He spoke openly about his life on the streets, apparently without covering up, deflecting, or mincing his words. On the day of the interview—like Dona Margarida's, not previously scheduled—he had just arrived from the city of Recife, in the northeast, 1600 miles away, where his mother was hospitalized due to a stroke. Eduardo is a member of Coorpel, one of the first and oldest cooperatives formed by homeless people in São Paulo. We met there several other times, discussing other aspects of his life on the streets, his work in the cooperative, and other topics.

I conducted the first interview with him at the cooperative's office. It was recorded on cassette tape and has some inaudible parts—the result of using a bad microphone, the noise of a truck in the courtyard, and a rolled-up tape. It is a sort of "dirty" interview: in just under two hours of recording, at least two other people, a friend and a social worker, interrupt Eduardo as we speak. Filled with short sentences, many of them not even complete, the answers' fragmentation becomes blatant when he talks about topics unrelated to his life on the streets—creating a contrast with his straightforward approach when it comes to this subject.

His story's starting point was the violence he experienced on the streets. Eduardo came from Recife at the age of 20, all alone; it took 23 days hitchhiking to reach São Paulo. He left his family behind. It is the story of a separation, of a life comforted by the hope of a return that never comes. What remained were memories of years of a life without much schooling and with many days spent away from home, on the canals of the "Brazilian Venice," as Recife is called, diving under the submarines moored at the port pier, small thefts, and much running away from the policemen who chased the "brats" by the iron bridge. Stories of crimes, involvement with drugs, and abuse by the police are mixed with his trajectory of wandering through Recife and the ways he had to find to survive.

Eduardo was in São Paulo since 1990; thus, when we talked, he had been homeless for 13 years. His first job was unloading trucks. Since then, he has lived on the streets, in a school turned into a squatter settlement, in a house he built (but abandoned, because of a failed romance), and in another squatter settlement in the city center coordinated by a branch of the housing movement, from which he was evicted. At the time of the interview, he lived in a kitchenette bought in another squatter settlement.

Eduardo's movement through São Paulo mixes the "two sides of life," as he himself says, pointing to a situation of liminality: a borderline experience between a life in order and in disorder, marked by arbitrary relationships (in work, with society, with the police). In the middle of all this, he is deprived of the possibility of envisaging a different future. The effects of the public understanding of poverty as disorder are experienced by homeless people on a daily basis, either because of police violence or because of its internalization, which distorts self-perception:

Eduardo: I was always beaten by the police. I mean, if they had a reason, I'd accept it. Now, when they didn't, I wanted revenge.
JB: Did you think the police were right when they beat you?
Eduardo: Like, if I gave them a reason, I'd even accept it. I mean, nowadays, I even accept it.
JB: But what do you consider to be a reason for the police to beat you?
Eduardo: Like, if I'm caught with drugs, or stealing, if there's a witness and I'm doing something wrong, being beaten is normal.
JB: Do you think it's normal for the police to beat people up?
Eduardo: No, if you make a mistake. Let's say, I get here, I take this object from you. Why not get beaten up to see if you learn? But one thing I've always told people, a beating doesn't fix anyone. (…) Stealing, putting yourself at risk is not so much about dying. 'Cause a bum isn't afraid of dying. (…)
JB: And at that time, you thought you were a bum?
Eduardo: If that's how society sees you, why not accept it?
JB: But you were working at the time.
Eduardo: No, but it's just that I was already a bit twisted, you know. (…) Like it or not, society doesn't accept [if you're a bit twisted]. Or what you constantly see is some person there, living honestly, maybe just to show what he never was or never will be tomorrow or the day after. It's no use.

Eduardo's self-perception of his life on the streets and his work as a waste picker is full of ambiguity. It is an ambiguity that is apparent in his narrating style: a chopped account, permeated with questions addressed to his interlocutor about the social judgment of his own acts, as well as in his insistent questions about my fear while keeping alive the bond of dialogue with someone who insists on "getting involved with drifters."

Eduardo: I don't really believe in this [contributing to the state pension fund], no; 'cause my mother is there with a stroke, and she's there in a hospital, in the middle of a bunch of people, all of them torn to pieces, pierced by bullets. What am I going to … you better have nothing. (…) It's just that people at your level, you believe too much in the future. (…) Sometimes, look … I play so much in the middle of the street that I, I don't know, for me, death can come at any second.
JB: But doesn't your work reassure you that …
Eduardo: No. If it were just work, maybe I'd even believe a little more. But, on the other hand, 'cause of what I do, no. (…) I don't know, I carry a lot of weight, I walk around a lot, I do things, even at work, things that shouldn't be done. You do it now and in the next minute you're in hot water. And maybe I'm not even lucky

	enough to get crippled. (...) If a guy tells me he's going to hit me, as long as he doesn't touch me, that's fine, but if he so much as pushes me ... then. I think it's a grievance, a grudge I carry with me, that I've been keeping. If you must die, you die; otherwise, you don't.
JB:	But haven't you said that the cooperative saved you, gave you a new life?
Eduardo:	It is a new life. But, as they say, it's on the professional side only. Now, like ... I don't know ... it's very sad ... even with this life that we lead [as a waste picker] (...) Sometimes, because of a bag just like this one, someone comes and stabs you, anyone can stab someone else.
JB:	It's still a jungle.
Eduardo:	It's the survival of the strongest. Ask any trolley puller—they'll tell you the same. In the streets it's the survival of the strongest. I mean, this here [the cooperative] is the last resort I found. (...) There are many who pull out a knife because of a sheet of cardboard. And there are others that don't accept it: that if you pull it out and don't stick ...

Eduardo recounts his life and his experience of the unpredictable work on the streets and also mentions its advantages. He employs the image of the streets as a jungle—and, therefore, brings to the table the fear, the strength, and the impossibility of a shared world in which he is welcome. But he also refers to his work as something that allows him to be "on this side":

> I really love being here [working at the cooperative]. Yet the day I have to leave, of hunger I won't die. And I'll head for the other side if they take my trolley from me. If they take it, anyone out there could be a victim for me. (...) The trolley is my life. (...) I don't lack disposition either to work or to mess up. I don't lack it. The disposition is the same. I've got some good experience of both sides. The one I'm in now is good. It's right, it suits me very well. 'Cause before, I had nothing, right? Everything I got, I ... it went up in smoke. Not this one now, this one ... What I want to build I get built. Both friendships and material things. But if you take the trolley from me ...

Eduardo's short sentences—which seem to mimic the brevity and precariousness of his living and working conditions, his going back and forth around the city—might make his story look like an unsuitable one as research material. And it demonstrates a clear disjunction with other interactions with Eduardo. While the interview went through piecemeal descriptions of the various situations of brutality he endured, our subsequent talks were about ordinary life, love, home, and daily work. For me, the unexpected was that Eduardo's account was so fragmentary, so difficult to interpret. For him, the unexpected was that the very situation of the interview (and the conversations triggered by it) had happened. He thought that dialogue was highly improbable and reacted by asking, "Ain't you afraid to be around a drifter like me?"

Violence always separated and denied Eduardo the possibility of having a future and a life close to others (whether his family members or the "non-drifter" society). Eduardo's question indicates the undoing of the separation he experiences daily, and the opening of a dialogue, of a situation of listening and speaking, of sharing, and of existence—of creating yourself in the relationship with the other, the otherness that every interview assumes and on which it is based. For him, the encounter of a researcher with a "drifter" seemed to be out of step—just as his short sentences, his crudeness, our tangled tape, the silences, and noises, all the things that we want to avoid in an interview, are out of step for oral history.

What is unexpected in encounters like the ones with Dona Margarida and Eduardo is that they are still necessary, otherwise the telling, the exchanging, and the establishing of meanings for experiences of pain, loss, and violence, through a constellation of fragments of life, would be harder—and they would be more prone to oblivion and silencing. When Eduardo asks, "Ain't you afraid to be around a drifter like me?" he is pointing out his amazement in the face of the interview as a situation where he can emerge as a legitimate subject, but, ultimately, to the interdiction of the possibility of a common world outside these provisional, artificial dialogues.

CHAPTER 32

Struggling Through Speech in the Midst of Grief: A Non-interview and the Indigenous Xakriabá Cosmopolitics

Juliana Ventura de Souza Fernandes

In this chapter, I will deal with narratives whose circumstances of production may be more contingent than is usual in oral history projects. These narratives reflected a certain level of planning and methodological guidance, but much of the design was changed as a result of my contact with the modes of sociability of the indigenous Xakriabá people, with whom I worked. Approaching indigenous history as a history created from the indigenous point of view implies creating bonds with the community and establishing a close dialogue between the practices of oral history and ethnography.

My reflections derive from the fieldwork carried out for my doctoral thesis, whose aim was to analyze the Brazilian military dictatorship (1964–1988) from an indigenous perspective. It was produced in dialogue with native concepts and with the sense of time of the Xakriabá—a people whose territory is located in the extreme northwest of the state of Minas Gerais, in Brazil. Differing from canonical historical studies of the dictatorship—which are generally guided by chronological perspectives, political landmarks, and State practices—my research demanded a reorientation of temporal categories and the presentation of the experiences in which the narrative was inscribed. This because, from the

J. V. de S. Fernandes (✉)
Instituto Federal de Minas Gerais (IFMG), Ribeirão das Neves, Brazil
e-mail: juliana.fernandes@ifmg.edu.br

© The Author(s), under exclusive license to Springer Nature Switzerland AG 2023
R. Santhiago, M. Hermeto (eds.), *The Unexpected in Oral History*, Palgrave Studies in Oral History,
https://doi.org/10.1007/978-3-031-17749-1_32

Xakriabá point of view, the things that were experienced during the "time of the struggle for land" or in the "time of war"—their ways of naming the events that unfolded in the indigenous territory between the 1960s and 1980s, that is, during the dictatorship—are connected to cultural repertoires that need to be considered over a long period of time.

From the Interview to a Non-interview

At the beginning of my research, I was guided by the chief of the territory, Domingos Xakriabá, to be hosted by his family members who had been direct victims of the conflicts that had occurred in the "time of the struggle for land." Because of this initial approach, I ended up getting close to the Xakriabá "elders," acknowledged by their community as the greatest and most knowledgeable narrators of those experiences. However, these approximations were rarely oriented toward recording a proper "interview," since the plan of creating a specific setting for it, when made without the prior constitution of a relationship with the interlocutors, may even impede or invalidate it. After all, we are dealing with a group that has been a victim of long-term violence, which often continues to be hovering nearby because of the presence of its perpetrators or their relatives. The fear of retaliation for complaining or disclosing information about these conflicts remains.

Not infrequently, the "elders" of Xakriabá themselves clearly remember having participated in or given "interviews." However, it is noticeable that the density of the dialogues they recall stems from the depth of the bonds and relationships that framed them—bonds and relationships that can be broader than the specific research situation. In other words, they are informed by a community's relation with researchers who preceded us, with scholars who are our advisors or whom we are close to, and even by networks of relationships established in everyday life with the Xakriabá people themselves. Eating from the same pot—participating in the community's daily activities—is a key element for building relationships within the territory.

In other words, whether because of the kind of listening required by indigenous narratives (which is related more to accompanying their everyday activities than to orchestrating a particular setting for the narrative sharing) or because of the time constraints and operations required for what we call an interview, it is not uncommon that interviews with native people turn out to be a sort of "non-interview." This was, indeed, my case. And that means that my own "interviews" implied overlooking, at least temporarily, some oral history tenets and assumptions about dialogue situations. The contexts in which most of my listening took place were created and established by my indigenous interlocutors, even though they were demanded by me. Notwithstanding, this does not mean that I assumed a passive role in the narrative performances resulting from our encounters: on the contrary, there is a space for active co-agency, marked by rules and specific social places in which I was included. Thus, some of this was oral history, some not. Some was unexpected, some not.

Because I had in mind listening to narratives about the period of the military dictatorship, my interlocutors, as noted above, were mostly "the elders"—a feature that accounted for certain aspects of our intersubjective and collective relationship. These elders were acknowledged by the community as persons who should be extremely respected given their vast knowledge about the territory, the Xakriabá culture, and its connection with indigenous ancestry. Thus, adopting an interview style with interruptions and much questioning could interfere with establishing a favorable situation for gathering their narratives. In addition, what I was told also resulted from the place assigned to me by the community.

The interviews—or non-interviews, as I put it—that I conducted had another unexpected trait: they were largely marked by a public character, rarely taking the shape of a transmission from the interviewee to the researcher alone. First, because when we talk to the elders, the younger members of the community are expected to come close and listen to them. Second, because we are often brought to the interviewees by their relatives whom we have met before. In the Xakriabá cosmopolitics, it is expected that the elders narrate in the company of their peers, so "one can trigger the other's memory," an experience that puts into question the notion of an interview as a creation centered on one individual only.

From this, it would be fair to assume that a research enterprise involving indigenous subjects, one that takes their perspective as central to the production of a narrative, is largely grounded in the unexpected. That said, I will now address a particular event in which the very encounter/interview was unexpected, at least from my point of view. For starters, because it actually happened, when I thought it would be canceled given the mourning experienced by the community due to the death of an important leader. This event alludes to unexpected—to me, again—forms of relationships to mourning, to the way in which collective mourning is connected to strategies of struggle, of knowledge transmission, and of the indigenous Xakriabá cosmopolitics.

The Practice

I was invited to the public activity that generated this encounter/interview a week earlier, at a meeting of indigenous leaders in the Brejo do Mata Fome village. I asked Seu Valdemar, the leader of the Silver village, if I could meet him to talk about my research. At that time, he was already aware of the purpose of my stay in the Xakriabá territory and suggested that I attend a "movement" (that is how he called it) that would take place at the Oaytomorin indigenous school on July 11, 2018. He said it would be a good opportunity to "exchange experiences." I never received further details about what would happen at that meeting, but I attended it. On the appointed day, Seu Valdemar facilitated a walk through the bushes, accompanied by children and adolescent students and a few teachers.

The unexpected death of Seu Valdin, leader of the Barreiro Preto village, a few days before the walk, helped to making the occasion quite moving, especially for Seu Valdemar. They had been companions for many years and nurtured a relationship of friendship and affection. As Seu Valdemar told me on the day of Seu Valdin's funeral, his late friend was a great fighter for the Xakriabá people; thus, to honor his memory, "the struggle could not be weakened." His unexpected death reinforced the need for the generational transmission of the struggle's torch, as well as the continuous need for the formation of new leaders among the younger community members. That is why Seu Valdemar decided that, despite these circumstances, the program (of the walk as well as our conversation) should be maintained. Proceeding with the activity during a mourning period might seem unexpected to some indigenous members and to me, but it was not exactly odd. Much of native education—what I call "pedagogy"—is done "traditionally through speech and movement," as several indigenous authors argue (Tukano 2018; Munduruku 2018; Xakriabá 2018).

Seu Valdemar's agile footsteps during the walk took us to the top of a hill. When we got to the peak, he pointed out a small concrete building, partially covered by vegetation. It was one of the milestones established by the National Indian Foundation (FUNAI) at the territorial delimitation made in 1979, when, in an unprecedented way, the Brazilian State finally acknowledged the Xakriabá as a proper native indigenous people. At that moment, Seu Valdemar also explained to the others that I was there because I participated in a "Truth Commission" and that, therefore, I was looking for "true stories"—he was alluding to my volunteer work as a researcher for the Working Group on Violations of Indigenous Rights of the Truth Commission in Minas Gerais (COVEMG), a work that took place in parallel with my doctoral research.

According to Seu Valdemar, the Silver village was named after its crystal clear, almost silvery sand. It is one of the closest villages to the town of São João das Missões, and it has worked as a boundary since the first official territorial shaping of the state of Minas Gerais. From that hill, one can see neighboring towns and areas of territorial "retake"—places reclaimed by the Xakriabá people, whose goal is to reinstate the territorial shape and the indigenous ownership recognized during the Empire (until 1889). It includes returning to the margins of the São Francisco River, which is important for their food and ritual sovereignty. Pointing to one of these areas, the indigenous land Dizimeiro, Seu Valdemar explained to the young people that they were not only participating in the same struggle of "the late Rosalino plus [chief] Rodrigão" (a leader killed in the Xakriabá massacre, in 1987, and a chief from the 1970s to the 1990s, respectively), but also in a much older struggle that he inherited from his grandfather, Geronimo, and his uncle. His statement is an example of a view that considers that struggles to guarantee territorial rights are still needed in the face of the constant violence to which native peoples are subjected. In their cosmovision, such struggles are, and must be, supported by reference to their indigenous ancestry.

"Memory," for Seu Valdemar, "is something you must have." However, he believes memory should be kept not only "in the heart." His experience led him to discover that "if you don't have the mind, the heart doesn't record anything." The non-overlapping of matters of the "heart" over those of the "mind" was a strategy learned from ancestors. He listened carefully and did not "let go" of what his grandfather and other elders said: "Everything stayed in my mind all my life; that's why I can tell [these things]." In his house, Seu Valdemar keeps copies of documents "with my history told, the way I told it"—documents that range from endorsements of the Land Donation Certificate, produced during the Empire, to a series of papers related to the acknowledgment of Xakriabá indigeneity, the 1979's land rights demarcation, and its ratification in 1987. Therefore, he knows the limits of the "first demarcation, when the land was donated, in 1728"—an event that resulted from contacts between the Xakriabá people and colonizers. For Seu Valdemar, understanding and creating a "true story" implies careful attention to the oral transmission by the elders and keeping documents. But his handling of these documents involves a particular form of relationship with the written text, one that I interpret as an indigenization of the colonial and neocolonial narratives they express. Given the history of violence against indigenous peoples (which also implies epistemic violence against their knowledge and ways of life), the handling of the "weapons" of the non-indigenous world has become a condition for survival. It is not fortuitous that the Xakriabá people usually affirm that they have been attacked by a weapon even more sophisticated than firearms: the pen. Through its use, decrees involving indigenous rights have been signed almost daily in the country.

Seu Valdemar's speech during the walk was not only an important moment of learning and transmission of knowledge. These situations of contact between the "younger" and "older," which I was able to take part in during my fieldwork and which constituted my "non-interviews," are also moments of construction of the ongoing struggle and teaching of techniques and strategies of existing and resisting. I call this complex set of practices "resistant pedagogy" (and not "pedagogy of resistance," for example) because it constitutes not only a *reaction* to the non-indigenous world but a particular form of know-how: knowing what to do with what the land, the beings that inhabit it, and your ancestors teach you. It is a "resistant pedagogy" also because, while it is a transmission, a teaching, an enunciation to others, it is in itself an act of existence, a Xakriabá way of life. It builds and establishes principles for a struggle for the land that is endless, since possible threats against the territory can always be lurking. That is why such a struggle, as Seu Valdemar tells us, brings together the "ancestors," the "older," the "younger," and "those who are yet to come or do not even know where they are." All this helps to explain why my fieldwork included more analyzing of everyday situations of knowledge transmissions rather than formal interview settings. Respecting the Xakriabá forms of expression demanded that I change what I had initially planned as my path to learning about, and from inside, the territory.

In this situation, an unexpected way of experiencing grief reactivated the Xakriabá cosmopolitics. Seu Valdemar's narrative connects different experiences of mourning (both the losses resulting from the 1980s' massacre and from the death of Seu Valdin) and different temporalities (shifting between the official time of the State and the time of the Xakriabá people). He deploys a series of elements that refer to the long history of violence his people have been subjected to. The central theme of his speech—the "struggle for land"—is both anchored in the strength and experience of the elderly, in the past, and constitutes a permanent commitment that guarantees the people's ownership of the territory, as well as the consummation of an ancestral "gift." Thus, in the Xakriabá cosmovision, this commitment to struggle includes future generations, the "little ones," those who "don't even know where they are."

The Xakriabá were seen, by Brazilian authorities in charge of repression during the dictatorship, as bodies liable to suffer. From the Xakriabá point of view, however, it was not only their bodies that were under attack—but also their "culture," their biome (the Brazilian *Cerrado*), and all the "sciences" implied in their community relations. This highlights the limits of the state's imagination in relation to Xakriabá's complex forms of existence and of constructing possible worlds, as well as the indigenous concept of damage, which is broader than the mere violation of rights. The territory, as the Xakriabá say, is what "sustains culture." Its degradation threatens the very possibility of continuing to exist.

Just as the mourning for Seu Valdin did not impede Seu Valdemar's walking, narration, and our "non-interview," the mourning for all these other losses is not carried out in silence, as someone coming from another culture could anticipate (just as I initially did as a researcher). They are reconfigured as a political action that shapes indigenous cosmopolitics: one that is supported by ancestral experiences but is at the service of the future, of Xakriabá becoming. Producing a "true story," "warring" against genocidal and epistemic ends of the world, and raising children and Xakriabá warriors in these spaces of transmission (of knowledge, experiences, and narratives) are some of the micropolitical acts that allow the very maintenance of life and land healing. In this context, mourning experiences are carried out in "movement" and through orality and can be expressed in the most traditional or the most unexpected ways, concepts that are not absolute.

References

Munduruku, Daniel. 2018. Educação Indígena: do corpo, da mente e do espírito. In *Daniel Munduruku*, ed. Kaká Werá, 67–76. Rio de Janeiro: Azougue.

Tukano, Daiara Hori Figueiroa Sampaio. 2018. *Uhushé Kiti Niíshé. Direito à memória e verdade na perspectiva da educação cerimonial de quatro mestres indígenas*. Master's thesis, Universidade de Brasília.

Xakriabá, Célia Nunes Correa. 2018. *O barro, o genipapo e o giz no fazer epistemológico de autoria Xakriabá: reativação da memória por uma educação territorializada*. Master's thesis, Universidade de Brasília.

CHAPTER 33

Ethnic Classification and Trauma During the Rwandan Genocide

Philippe Denis

My interview with Malachie was not what I expected. Not that it went wrong. In fact, it went extremely well, far better than I had anticipated. But Malachie took over the process. He hijacked the interview. In the end, I was the main beneficiary both at the personal level and from a research point of view.

Malachie is a Presbyterian pastor who narrowly escaped death during the three months of the Rwandan genocide, during which an estimated 800,000 mostly Tutsi people were brutally slaughtered under the pretext that they were "accomplices" of the Rwandan Patriotic Front (RPF), a "rebel" army which had invaded Rwanda four years before. The shooting down of President Habyarimana's plane, almost certainly a feat of the Hutu extremist faction within the government, was the trigger. Between April and July 1994, men, women, and children were killed in great numbers by the Interahamwe, a state-sponsored Hutu extremist militia, with the assistance of neighbors, colleagues, and sometimes even family members and with the logistical support of the Rwandan government and the Rwandan army (Des Forges 1999). It is estimated that three quarters of all Tutsi living in Rwanda at the time were massacred. Heavily traumatized, Malachie relocated to the United Kingdom in August 1994 where his wife, employed in an international church organization, had been residing since January of the same year. Today he no longer works as a full-time minister of religion and rents a house belonging to an

---

P. Denis (✉)
University of KwaZulu-Natal, Pietermaritzburg, South Africa
e-mail: Denis@ukzn.ac.za

© The Author(s), under exclusive license to Springer Nature Switzerland AG 2023
R. Santhiago, M. Hermeto (eds.), *The Unexpected in Oral History*, Palgrave Studies in Oral History,
https://doi.org/10.1007/978-3-031-17749-1_33

association of retired pastors in Wolverhampton not far from Birmingham. I visited him there in March and again in October 2019.

I am a historian by training. I see my research as a contribution to the emerging field of memory studies. The Christian churches have been widely criticized for their silence, if not their complicity, during the genocide despite numerous acts of courage and solidarity on the part of individual church members (Rittner, Roth and Whitworth 2004; Denis 2022). Using a combination of oral history and archival research, I try to see how they dealt with the memory of the genocide after the defeat of the Rwandan army in July 1994 and the installation of a government of national unity led by the RPF. This is a sad history because the genocide against the Tutsi triggered a cycle of violence in the Great Lakes Region, which tore apart society in many areas for years. The tragedy is that the officials who prepared and executed the genocide against the Tutsi never expressed remorse. They lived in denial, putting all the blame on the RPF, accused of having destabilized the country by starting a war in 1990. Unlike apartheid in South Africa or Nazism after the Second World War, the genocide against the Tutsi never formally ended. Despite the work, limited though valuable, of the International Criminal Tribunal for Rwanda in Arusha, there has not been any real closure. The history of Rwanda has always been and remains contested (Denis 2020).

Because this is a vast and complex subject, I elected to focus on two churches, the Roman Catholic Church, long associated with the previous regime, which struggled to come to terms with its contested legacy (Denis 2018), and the Presbyterian Church, also compromised, but which took, during a general synod held in December 1996, the unprecedented step of confessing its participation in the genocide and asking for forgiveness (Gatwa 2005). They exemplify two very different ways of relating to the memory of the genocide.

I had read in a book written by Gerard van 't Spijker (2007), a Dutch Protestant missionary present in Rwanda before and after the genocide, that Malachie had been the general secretary of the Presbyterian Church between February and December 1995. He had agreed to return to Rwanda for one year. At the time, the Presbyterian Church was divided between those who had remained in Rwanda after the genocide and those who had fled to neighboring Kivu, with the government and the army involved in the genocide, and stayed there in refugee camps until the end of 1996. That created a complicated situation. In Rwanda the majority of church members, those who were burying the dead and were looking after the orphans, fully accepted the reality of the genocide. In the refugee camps, many harbored resentment against the new Rwandan government, guilty, according to them, of crimes worse than those of the genocide period. It was a case of divided memories. I wanted to know what Malachie thought about this situation.

It took me a while to find Malachie's contact details. I knew he was living in England, but nobody could tell me exactly where. In December 1998, Elisée, another interviewee, told me that Malachie was in Kigali. I had arrived there a few days earlier from South Africa where I live and teach. I managed to call

Malachie who was staying with some friends, but he was not available. He advised me to come and see him in England. Luckily, I had been invited to travel to this country for another research project in March 2019, all expenses paid. One morning I took a train from London to Wolverhampton. Malachie was waiting for me at the station of this middle-size industrial town close to Birmingham. The conversation started in the bus going to his home, in the outskirts of the city. His wife Julienne—who was absent on that day—had prepared a bed for me. That showed that I was expected. Three big folders, full of documents, were waiting for me on one of the tables.

What I did not expect, first of all, was the length of the interview. We started the interview around 11 am. By 4 pm, it was still ongoing. We did not see the time passing. Both of us forgot to eat. We had supper in the end, I must say, in an Indian restaurant in town. As a matter of principle, I never use a tape recorder for this type of research in order to avoid suspicion. I take notes in shorthand on my laptop. The transcript is 11,000-word long. Revisiting it as I set out to write this chapter, I realize that I asked Malachie to accelerate the pace a few times. I now regret it. More details could have been added to the story.

But it was not only the duration of the interview that made it unique. As is often the case in oral history, the process counts as much as the content. Malachie re-enacted in front of me the genocide. He was at the same time precise and articulate and—in a controlled way—emotional. At key moments, he would interrupt the narrative, struggling to contain the pain that the memories of the genocide revived in him. We would keep silent and then he would carry on talking. The interview started in English, to both of us an adopted language, before imperceptibly shifting to French—my mother tongue and, for Malachie, a language he has spoken since childhood. English words would reappear from time to time.

I had come to talk about the reconstruction of the Presbyterian Church in Rwanda after the genocide. Malachie did touch on this subject. I shall come back to it. More pressing for him, however, was the urge to share his story of the genocide. Towards the end, I asked him how he felt. "It was hard," he responded. "The time of the commemoration is coming soon. We must keep this memory. I shall carry it all my life." In Rwanda April is the month of the genocide commemoration, with gatherings all over the country, some of them with thousands of people. Genocide survivors apprehend this moment because it brings back painful memories, but they would not miss it for any reason. That year we were commemorating the 25th anniversary of the genocide.

The Ordeal of a Man of Peace

Malachie started by explaining that the first travelers, anthropologists, and geographers who described Rwanda in the nineteenth century gave a false image of the country's social structure. He was referring to the Hamitic theory according to which the Tutsi had come from Ethiopia or further north and were therefore strangers, an argument used by the Hutu extremist propaganda during the genocide to justify the killings (Chrétien and Kabanda 2013). Malachie then told his story. Born in Rugalika, south of Kigali, he had trained for the ministry before going to Germany to work on a thesis, a project he was forced to interrupt after a car accident. Back in Rwanda, he was seconded to African Evangelistic Enterprise (AEE), a Christian organization campaigning for peace at a time when Rwanda was bracing for a violent ethnic confrontation. When narrating the events that unfolded after April 6, the day of the shooting of President Habyarimana's plane, Malachie frequently came back to this period. He felt in danger because he had challenged the political and religious leaderships several times for their refusal to oppose the mounting violence. He had used the parable of the bramble as told by Jotham in the Book of Judges to make the point that one had to take risks in difficult circumstances. The following day somebody threatened him over the phone. The fact that his wife, also involved in peace efforts, had accompanied church leaders to the headquarters of the RPF in the north of Rwanda when she was still in the country to negotiate a political settlement which was considered by the Hutu extremists as a betrayal.

It was then that Malachie started to describe, with a great wealth of details, the genocide in Gikondo, a district of Kigali, in April and May 1994. On 7 April, he had a conversation over the phone with Israel Havugimana, the AEE team leader, an hour or two before he was murdered with his family. Malachie thought that he would be the next victim. All he could do was to pray. On 11 April, a crowd of 400 Interahamwe arrived in the neighborhood. Malachie and his children, as well as Olivier, a friend and confident, and his family, and two other families, were told to stand in the street with their households. Despite the brainwashing they had been submitted to, the people gathered there hesitated to kill. A participant then told a young man "*Kora*," which means "Work," the infamous euphemism for exterminating the Tutsi. He stabbed to death Alphonse and Béatrice, two Tutsi friends and fellow worshippers whom Malachie was hosting in his house. The killers also wanted to murder their children, but a woman assured them that the couple had no children, miraculously saving their lives. In the middle of this horror, gestures of human compassion were still possible.

Malachie was then pushed into the house. A soldier was about to shoot him when the crowd came in to loot what was inside the building. The killer was distracted. Malachie escaped death for the second time when a few moments later, a youngster who used to visit his house when he was a child told the murderers that Malachie was not the owner of the house and that he would not hesitate to kill them if they touched his pastor. There was something hazardous, almost irrational, in the genocide. Some would die and others not, for no apparent reason.

Two or three days later, Malachie managed to send his children to his father's place in Ragalika, and he stayed behind in Gikondo. The RPF being at a short distance, there were rockets flying around, and he was nearly hit by one of them. On 20 May, he found a vehicle that was traveling to Remera-Rukoma, an important Presbyterian mission, near Gitarama, in the south. He changed his mind on the way, going to see his family in Ragalika instead. This last-minute decision saved his life. Two days later a group of Presbyterian ministers and several lay people, including his friend Olivier and his family, were massacred in Remera-Rukoma. Then in June, as the RPF was approaching, he left his father's place and wandered with a group of people, not knowing where to go. There again he could have died because the Interahamwe still wanted blood. They ended up in a refugee camp under the protection of the RPF and eventually returned to Kigali.

A Case of Mistaken Identity

When listening to this story, I was convinced that Malachie was a Tutsi. He was hunted down and owed his life to luck—or rather to prayer, he would say, because he prayed a lot, while wondering why God had spared him and his children when so many family members, friends, and colleagues had been assassinated. He spoke as a survivor, a real survivor, somebody who did not now know why he was still alive. He almost felt guilty to be there to tell the story.

It was only later that I discovered that, in fact, Malachie was not a Tutsi. The killers thought he was because of his high stature. According to a stereotype spread in Rwanda since the colonial times, being tall proved that you were a Tutsi. As it happened, Malachie was neither a Hutu nor a Tutsi. He was from a Ugandan background, his forefathers having been brought into Rwanda as a booty of war by King Mazimpaka or his successor in the seventeenth century. For no particular reason his father had been classified as a Hutu during the Belgian colonial rule.

Towards the end of the interview, he mentioned that, on arriving in England in August 1994, he had described his ordeal in a 17-page typewritten document that he allowed me to photocopy in a stationery close to his home. In this text—which provided details that were not included in the interview, the two sources complementing each other—Malachie had pointed out that, on 11 April, the Interahamwe had asked him to produce his identity card and discovered, frustrated, that he was listed as a Hutu. They did not believe it, claiming that he had falsely represented himself as a Tutsi and that he deserved to die anyway because he had sheltered Tutsi people.

I came back for a follow-up interview in October 2019 and used this opportunity to probe the issue. This is how I discovered that Malachie was from a Ugandan background, that he was neither a Hutu nor a Tutsi, and that he had been classified as a Hutu. The interview was unexpected in the sense that, on discovering that he was not a Tutsi after all, I felt compelled to reinterpret his story. He was not a Tutsi survivor, perhaps, but a survivor all the same. There we had a man who refused to embrace an ethnic identity. When he said that he was neither Hutu nor Tutsi, he meant it. He refused such categorization. He had no time for the colonial-born Hamitic theory which, by starkly opposing Hutu and Tutsi, had led to the genocide.

There has been a tendency among Tutsi survivors, in the immediate aftermath of the genocide, of globally condemning the Hutu people, out of grief, anger, and frustration. Many crimes of revenge took place, and a certain number of people were sent to jail under false pretexts. The poison of internalized ethnicism did not only contaminate the perpetrators but also the victims or at least some of them initially. Malachie's story made me realize, in an emblematic way, that the problem in Rwanda was not ethnicity, a dubious concept that many historians and anthropologists question today, but the ideology built around ethnicity.

Malachie's irenic and profoundly Christian attitude did not change after the genocide. As mentioned earlier I wanted to see how he had experienced the tension that nearly destroyed the Presbyterian Church after the flight of many pastors, including Michel Twagirayesu, the president, and thousands of church members to refugee camps in Kivu in July 1994. It was a challenge because of the physical and ideological proximity of this part of the Presbyterian Church with the genocide perpetrators. In the last part of the interview, Malachie spoke without passion nor resentment of this period. At an extraordinary synod held in February 1995, he was elected as general secretary of the church for one year. He was one of those who tried to keep the link with the Presbyterians in Kivu and other places of refuge such as Nairobi, hoping to persuade them to come back home.

Malachie was not the first genocide survivor I interviewed. I must have interviewed 20 of them, if not more, between 2015 and 2020. Some had been referred to me by fellow church members. Others had been introduced to me by Emilienne, my research assistant, who was a genocide survivor herself.

These interviews were memorable. Every time I felt humbled to gain the trust of people who, after having suffered so much, saw in me a brother who could receive the gift of their story. So big was their desire to talk that they faced the risk of being exposed again to the pain of the genocide when narrating the events that carried away part of their families and part of their lives. I knew I might suffer from vicarious trauma myself. I was rescued from it by the extraordinary sense of connectedness the interviews developed in me. They changed my way of looking at the world. I touched the worst that the human species can produce but also the best. To use the language of the existentialist philosopher Karl Jaspers (1947) in a book written shortly after the Second World War, I felt metaphysically guilty of the genocide in the sense that human beings like me committed horrible deeds but at the same time those like Malachie who developed resilience in the process gave me hope in the future of the human destiny.

Before I conclude, let me share another surprise, one of a different kind. Finding written documents on the history of the Presbyterian Church of Rwanda during this tumultuous part of its history had proved fairly difficult. Quite understandably given the chaos reigning after the genocide, the

Presbyterian Church in Rwanda has not been very good at preserving its archives. The headquarters of the church in Kigali and the Protestant University in Huye (formerly known as Butare) do not have much to show to the researcher. For two or three years, I had been at a loss.

All changed when I visited Malachie in Wolverhampton. There, on the table in the lounge, was a folder with dozens of letters and reports pertaining to the history of the church in 1994, 1995, and 1996. The older folders kept press clippings, which were also interesting though not as unique as the church's archives. In short, this was a real trove! During my first visit, I did not have the time to go through this remarkable collection. When I came back in October 2019 for a follow-up interview, I spent time consulting these documents. Malachie graciously gave me permission to borrow them, scan them, and return them to him.

Both in terms of oral history and of archival research, this encounter was a great moment in my life as a historian.

References

Chrétien, Jean-Pierre, and Marcel Kabanda. 2013. *Rwanda. Racisme et génocide. L'idéologie hamitique.* Paris: Belin.

Denis, Philippe. 2018. Grief and Denial Among Rwandan Catholics in the Aftermath of the Genocide Against the Tutsi. *Archives des sciences sociales des religions* 183: 287–307.

———. 2020. Contested memories and Competing Narratives of The past in Post-Genocide Rwanda. In *Memory Work in Rwanda. Churches and Civil-Society Organisations Twenty-Five Years After the Genocide Against the Tutsi*, ed. Tharcisse Gatwa and Philippe Denis, 21–32. Pietermaritzburg: Cluster Publications.

———. 2022. *The Genocide Against the Tutsi and the Rwandan Churches. Between Grief and Denial.* Woolbridge, Suffolk: Boydell & Brewer.

Des Forges, Alison. 1999. *Leave None to Tell the Story. Genocide in Rwanda.* New York: Human Rights Watch.

Gatwa, Tharcisse. 2005. *The Churches and Ethnic Ideology in the Social Crises 1900–1994.* Oxford: Regnum Books International.

Jaspers, Karl. 1947. *The German Guilt.* New York: The Dial Press.

Rittner, Carol, John K. Roth, and Wendy Whitworth, eds. 2004. *Genocide in Rwanda. Complicity of the Churches.* St Paul, MN: Paragon House.

van 't Spijker, Gerard. 2007. *Indicible Rwanda. Expériences et réflexions d'un pasteur missionnaire.* Yaoundé: Éditions CLÉ.

CHAPTER 34

Commentary: How Do We Face the Unexpected? Constitutive Practices of Oral History

María Laura Ortiz

How could we not rethink what to do with the unexpected in our research in a world awash in COVID-19? This pandemic could be cataloged as a world tragedy, and as such, it is associated with the idea of a radical change, a threat to civilization. We usually connect these notions with the irreparable action of death—not only regarding the withering away of living beings, but above all, extinguishing certain ways of living and feeling. Tragic facts do not exist by themselves—they are named as such when they are interpreted as something that is more than a mere accident, that is, as part of a set of events that tends to imply a tragic disorder (Williams 2014). Thus, there is no better time to reflect on the unexpected than at a conjuncture in which the entire planet was forced to live in completely unexpected situations, without being able to plan almost any aspect of our lives accurately. This circumstance is also reflected in the academic world. We cannot anticipate whether universities will be open or work in digital environments, if conferences will be in person, and if archives and libraries will open, among an extensive list. How many of us had to adapt our research goals to the actual current conditions of access to documents, interviews, and fieldwork? How many students and graduate students have we advised to do the same? Is there, then, there a more opportune time to think about the unexpected in research?

M. L. Ortiz (✉)
Universidad Nacional de Córdoba (UNC), Córdoba, Argentina

© The Author(s), under exclusive license to Springer Nature Switzerland AG 2023
R. Santhiago, M. Hermeto (eds.), *The Unexpected in Oral History*, Palgrave Studies in Oral History,
https://doi.org/10.1007/978-3-031-17749-1_34

In this commentary, I will reflect on four chapters that examine different unexpected situations that occurred during oral history research. Present in all of them is the discussion about the extent to which unforeseen events are the result of planning failures—an assumption shared by many researchers who find themselves in this type of situation. They would be the product of poor planning that would have resulted in a chain of bad decisions that, in turn, would have produced defects, errors, and misunderstandings, which is why things did not turn out as intended. If we connect this with Raymond Williams' observation, these unforeseen events would be considered part of a "tragic disorder" in research. But the works discussed here make it clear that all those who resort to oral history must learn to live with unexpected situations. I strongly endorse this idea, suggesting that the unexpected is a constitutive practice of oral history work, as it integrates the humanity with which we all work, we historians who approach the orality of memories.

Taking the Western philosophical tradition as a reference point, the academic world defined the scientific method as an intellectual activity composed of a program that establishes, in advance, a series of non-modifiable operations that, when carried out, guarantee access to true knowledge. In fact, the etymology of the term "method" refers to the notion of "a way to be followed," a succession of acts that aim to achieve a goal. The trail starts when a problem is defined; then the goals come; then a theoretical framework is delimited; hypotheses are elaborated; a methodology is determined to collect data and control the hypotheses, which are finally verified or rejected (Mastrángelo 2020). However, this idea has been questioned in recent decades, especially in the social sciences and humanities. We have debated if we must be governed by a single method, given that we are to approach so many heterogeneous problems. We no longer consider that the method must be a stable, unidirectional, and definitive "way to be followed"—for this would offer little space for the diversity of knowledge, as well as for the exercise of the creativity necessary for its crystallization (Marradi 2018).

Some authors connect the research method to decision-making, according to the conditions presented in each specific context. In such cases, the decisions made at the beginning can be revised, demonstrating that flexibility is welcome when you reflect on the research process (Aceves Lozano 2017), especially if you have found data that forces you to a reorientation or if a pandemic, for example, limits your fieldwork. Research decisions are social practices that constitute the construction of knowledge—in this case, of historical knowledge. This is a key element in the article by Mônica Rebecca Ferrari Nunes, whose suggestion is that oral history research is a sort of outing. For her, research is a journey in which the itinerary is decided according to the needs and possibilities that arise; thus, it is essential to reflect during the very process, especially when your research is carried out in your own urban context—in such a situation, researchers must inquire about themselves and their own culture, to objectify their own position and make decisions about it. For many years, such an approach was considered unscientific by hegemonic nuclei, who defended the image of a neutral researcher who analyzed a distant object. But the static idea about the historian's craft has been transformed in the last five decades, and we have come to recognize that we are human beings and cannot separate ourselves from this condition while doing research, especially when our sources are other people. This set of ideas refers to the humanity that characterizes the scientific method that we, historians who work with oral sources, use. Our practice of connecting with people like us—but who are also different from us—forces us to question our own position, without forgetting that our subjectivities, which are bridges with others, can also imply distances.

Especially in the field of oral history, the use of in-depth interviews impels us to recognize spoken language as the protagonist of our method. Orality constitutes a form of enunciation of cultural belonging and represents structures of feeling that memories then manifest (Laverdi 2010). For this reason, in our conversations, there is always a cultural dialogue, which requires empathy and respect for the other. It is from this perspective that one can read the work of Juliana Ventura de Souza Fernandes, who recovers the indigenous cultural inscription of the Xakriabá people, in Minas Gerais, Brazil, based on their own native categories and their way of maintaining alive long duration of past time in their collective memory. In her work, one can see that an empathic dialogue with others opens paths for the emergence of the unexpected.

However, advance planning is not always possible in interviews. Even if you design a long-winded list of questions, aiming to create a semi-structured open-ended interview, the moment of dialogue can lead to unforeseen events. Sometimes, feelings interrupt the narration, and the recorder must be turned off. In other cases, people's occupations make some encounters hard while facilitating unexpected ones. In still others, failures in recording equipment may occur, or the audio may get ruined over time. Even when everything seems to be working out well, we can never fully anticipate the development of an interview before it unfolds. Each question, each gesture, and each answer can trigger a tsunami of surprising events, unnoticed twists, forgotten memories, thoughtless words, and overlooked turns. All this sudden development is unpredictable, and it is an integral part of our craft. Uncertainty is our companion, but since do not give it the place it deserves, we feel that it gets in our way.

This in no way implies that the method is useless or that planning is unnecessary. Nothing is further from my point. Before starting fieldwork, or looking for empirical data in existing collections, or carrying out interviews, one must plan, having in mind clear research goals. Considering that the first steps of any research project generate anxiety and fear, especially in young researchers, it is important to highlight that such planning can alleviate concerns regarding "what" and "how" to pursue the research. Nonetheless, it is good to start by accepting that, along the way, unforeseen events will occur and that we must discuss how to deal with them.

Nunes recounts her difficulties in getting young cosplayers from southeastern Brazil to accept the formality of an interview. One of her first explanations is a stereotype that dominates the population she works with, "People from Minas Gerais always distrust you." But she questions this and thinks of other reasons. Indeed, if there is a salient feature in oral history, it is the obligation to reflect, not only on the common sense that floats in the testimonies, but especially on those that make up our own prejudices, as researchers. Something similar happens with Fernandes, who seeks to understand the "resistant pedagogy" of the Xakriabá indigenous people mainly through the sharing of daily practices—and not through recorded interviews. This was due to the group's memory of researchers who acted as interviewers but were also participants in a sequence of structural violence that anchors their experience between the eighteenth century and the present. And reflecting on the back-and-forth of dialogues, of the preconceptions that cross each other on such occasions, is also part of our craft (Grele 1991). In addition to this observation, which at this point in the development of oral history is somewhat obvious, I believe that this work compels us to scrutinize the formalities of the interview moment. We increasingly discuss which are the best instruments to protect the rights of the interviewees and the ownership over the testimony, to give legitimacy to recordings as historical sources, but we have not discussed whether accounts such as those produced by Nunes are ideal interviews for oral history work. Suppose you cannot turn the recorder on and just write down a few responses. Is this a valid interview, or you must have an audio register? If the recording is inaudible due to music, screams, and noises that are common at a crowded fair, does it qualify as a source? If you could not log the full names of the persons who answered your questions, can their account be used? And in this case, how should you cite it? If they did not sign a release form, is the interview legitimate? And if we do not get to record the dialogue, but soon after we meet again and try to record the same words as before, we discover that this is an impossible mission because each interview is unique and unrepeatable, even if we present the same questions to the same person.

These are questions of method—again, it all depends on the decisions taken during the research development. Even if such situations seem unforeseen and offer a glimpse of spontaneity, they are the very reality we find ourselves in when we go out for interviews. In her article, Nunes asks herself when the fieldwork begins: in her case, as she views it, it was when she arrived in her destination city, not just when she started the (frustrated) interviews. For others, however, oral history starts when the recorder is turned on—despite knowing that some of the richest and most meaningful memories tend to appear when the record button is turned off. In this dilemma about what the oral source is—if only the recording or everything that accompanies it—practices from different disciplines are intertwined. It is in this transdisciplinary dialogue that oral history gains potency.

The Ability to Listen

In the four preceding chapters, the ability of the oral history method to access voices from marginal sectors of history, whose records are not in traditional archives, is attested. But these chapters also show how such access is often fragmentary. Despite the availability of techniques for carrying out formal interviews, there are times when we must be flexible enough to admit informal conversations, recorded at an anime event or on the streets, with their characteristic clatter. In such contexts, the interview arises unexpectedly, and you must be willing to turn on the recorder not when you feel you are ready, but when the other person wishes to talk. In this flexibility and in this empathic disposition lies the heart of our method: the ability to listen.

Catalan historian Mercedes Vilanova recalls that one of the most important lessons about her craft, given by the great master Ronald Fraser, is that "it is worth doing history if we know how to ask and listen" (Vilanova 2008, 6). The willingness to listen is not limited to the sound file; it comprises a broader attitude that begins with the first contact and never ends, as long as we keep reflecting on what was said. This practice is clear in Joana Barros' work, where the researcher's interests are contrasted with those of the person who tells his or her own life story. Barros first wanted to establish a chronology that could explain causalities about living on the streets, but the interviews were not useful for this purpose: her narrators would not interconnect facts and temporalities as she expected they would. And how many of us have walked away from an interview thinking it does not serve our purposes? But Barros recognizes that a specific narrating style, while negating or ignoring certain events, did offer interpretive keys to the causalities she was seeking; it merely happened in terms different from those she had suggested. People who are homeless spoke to her in a labyrinthine narrative, which she initially thought indicated defects in their memories. After analyzing their speech, she recognized the parallelisms between their ways of expressing themselves and their wandering lives. If people talk as they live, then, we are back to the topic of an interview's context: these four chapters show us that oral sources may be merely recordings, but their interpretation requires a link with the context in which they were produced; the inclusion of what was said before and after; what happened during the conversation; the jokes, the looks, and the repeated questions; and the "nothings" that reflect significant absences.

Our ability to listen is never neutral, for it emerges from our tentative hypotheses and from the preconceptions that come into play in interviews. This is equally evident in the four chapters of this section: in all of them, interviewees and interviewers have suspicions and prejudices. They come from young, poor, and Black cosplayers; from the academic who presents herself on the pedestal of a university; and from people who live on the streets toward a professor who is involved with drifters. They are also present in the ethnic attributions of the survivors of Rwanda's genocide who talk to Philippe Denis. They are conflicts related to gender, class, age, and ethnicity. The contentious character of memories (Pollak 2006) is reflected in at least three dimensions: (1) between different communities of memories, whose memories of the same event do not converge; (2) in those who testify and whose memories can generate internal conflicts through the intervention of emotions, trauma, pain, and others; and (3) between those who research and those who are researched, who do not always share expectations, desires, interests, and needs.

In its traditional sense, memory conflicts happen because different communities are doing the remembering. This hovers in Barros' work, but also in Denis', in which differing memories about the genocide are presented: those of the perpetrators and the survivors. For the latter, every remembrance brings back the terror and the pain of loss, because they include another dimension of conflicting memories. But recollections of this kind of traumatic experience generate internal conflicts which stir up their deepest feelings. And this brings us back to the question, What is the point of remembering?

The most accepted answer seems to be that memory prevents these types of events from happening again, but even if this notion of *historia est magistra vitae* seems to fall apart every time a new far-right movement appears, a coup d'état takes place, or other types of violence are repeated. Would it, then, be enough to claim that remembering allows individuals to process their own experiences? That seems to be a less promising goal—but for survivors of these kinds of circumstances, it is not a detail. I think of those who survived the last civil-military dictatorship in Argentina and were unable to talk about their fears and sufferings, even with their families, for decades. When speaking, with the reflection that necessarily accompanies listening to yourself talking aloud, one can build a space that conduces to understanding the social meaning of what was first conceived as a solely individual, isolated experience. But then: if the purpose of remembering is to be able to digest an experience, whether it is more or less painful, it should arise from the interest of the survivor—not from scholars who need to gather sources in order to solve a research problem.

It is here that a third dimension of the conflict of memories is presented: it occurs between the goals of the research and the individuals who remember. It would be ideal to coordinate these expectations, but this is not always possible. Conflicts can arise even when the interviewees seek out the researcher because they need to talk, remember, and report their experiences. As Denis suggests, testimonies should be considered as a gift, especially when, by narrating, the interviewee relives a horror. There is a saying that when we share pain, it divides; and when we share joy, it multiplies. Something of this kind runs through all interviews, including those not limited to traumatic experiences. In addition, as Denis comments, this gift—the sharing of memories—can also be accompanied by other benefits, such as documents that seemed lost and writings or images that do not exist in official collections and that, for assorted reasons, ended up in the hands of private individuals. To access this legacy, it is not enough to feel empathy or persevering, although both are necessary conditions. What is the role of intuition in these moments—when something that naturally emerged from the dialogue opens a treasure of unexpected information and, in turn, provides new questions? Despite all the uncertainty that constitutes this type of situation, we always open an interview knowing that, when we leave, we will not be thinking and feeling as we did before.

In short, the chapters in this section demonstrate how unforeseen situations make us uncomfortable, leaving us in a state of temporary incomprehension. But they are also useful to remind us of the importance of reflecting on our practices and making decisions that allow us to continue. While the scientific method is a path to be followed, it should not constitute a limit; on the contrary, it must be complemented by the humanity that fills our work with life. The diversity of voices that we choose to incorporate in our investigations about the past and the present is much more than an illustration for our hypotheses. They are the core of historical experiences; they overflow diversity, identities, emotions, ideas, and desires. In the same way, the unforeseen is not necessarily a tragic disorder—it constitutes our social life and, as such, is constitutive of the humanity with which we work in oral history. It is about time to recognize that unforeseen events are not exceptions; they are the rule of our method, and are often the trail that allows us to access interpretations that would otherwise remain undiscovered.

References

Aceves Lozano, Jorge. 2017. La historia oral y su praxis actual: recursos metodológicos, estrategia analítica y toma de decisiones. In *Entrevistar ¿Para qué? Múltiples escuchas desde diversos cuadrantes*, ed. Graciela de Garay Arellano and Jorge Eduardo Aceves Lozano, 64–90. México: Instituto Mora.

Grele, Ronald. 1991. La historia y sus lenguajes en la entrevista de historia oral: quién contesta a las preguntas de quién y por qué. *Historia y fuente oral* 5: 111–129.

Laverdi, Robson. 2010. Raymond Williams y la historia oral: relaciones sociales constitutivas. *Palabras y silencios* 5 (2): 21–32.

Marradi, Alberto. 2018. Método, metodología, técnicas. In *Manual de metodología de las ciencias sociales*, ed. Alberto Marradi, Nélida Archenti, and Juan Ignacio Piovani, 51–67. Buenos Aires: Siglo XXI Editores.

Mastrángelo, Mariana. 2020. Herramientas claves para pensar y elaborar un proyecto de investigación en Humanidades. In *Haciendo historia: herramientas para la investigación histórica*, ed. Pablo Pozzi et al., 57–92. Buenos Aires: CLACSO.

Pollak, Michael. 2006. *Memoria, olvido, silencio. La producción social de identidades frente a situaciones límite*. Buenos Aires: Ediciones Al Margen.

Vilanova, Mercedes. 2008. Ronald Fraser, historiador y maestro. *Historia, Antropología y Fuentes Orales* 40: 5–10.

Williams, Raymond. 2014. *Tragedia moderna [1966]*. Buenos Aires: Edhasa.

Afterword: Expecting the Unexpected

Alessandro Portelli

The very roots of my fascination with oral history lie in an unexpected interview: I have been intrigued by the discrepancy between the event of the killing of Luigi Trastulli in 1949 and the stories that people told in 1953. On that occasion, I had thought that I would do a project on working-class struggles in Terni covering the time span from 1949 to 1953. But what happened was that the very first person I interviewed—one of the workers that had been laid off in 1953—was telling me the story of working conditions, strikes, and everything interesting, and, unexpectedly, her wife grabbed the microphone.

In any interview situation, you have a researcher who is looking for a story, and you have somebody that has a story they want to tell—and they don't necessarily coincide. So, being open to the unexpected is the basic rule for whoever does fieldwork—in a way, for whoever does research, because it is what allows you to *not* find what you were expecting to find or what you already knew you would find.

In this case, she grabbed the microphone and told me the story of her great grandfather, in 1860 or so. He came from a good family, but he had married a poor woman, and they were living in Romagna, between Bologna and the sea. On the day they got married, he took his bride home and said, "I'm going out to buy some meat for lunch." And he locked her in the house and went out to buy meat. On the way to the store, he ran into Giuseppe Garibaldi, who was marching with his troops to liberate the south of Italy. He then joins Garibaldi, goes to Sicily with him, and comes back four years later or so, after he has liberated Italy, and finds his bride again.

A. Portelli (✉)
Università di Roma, Rome, Italy

This is an incredible story, of course. So, what do you do? You are doing a project on the working class between 1949 and 1953, and here comes a story that is way out there. Do you say that it is interesting but, however, it is not within the scope of your project? Or do you change the project? The final result is that my book, which was supposed to be 1949–1953, turned out to be 1831–2014.

Of course, that story is an incredible counter-mythical narrative. Garibaldi is the founding myth: a hero of two worlds, Porto Alegre and Genova. Any family with an ancestor who fought with Garibaldi has a proud family heritage. And in fact, I started looking for these stories. Terni is not just where I did my oral history, but also where I grew up and went to school, and throughout my school career, nobody had told me that it had been a stronghold of Garibaldian activism in the 1860s—basically, because Terni became a sort of a border town between the new kingdom of Italy and what was left of the Pope's states. All the efforts to liberate Rome started from Terni. Still, nobody mentioned that in school—local history was not a part of what you were taught back then, in the late 1940s, early 1950s.

After that interview, I found a number of people who brought up stories of their ancestors who fought with Garibaldi. They are all stories of family pride—and yet, they all started out as rebellions against or breaks from the family. In my own parish there was a famous Garibaldi hero who destroyed his family's fortune because he spent all their money in the fight to help Garibaldi. There are a lot of stories about people who leave the family and run away from home to join the independence movement. And then you had this other image of Garibaldi himself, the founding father, who was sort of an *On the Road* hero—he had long hair, incidentally—and the people who joined him were rebels. But these rebels only became the nation's and the families' heroes because they won! If they had lost, of course, you will be abandoned like those who rose in the south after the mid-1860s.

So, this is the most unexpected interview because it was not even an interview. And it taught me some of the basic rules. Number one: you listen. And number two: you are flexible, because you are dealing with memory, and memory does not have time limits, time boundaries. Memory goes indefinitely into the past and lasts indefinitely into the present. So, being flexible and open is part of the art of listening.

And there is another interview, which again was not even an interview. This must have been 1972 or 1973. This young man, from a small town near Rome, Giulianello, for some reason gets in touch with me and says: "I know you're looking for folk songs, and we have a number of people who sing folk songs in this village. If you'd like, we can do some recordings." I went and for some reason we failed to find the singers. We were sitting in the car with him, and it was raining, pouring, so we just started talking. Back then, the idea of interviewing young people had not occurred to me yet—that was the beginning. And he started talking about what it was like to grow up in this semirural village. It was fascinating, because he talked about how very small towns, within

10 or 15 miles from where he was living, were like Paris: places where you went out, you went dancing. He told me the fantastic story of the "liberating power of the Beatles," and this was the first time I used that expression.

He talked about how he managed to grow his hair to cover his ears. He said there were two barbers: one in his village, and one in the next village, Cori, five miles away, which is bigger, so the barber in Cori was a little bit more progressive. So, every time he went to have his haircut, he went to Cori and had his hair cut just a millimeter longer, so that his father could never say anything until finally he had covered his ears.

And then he told me other stories. He said, "There's a whole generation before mine that never got married. The reason is, this is a rural village. In the 50s, finally, we had land reform, and farmhands and landless peasants were finally given pieces of land. However, it came too late. Young women from Giulianello, who had been influenced by Cori, by Artena, by Velletri (all small towns within a twenty-mile radius) would no longer marry a poor farmer, a peasant." These people had the land too late—and it tells you, in a way, the cultural failures of land reform in Italy.

From that conversation—which I didn't record, but I quickly went home and wrote down—my whole outlook changed again. Number one: young people have a history. And I've been working on that for a long time. Number two: back then, we were strictly class oriented. Suddenly you discover generation, gender, politics of private life, youth culture, and the impact of mass culture, all things that a strictly class-oriented approach had ignored. Back then, feminism was also beginning to have an impact, and you don't have to be a woman to realize that they were absolutely correct: feminism changed the perspective for everyone. Incidentally, this was a conversation with a young man, but clearly the themes came from a whole different history than the one I had been looking for.

And then, a third story, which was another sort of an unexpected interview. It was during my first visit to Harlan County. I was staying with a family of a friend, an African American sociologist. Part of this idea, which never worked out, was that both he and I would interview people in the community and see how they spoke differently to a local boy and to a white outsider. This project never happened, but I interviewed all his family members. He had me interview his grandmother, a very wise woman, who was back then in her early 90s—she lived to be over 100. When I went into people's homes, they always had their television on, and I was too shy to ask them to turn it off. It of course intrudes on the sound quality, but then you go back and have a fantastic documentation of what people were watching on television. She was watching one of those white fundamentalist preachers. We sat down.

I knew she was from Alabama and had worked in the fields as a sharecropper, before the Great Migration north. So, I wanted to ask her about what that was like, what her experience was, and what did she remember. She was absolutely intrigued by the fact that what she said was going to be heard by white people—not only that I was white, because I came with good recommendations, as a guest of her grandson. "But then, when people hear this story in Italy, they'll say that Miss-So-And-So said these things...." And she just pulled me around her little finger for two hours and didn't tell me anything.

At the end, I realized this was much more meaningful than what I expected. After all, I had read dozens of novels, history, sociology, and anthropology books about African American sharecroppers in Alabama at the turn of the twentieth century. Whatever she might have told me might have borne the imprint of personal experience but would not have been anything that we did not already know—it would have been a personal, intimate take on something we already knew. What we do not know from reading those books is that 70 years later she was still concerned that the white people might punish her and hurt her for telling the truth about what happened in 1910 or 1911.

And that leads me back to fourth interview, exactly with the same generation. This was a leader of the farmworker strikes in the Roman hills in 1910 or so. I interviewed him three times. Actually, twice—in the third one, he told me to turn the tape recorder off. It was when he told me that they actually used sabotage. These were vineyard workers; proud of their work and of the local wine, some of them had small plots of their own, so they had an affectionate relationship to the land, the vineyards, and the wine. Cutting the vineyards was something painful, but also a crime, and 60 years later he still would not talk about it openly. I said: "Look, it's been 60 years." I explained the statute limitations, and he finally said: "Okay, go ahead." What I learned from both these interviews, but especially from the black lady in Lynch, was the real meaning of a phrase I quoted at the beginning of my Luigi Trastulli article, from Walter Benjamin: "A lived event is complete on every aspects, as it is finished in the past; a remembered event is to be completed, because it is a key to connections to facts before and after it happened." The events of 1910 in the vineyards of the Roman hills or in the cornfields of Alabama still lived on 1970 and 1980. That was unexpected to me.

* * *

When Gianni Bosio handed me my first portable tape recorder, I had no training at all. The only training I got was one piece of advice from him, "Never turn it off." Never turn it off for two reasons. One, "It is bad manners." If somebody is talking about something and you turn it off, you are telling them: what you are saying is not interesting. Sometimes it is not interesting indeed, but it may turn out to be interesting to others, or you may realize years later that it was interesting all the time, perhaps for reasons you didn't know at the time. So just be patient and keep listening.

When you take somebody to a studio and interview them, and rehearse them, you more or less know what is going to happen. When you go into a place and just start listening, it is totally unpredictable. In a social context, you cannot plan ahead. So, in a way, expecting the unexpected, hoping for the unexpected, is at the root of all this. This is why I got the stories on tape when I started to collect folk songs.

The traditional ethnomusicological approach was to record only the songs, because that is what you are interested in. My dearest friend and Italy's greatest musician, Giovanna Marini, also went around recording things to build her repertoire, and she gave me all her tapes for our archive. It is fascinating because, when people were not singing, she would turn it off. Back then, tape was expensive. I was paying my own way, and so was she; she could not afford to waste money and tape. So, the result is half the times the first syllable and the first note of the song is missing, because people would start singing unannounced, unexpectedly. She rushes to push the red button, but…

So, the lesson I learned is: "Listen patiently to the small talk, to the stories and everything between the songs." This is how I finally managed to have those stories on tape—stories I was not looking for. In fact, I had never heard of oral history back then, so I did not really know what to do with these things. Our only outlet were records, which were not good for spoken words. So, these things were unsought for and I didn't know what to do with them. It took me sometime before I was able to figure out what it was that I was getting.

So, the whole thing is unexpected. Of course, you must keep being flexible and open enough to realize: "I'm not looking for this, but this is wonderful, so let me change." By the time I started the 1949–1953 project, I already knew that I was going to work with stories. But, before that, I had to shift from being an amateur ethnomusicologist to being an amateur historian.

* * *

Because I was not only paying my way but also doing all my transcripts—which is one of the reasons I have a bad back these days—there were moments in my oral history research in Terni when people told me things that I thought I was not interested in. I let the tape run, but I skipped them when I came to transcribe. Later, it occurred to me that basically I had skipped two types of stories. One was the stories of men about military service and the war. The other was stories of women about when their husbands were sick in the hospital and they were taking care of them. The reason I was not interested in those stories—and it was a basic mistake—is because I thought they were the same everywhere, they were not specific to Terni. That was a mistake: the culture and history of a town is made both of specific, unique traits and of traits and experiences shared with other places. But I was only a beginner then.

And after a while, I also thought that if these were the stories I skipped, perhaps they had something in common. And I realized it is the same narrative: leaving home, facing an institution, and dealing with hierarchies and technology. These include two very parallel stories: common soldiers that explain to the officer why he is getting something wrong and ladies that explain to the great doctor what is really the matter with her husband. And then, they are both about life and death.

That was not just unexpected; it was totally unwanted. I kept hoping that they would shut up about the war, shut up about the hospital. But when I went back to the tapes years later—of course, I didn't have transcripts!—they turned out to be fascinating. One of the things you get in the stories of these women, both in Kentucky and Terni, is that you have this male chauvinist husband, fascist, and authoritarian, and suddenly he is like a baby in your hands: you powder him, you clear him, and you have power over him. It is fascinating from this point of view.

* * *

The other story that has to do with the cost of the tape is from when I was doing the Fosse Ardeatine project. I had originally worked on the reel-to-reel, then I shifted to a Sony cassette tape, and then I had shifted to DAT, a wonderful, very expensive technology. I am interviewing this lady who turns out to be the most important character in my Fosse Ardeatine book. Each chapter begins with her story. I had things that I wanted to know; she had stories that she wanted to tell. So, when I think I heard all that I was looking for, and by the time she thinks she has told me all that she usually tells, I still have about 30 minutes of tape and do not want to waste that.

Also, how do you end an interview? When do you tell the person that that is done? This has always been a problem to me. And, in fact, often the really interesting things crop up later—you are still there and have to turn the machine on again, or, worse, you have already said goodbye and closed the door, you are walking down the stairs, suddenly you think of something you should have asked, and you must go back and knock on the door again—what the French call *l'esprit d'escalier*. In this case, I also lingered because it is always awkward to tell people that the interview is over—they have nothing more of interest to say to you....I had tape space left, so we started talking, just small talk. And what did she talk about? About what we old folks talk about: her health and her pension. She complained that her pension was not as good as those of people who had suffered less, and then she said: "And to think of all the things that I had to do to get that pension!"

That had not occurred to me before. "Yes, what did you have to do?" I asked. This was a time when women were full black in mourning, and the widows of the men killed at the Fosse Ardeatine went all over town, climbing the stairs of public institutions, churches, and welfare office, looking for work or some means of support....There was the sense of wandering around the city carrying death with them, but also the humiliation of begging. And she says: "And everywhere you went – but even later when I finally have a job, people thought that you were at their disposal..." I said: "Madam, what do you mean?" She says: "I mean what you know I mean." She was 24; her husband had just been killed. She did not have the words for sexual harassment, but sexual harassment has existed before there were words for it. To me this was really painful. As for the massacre of Fosse Ardeatine, you can distance yourself from it—because it was fascist, Nazi, and I am not a fascist or a Nazi. But that? Even though this is not what I learned from my father, it runs in the culture of masculinity, and I am a male. One thing that happens unexpectedly in interviews is that sometimes you suddenly realize: this is about me.

Then, of course, there was the typical question that is asked of oral histories: how do you generalize? Was it just her or not? I was still doing interviews, but you do not ask an elderly lady, "Mama, were you sexually harassed in the 1940s?" On the other hand, an oral history interview is not a question-and-answer. I have a football metaphor: it is like an assist. You pass open a space and pass the ball. So, I would just make a comment: "It must have been very difficult for young women back then." And they all knew what I meant. And they all had stories. What did this reveal to me? On one hand, the pain that was wrought upon these women that I had not thought about. And on the other hand, the discrepancy between what we, as historians, know as history and what this lady, who has a third-grade education, did know.

Clearly these women had shared stories among themselves about this, but it had never occurred to them that they were history. In their education there was no such thing as gender history, the history of sexuality, and social history. History was war, kings, generals, and massacres; the story of the Fosse Ardeatine was about their husbands. It had never occurred to them that it was also about themselves. And that is the other thing that I learned. So, I guess, all my education has been the result of unexpected encounters and narratives, from the very beginning.

*   *   *

I taught a number of classes and seminars, and I can think of some aspects of oral history work that can be taught. On the other hand, it is really a thing you learn by doing, and you make your own mistakes. I am still learning.

But there is no real technique—the only technique is good manners. And also, there is a mistaken mythology where the great interviewer is the one that extracts more information and makes a person tell things that they would not tell otherwise. As for me, I believe you should never violate a silence—both because silences contain much deep information and because, sometimes, when people realize that you respect them and are not intrusive, they might trust you with stories. It has happened to me a couple of times.

So, oral history is about good manners and respect. And then there is a matter of attitude about what you really want to know about a person. In this case, I have an advantage: I was never funded to do a project, meaning that I could do whatever I wanted. If I had been funded to do the Terni project, I would have left that story out. So, I was able to follow my curiosity and go where the narrators took me. I have often talked about the interview as akin to ballroom dancing, to tango. As in the dance, there is a relationship between your steps and the other person's steps, and you do not step on your partner's feet. So, these are things that you do not teach or learn in the abstract, or from a "how-to" manual. You need to develop these attitudes, good manner, respect, and authentic interest in the other person, within yourself.

I would not tell people to interview as I do. You develop your own style, and it really depends on what you are looking for. Oral history is a complex phrase because it implies a relationship between two poles of a continuum: events—"history"—on one hand and a way of talking about them, "orality." Where you place yourself in this continuum?

There is a difference between what was called the use of oral sources in historiography and what I call oral history. Typically, historians are about finding out what happened, so I see the point in needing to ask a person a specific question. But I am not a historian; therefore, I am more oriented toward the oral. I want my information to come in the first place from the interview—I want *that* to be my primary source because a great deal of the information I am looking for is couched not in the contents of the story but in the way in which the story is told (and in the fact that it is told at all).

When I was doing the Fosse Ardeatine project, I decided that I needed to interview fascists, which was a fascinating experience, because in that case the unexpected was for them: "Here comes this communist historian and he wants to talk to me." Usually (and unexpectedly), they were very forthcoming. So, I interviewed this person, who turned out to be an acquaintance of my father-in-law. He had actually been on the spot of the partisan's attack to which the Nazis retaliated by carrying out the massacre at the Fosse Ardeatine. It is a two-hour-long interview. Then, incidentally, I was on the beach at Copacabana reading a book on the war years in Rome and here comes his name, and it turns out that he had been tried for the murder of a young antifascist student. He has not mentioned this to me—and of course, I did not ask him, because I did not know.

For a historian this is a mortal sin: you ought to be prepared before you go into an interview. But being prepared is exactly one of the things that get in the way of the unexpected. And in this case what I did not expect was his reticence and silence—which you can discover if you go back to the written record *after* the interview rather than before. So, I went back, and he gave me his version. So, what did I gain by focusing more on his *oral* story than in the *history*? I gained the silence: I learned that, if not challenged, he would not talk about that episode. And, to me, oral history is where the oral narrative is your first source of information. So, if I am going to interview a coal miner, that is enough to know that he worked in the coal mines. I may miss a lot of actual, precise information, but I gain a degree of perspective.

Another thing I do that I would not suggest others imitate is that I prefer to expand the range of interviews rather than conduct several interviews with the same person to go deep into a life story (this is not an absolute rule anyway—there have been exceptions, and I am just at this time writing a book on a person's life after more than 30 hours of interviews). But I am infinitely more fascinated by meeting other persons and exploring other differences. Perhaps, it is because the more people you meet, more surprises you get.

Index[1]

A
Ação Cívico-Social (Aciso), 158, 159
Ação Popular (Brazilian guerilla group), 199
Accessibility, 37, 40, 41
Aceves Lozano, Jorge Eduardo, 111, 250
Activism
  Communist, 30, 32, 35
  cultural, 61
  Garibaldian activism, 258
  labor activism, 30, 179, 199, 201, 202
  left-wing, 30, 31, 48
  Republican activism (in Northern Ireland), 161, 162, 165, 166
  student activism, 197, 210, 211
Adebaldo, 73
African Evangelistic Enterprise (AEE) (Rwanda), 244
Agency, 18, 36, 51, 55, 218, 236
Alberti, Verena, 9, 12, 93, 111, 128, 129, 136, 143, 144
Aleksiévitch, Svetlana, 56
Alfredo, 149–153
Alfredo, Mr., 23
Alípio, Dr., 21, 22
Alphonse, 244
Alves, Maria das Dores, 72
Alzheimer's disease, 23
Amado, Janaína, 5, 7–9, 11, 56, 59, 76, 80, 82
Amato, Gabriel, 179
American Family Association (AFA) (USA), 41
Anachronism, 48, 129, 134
Andrade, Oswald de, 123
Andrade, Rudá de, 123
Annales School, 81
Anthropology, 50, 130, 139, 208, 222, 243, 246, 260
Archival research, 2, 5, 9, 131, 138, 139, 148, 161, 162, 173, 242, 247, 249
Archives, 138
Argentina's dictatorship, 144, 148, 151–154, 254
Argentine Psychoanalytical Association (APA), 85
Arp, Agnès, 4
Assmann, Aleida, 193
Atheism, 35
Aula, Inkeri, 191
Autobiography, 18, 84–86, 98
Autoethnography, 111, 136
Azaustre, Manuel, 4, 5

---

[1] Note: Page numbers followed by 'n' refer to notes.

B

Barela, Liliana, 216
Baremblitt, Gregório, 83–86, 102, 103
Barros, Joana, 216, 217, 253, 254
Barros, Manoel de, 104, 178
Basaglia, Franco, 80
Batucada, Miriam (Miriam Angela Lavecchia), 58, 89–92, 94, 95, 99, 100
Baudelaire, Charles, 219
Baum, Willa, 2
Béatrice, 244
Benjamin, Walter, 5, 11, 99, 104, 220, 260
Bhaduri, Tarun Coomar, 181
Biography, 18, 58, 84, 90, 91, 96, 99, 100
  generational sensobiography, 191
Bloch, Marc, 155
Body, 143
  body language, 24, 25
Bornat, Joanna, 174, 178
Bosi, Ecléa, 46, 110
Bosio, Gianni, 260
Bossa nova, 63
Botz, Gerhard, 4
Brazilian military dictatorship, 18, 60, 61, 63, 65, 80, 145, 156, 159, 179, 197, 209–212, 235, 240
  censorship, 61, 62
  opening, 60
Brazilian Oral History Association, 46
Buarque, Chico, 60, 62–66
Burke, Peter, 56

C

Camisasca, Marina, 211
Camp Trans (festival), 39
Campos, Irany, 179, 199–204, 200n2
Campos, Rui, 131, 133
Candomblé, 85
Caparaó guerrilla (Brazil), 156
Carr, Walter S., 170
Carvalho, Ana Emília de, 72
Carvalho, José Murilo de, 71, 74
Carvalho, Maria Angélica de, 71
Carvalho, Maria Selma de, 72
Cazuza, 83

Children's literature, 181
Chowdhury, Indira, 179, 211, 212
Chronology, 48, 217, 228, 230, 235, 253
Cícero, Antonio, 109
Clandinin, Jean, 98, 99
Clark, Septima, 173
Class, 10, 144, 259
  working class, 18, 29, 41, 61, 148, 154, 211
Cold War, 158–160, 172
Colonialism, 182, 185
Comando de Libertação Nacional (COLINA) (Brazilian guerilla group), 199
Commemoration, 243
Committed art, 61, 62
Common sense knowledge, 215
Communist Party of Canada, 31, 32
Concentration camps, 4, 79
Connelly, F. Michael, 98, 99
Connerton, Paul, 50
Consumption, 150, 224
Cordobazo, 148
Corrêa, Thedy, 60
Cosplaying, 217, 219–224, 251, 253
Coutinho, Eduardo, 82, 102, 103
Covid-19, 20, 40, 49, 76, 138, 249
Cowans, Julia, 169
Creativity, 8, 47, 80, 178, 208, 250
Cristina, Paula, 223, 229
Cruz, João Manoel da, *see* Lotera, João
Culture, 208
  class culture, 46, 150, 153
  folk culture, 8, 57, 69, 73–75, 101, 258, 261
  labor culture, 144
  mass culture, 259
  pop culture, 220, 221, 223, 224
  urban culture, 261
  youth culture, 259
Curiosity, 66, 125, 139, 157, 201, 263
Cvetkovich, Ann, 19, 20, 49–51

D

Da Costa, Cléria Botelho, 144
Dacoity, 181, 183, 185
DaMatta, Roberto, 130

Deleuze, Gilles, 79, 83, 122
Denis, Philippe, 216–218, 253, 254
Department of Political and Social Order (DOPS) (Brazil), 199
Devi, Phoolan (The "Bandit Queen"), 182
Diary
  personal diary, 30, 31, 35
Digital history, 138
Distortions, 9, 36, 57, 58, 93, 95, 99, 201
Dona Margarida, 227–231, 234
Douglas, Jessica, 170n1
Drexler, Jorge, 144
Dublin, Thomas, 170

E
Eco, Umberto, 218
Eduardo, 230–234
Education, 182, 183, 185, 212, 263
  adult education, 34–35
  alternative education, 80
  higher education, 113, 116, 197
  indigenous education, 238
  popular education, 143, 173, 174
  self-education, 163, 165–167
Elisée, 242
Emerson, 229
Emilienne, 246
Environment, 179, 190, 240
Ethnicity, 10, 18, 218, 244–246, 253
Ethnography, 13, 39, 138, 170, 217, 220, 235
Eysenck, Michael W., 110

F
Fábio, 57, 59, 62–67, 100, 101
Facebook, 20, 40, 50, 76
Family bonds, 190
Family history, 23–24, 46
Family stories, 191, 193, 194, 258
Fascism, 18
Federal University of Minas Gerais (UFMG), 22, 24, 25, 60, 66, 197–204
Feminism, 10, 37–39, 38n2, 41, 42, 49, 259

Fernandes, Juliana Ventura de Souza, 8, 216, 217, 251, 252
Ferreira, Bibi, 60, 62, 64, 65
Ferreira, Marieta de Moraes, 5, 56, 76, 80
Ferteco (Brazilian mining company), 192
Fiat, 144, 148, 149, 151–153
Film, 82, 97, 98, 101, 103, 124, 181
Flânerie, 217, 219–222
Forgetting, 73, 74, 82, 94, 95, 102, 109, 194
Forgiveness, 46, 242
Formoso uprising, 8
Foucault, Michel, 83
Foundation Remembrance, Responsibility and Future, 5n4
Francesco, 149–152
Fraser, Ronald, 3, 253
Freire, Paulo, 143, 173
Friedrich-Schiller University Jena, 3
Frisch, Michael, 10, 172
Frondizi, Arturo, 47
Fukuyama, Francis, 48

G
Gagnebin, Jeanne Marie, 109
García Conde, Luis, 216
Gardner, Kay, 43
Garibaldi, Giuseppe, 257
Gascón, María, 4
Gaspar Garcia Center for Human Rights (São Paulo, Brazil), 228
Gender, 10, 22, 24, 179, 212, 259, 263
Genealogy, 72, 74
Generation, 190, 191, 194, 259
Genette, Gerard, 11
Ginzburg, Carlo, 84, 147, 155
Glória, Dona Maria da, 27
Gluck, Sherna Berger, 10
Grahn, Judy, 40
Great Depression, 30
Grele, Ronald, 252
Grief, 240, 246
Grupo Plataforma, 83, 85, 86
Guattari, Felix, 79, 122
Guerrilla, 145, 152
Guimarães, Plínio Ferreira, 144, 171, 172

H

Habyarimana, Juvénal, 241, 244
Hansen's disease, 19, 21–23, 26, 49
Havugimana, Israel, 244
Helena Junior, Alberto, 131
Heller, Agnes, 122
Hermeto, Miriam, 1, 2, 23–25, 57, 97, 100–104
Heroism, 81, 82, 144, 147, 148, 151, 153, 164, 171, 179, 187, 212, 258
Hesitation, 9, 32, 95, 122, 207, 223, 244
Heymann, Luciana, 12, 111, 129, 136
High, Steven, 19, 20, 48, 51, 172
Historia est magistra vitae, 254
Historical sources, 4, 61, 120, 159–160, 162, 209, 246, 247, 254
  letters, 74, 75
Historical studies, 144, 160
History, 264
  social history, 263
Hoffman, Marella, 179
Hollanda, Bernardo Borges Buarque de, 111, 128, 136
Homeless people, 227, 229, 231, 253
Horton, Myles, 173
Humor, 8, 18, 84
Huyssen, Andreas, 19

I

Identity
  personal identity, 24
Illiteracy, 4, 5, 75, 116
Imperial Order of the Daughters of the Empire, 29
Inclusion, 224
Indigenous history, 235
Institutional Analysis, 79
Institutionalization
  of leprosy patients, 26, 27
Interahamwe (Rwandan militia group), 241, 244, 245
International Criminal Tribunal for Rwanda, 242
International Oral History Association (IOHA), 4
International Psychoanalytical Association (IPA), 80, 83

Intersubjectivity, 9, 35, 83, 98, 138, 143, 154, 237
Interview
  body language, 166, 167
  encounter, 24, 25, 47–49, 99, 103, 123, 125, 135, 144, 148, 149, 170, 237
  ending an interview, 76, 95, 117, 167, 170, 207, 228, 243, 245, 262
  first experiences interviewing, 24, 30, 49
  in family, 24
  follow-up interview, 245, 247
  informal interviews, 39, 91, 102, 220, 230
  interview setting, 111, 114, 167, 236
  job interview, 9
  non-interview, 216, 236–237, 239
  nonrecorded interviews, 118, 216, 227, 252
  off-the-record interviews, 82, 91
  pre-interview, 31
  public interview, 50, 211
  recruiting interviewees, 61, 66
  restricted access interviews, 31
  revisiting old interviews, 30, 114, 135, 136, 139
  self-interview, 83
  types of interview (informal), 253
  types of interviews, 170
  types of interviews (collective), 237
  types of interviews (directive), 136
  types of interviews (in-depth), 216, 251
  types of interviews (life story), 13, 29–31, 36, 49, 90, 149, 153, 157, 163, 264
  types of interviews (semi-structured), 190
  types of interviews (structured), 136
  types of interviews (thematic), 13, 66, 90, 131
Intuition, 13, 103, 104, 144, 254
Irish Republican Army (IRA), 163, 164

J

James, Daniel, 169
Janov, Arthur, 34

Jaspers, Karl, 246
Jesus, Maria Cecília de, 71, 72
Jesus of Nazareth, 114, 115, 117–119
Journalism, 17, 56, 62, 63, 65, 91, 103, 127, 131, 132, 181, 201
Judaism, 111, 121, 122
Julienne, 243

K
Kerr, Daniel R., 173
Kilomba, Grada, 74
Kind, Luciana, 57, 58
Klein, Melanie, 85
Koselleck, Reinhart, 49
Kossoy, Boris, 128, 133, 134
Kurt, Elvira, 40, 41

L
Labor history, 29
Langer, Suzanne, 85
Lapassade, Georges, 79
Lavecchia, Mirna, 90
Laverdi, Robson, 251
Leão, Nara, 63
Lejeune, Philippe, 84
Leprosy, *see* Hansen's disease
Lesbianism, 58, 95, 96, 99, 100
Levi, Primo, 82
Lévi-Strauss, Claude, 222
Lie, 8, 55–57, 59
Lima, Ana Cardoso Maia de Oliveira, 115n2
Lima, Paulo, 115n2, 118
Lima Filho, Agripino de Oliveira, 111, 113–120, 115n2
Lisa Vogel, 38
Lispector, Clarice, 63
Listening, 50, 98, 100, 124, 125, 137, 144, 171, 217, 223, 236, 253, 254
  active listening, 41
  attentive listening, 7, 24, 73, 258, 261
  importance of listening, 260
Local history, 20, 30, 36, 48, 57, 190, 191, 194, 258
Los Del Rio, 221
Lotera, João, 71
Lourau, René, 79
Louzada, Silvana, 47

M
Magaldi, Sábato, 64
Malachie, 217, 218, 241–247
Maltoni, Luís Augusto, 131
Maravilha, Tutti, 63
Mariano, César Camargo, 63
Marini, Giovanna, 261
Marradi, Alberto, 250
Marxism, 35
Mastrángelo, Mariana, 250
Matt, 165–167, 171
Mauad, Ana Maria, 19, 20
Maurice, 164–166
Mauthausen Survivor Documentation Project (MSDP), 4
McDonald's, 223
McLaren, Peter, 220
Meihy, José Carlos Sebe Bom, 130
Melgaço, Carlos, 211
Memoir, 39, 44, 148
Memory, 46, 48
  autobiographical, 8, 25, 35, 60, 156, 165, 167, 192, 202, 220, 258
  collective, 62, 74, 81, 111, 127, 182, 184, 185, 251
  communities of memory, 254
  composure, 82
  conflicting memories, 254
  cultural memory, 8, 193
  disputes, 204
  divided memories, 81, 242
  false memories, 34, 110
  hidden memories, 20
  as a historiographical issue, 46
  history of memory, 67, 86, 110
  individual memory, 56, 110, 194
  intergenerational transmission, 237–239
  mediatic memory, 220
  memory conflicts, 254
  memory framing, 19, 20
  memory operations, 209
  memory structure, 189
  memory studies, 242
  memory transmission, 194
  memory work, 46, 51, 73
  misconceptions, 50
  mnemonical operations, 110
  mnemonic operations, 110, 111
  nostalgic memory, 192

Memor (*cont.*)
  official corporate memory, 179
  official memory, 198, 200, 202–204
  public, 61, 144, 211
  social, 17, 56, 158, 194, 220
  underground memories, 19, 48, 51, 74, 209
Memory studies, 18
Memory work, 49–51
Meneses, Ulpiano Toledo Bezerra de, 46
Meringolo, Denise D., 173n3
Methodological dogmatism, 7
Michigan Womyn's Music Festival (Michfest), 20, 37–44, 49, 50
Microhistory, 147, 155
MI5 (British Security Service), 163
Miguez, Mercedes, 216
Mining, 190, 191, 194, 212
Mitterrand, François, 119
Mlodinow, Leonard, 177
Monteiro, Elmira, 57, 69–76, 101–103
Monteiro, Lívia Nascimento, 57, 97, 101–104
Mourning, 24, 179, 217, 237, 238, 240, 262
Movimento Nacionalista Revolucionário (Brazilian guerilla group), 156, 157
Mühlhaus, Carla, 56
Museum of Image and Sound (MIS) (São Paulo, Brazil), 123, 127–131, 133
Music, 37, 58, 61–63, 65, 75, 89, 90, 94, 123, 124, 221, 252, 261
Myth, 81, 215, 258

N
Nambikwara (Brazilian indigenous people), 222
Narayan, Jayaprakash, 182
Narrative, 9, 10, 99, 143, 208, 229, 232, 233, 236
Narrative research, 99
Nascimento, Afonsina, 69–71, 73, 74, 76, 101–103
Nascimento, Darci, 70
National Council for Scientific and Technological Development (CNPq) (Brazil), 219
National Indian Foundation (FUNAI) (Brazil), 238
Nazism, 81, 242
Neves, Lucilia de Almeida, 178
Neves, Tancredo, 73
1968, 161, 211
Nogueira, Marina, 209, 210
Nora, Pierre, 46
Northern Ireland conflict ("The Troubles, 161, 162
Nunes, Mônica Rebecca Ferrari, 216, 217, 250–252

O
Oblivion, 22
Olivier, 245
Oral history, 44, 46, 49
  activist oral history, 39
  as an art, 178
  authority, 13, 25, 36, 99, 144, 172, 201
  authorship, 10, 82
  in Brazil, 7, 46, 128
  collections, 12, 119, 121, 123, 127, 133, 138, 173
  commissioned projects, 113, 119, 179, 182, 212
  dialogue, 98
  disagreements between interview participants, 100, 102
  in education, 178
  encounter, 128
  epistemological status, 80, 136, 137
  ethics, 30, 36, 38, 137
  expectations of narrators, 179
  expectations of researchers, 36, 149, 154, 159, 171, 178, 211, 212, 253, 254
  as an experiment in equality, 4
  field notes, 13, 136, 220
  generalization, 145, 171
  generalization and interpretation, 263
  history of oral history, 3, 178, 216
  informal encounters, 83
  intellectual culture, 178, 179, 208, 210–212
  interdisciplinarity, 56, 102

interpretation, 2, 12, 13, 86, 110, 111, 119, 127, 136–138, 172, 202, 245, 253
interviewers' expectations, 99
interviewing, 82, 223
legitimacy, 138
manuals, 9, 24, 128
as memory work, 93
as a method, 38–40, 50, 76
as a methodology, 7, 30
off-the-record interviews, 243, 260
oral history in Brazil, 12
pedagogy, 216
performance, 10, 50, 114, 116, 117, 136, 148, 208, 236, 243
practice, 13
preparation for interviews, 99
as a profession, 26, 30, 31, 48
psychological support during interviews, 30
recordings, 172, 227
recruiting interviewees, 101
as a relationship, 178, 201
reliability, 55
researchers' expectations, 17, 29, 100, 257
research planning, 125, 126, 128, 135, 136, 155, 156, 162, 165, 167, 171, 182, 208, 211, 219, 222, 227, 235, 250, 251
re-use of interviews, 119
reuse of old interviews, 2, 127, 129, 133
revisiting old interviews, 119
social meaning, 124, 172, 173
social purpose, 145
tape recorder, 80, 93–96, 118, 165, 221, 231, 243, 252, 260, 262
theory, 9
training, 9, 216, 263
training (lack of), 29, 31, 260
transcribing, 2, 261
transcripts, 80, 111, 118, 122, 171, 243, 262
types of interview (life story), 129, 167
version, 44, 55, 59, 81, 86, 93, 96, 100, 143, 144, 264
Oral history collections, 2
Orality, 102, 250, 251, 264
Oral tradition, 217, 237

Orkut (social network), 61, 101
Ortiz, María Laura, 3, 216, 218
Our Lady of Aparecida, 118

P
Participatory research, 9, 215, 236
Passerini, Luisa, 18, 93, 152
Patai, Daphne, 10, 98, 178
Peebles, Lucy, 170, 170n1
Pennsylvania State Archives (USA), 173
Pereira, Francisco Manuel (Chico Padeiro), 21
Pereira, João Batista, 19, 21–27, 48, 49
Pereira, Maria da Glória, 21
Pereira Junior, Rufino, 21
Perelmutter, Daisy, 111, 136
Performance, 37, 38, 38n3, 40, 40n6, 43
Philosophies of Difference, 122
Photography, 20, 25, 39n4, 45, 46, 103
Place, 191
Poe, Edgar Allan, 219
Política Operária (Brazilian guerilla group), 199
Pollak, Michael, 19, 46, 49–51, 56, 74, 79, 209, 254
Pontes, Paulo, 60, 62
Portelli, Alessandro, 4, 9, 10, 17, 70, 73, 80, 82, 84, 93, 98, 101, 102, 110, 124, 148, 169, 171, 172
Porto, Guiomar, 23–27
Porto, Luiza, 3, 19, 48, 49, 51
Poverty, 5, 33, 223
Power, 10, 32, 46, 56
Poy, José, 131, 132
Presbyterian Church, 242, 243, 246, 247
The Primal Scream, see Arthur Janov
Primal therapy, 34, 35, 48
Protestant Church, 163
Psychology, 79, 102, 110
Public history, 100, 110, 137, 173

Q
Quadros, Jânio, 47
Qualitative research, 56, 98, 103
Queer
queer culture, 37, 39
queer oral history, 178
queer theory, 38

R

Race relations, 72, 74
Racism, 37, 76, 119, 124
Rajão, Raphael, 136
RCA Victor (recording company), 60
Regina, Elis, 63
Reguillo, Rossana, 194
Reinisch, Dieter, 144, 145, 171, 172
Reluctance, 2, 25, 145, 157, 162, 166, 167
Remembering, 109, 189
Reparation, 23, 49
Republican Sinn Féin (Northern Ireland), 164, 165
Republicanism, 164
Research design
    hypotheses, 2, 5, 9, 13, 86, 110, 122, 144, 147, 148, 152, 154, 155, 165, 198, 250, 253, 255
Research methods, 5, 162, 163, 167, 180, 207, 215, 220, 250
Resende, Valério de, 22
Resentment, 27, 81, 109, 124, 185, 242, 246
Ribeiro, Djamila, 76
Ribeiro, Raphael Rajão, 111
Richard, Florence, 19, 29–34, 36, 48
Richard, Norman, 30, 36
Ricoeur, Paul, 19
Ritchie, Donald A., 9
Robertini, Camillo, 144, 171, 172
Rodrigão, 238
Rodrigué, Emílio, 83–86, 102
Rodrigues, Heliana de Barros Conde, 57, 97, 98, 102–104
Rodrigues Filho, Mario, 130
Roman Catholic Church, 75, 115, 118, 162, 199, 242
Rosalino, 238
Royal Ulster Constabulary (RUC), 163
Rukmini, 186, 187
Rwandan genocide, 217, 241–244, 246, 253, 254
Rwandan Patriotic Front, 241, 242, 244, 245

S

Sampaio, Sérgio, 89
Santana, Antônio, 193
Santana, Marco Aurélio, 18
Santhiago, Ricardo, 1, 2, 57–59, 97, 99–104
São Paulo Museum of Image and Sound, 111
São Paulo Soccer Club (São Paulo, Brazil), 131–133
Schneider, Erno, 47
Scientific method, 3, 147, 215, 250, 251, 255
Seeman, Jörn, 189, 190
Seixas, Raul, 89
Self-reflexivity, 10, 60, 101, 102, 120, 136, 148, 185, 209, 210, 250, 255
Semprún, Jorge, 4, 5n4
Seu Valdemar, 217, 237–240
Seu Valdin, 238, 240
Sex, 41
    BDSM, 41, 42
    radical sex cultures, 42, 43
    sex wars, 41, 42
    sexual freedom, 42
Sex-positivity, 37
Sexual harassment, 262, 263
Sheftel, Anna, 11
Shopes, Linda, 9, 144, 145
Sign language, 40
Silence, 9, 18, 19, 27, 32, 49, 74, 76, 95, 102, 125, 167, 171, 203, 243, 263, 264
    breaking the silence, 18, 19, 24, 51
Silva, Iara Souto Ribeiro, 179, 211, 212
Silva, Leônidas da, 131
Silva, Regina Helena Alves da, 179, 191, 211, 212
Silveira, Joel, 56, 57
Singh, Gyan, 182–187
Sippy, G.P., 181
Soccer studies, 128, 130
Sociability, 26, 221, 224, 228, 230, 235
Social cartography, 190, 194
Social history, 147
Social justice, 173
Sociology, 130, 139, 260
South Africa apartheid, 242

Spanish Civil War, 3
Sports, 127–130, 133, 145, 166, 167
Srigley, Katrina, 10
Star, Edy, 89
Stereotypes, 42, 222, 225
Stigma
  of leprosy, 22, 23, 25, 27, 49
Storytelling, 32, 40, 41, 102
Strohl, Tom, 170
Subjectivity, 10, 47, 48, 76, 82, 147

T
Tagore, Rabindranath, 181
Television, 90, 129, 259
Terrorism, 153, 161
Theater, 60, 100
  Brazilian theater, 66
Thiago, 224
Thompson, Paul, 56, 174
Thomson, Alistair, 9, 18, 82
Thunder Bay Museum (Ontario, Canada), 29, 30
Tilly, Louise, 171
Torture, 185, 199, 200, 202
Totalitarianism, 56
Transexuality
  trans-inclusion, 37, 39
Transitional justice, 211
Trastulli, Luigi, 10, 81, 257, 260
Trauma, 34, 90, 109, 178, 179, 189, 191, 192, 194, 241, 246, 254
TripAdvisor (website), 118
Troiani, Igea, 91
Trust, 76, 82, 156, 157, 164, 165, 184, 222, 225, 246, 263
Truth, 6, 19, 20, 39, 55, 56, 59, 80–83, 85, 86, 99, 102, 103, 260
Truth Commission in Minas Gerais (COVEMG) (Brazil), 238
Truth commissions, 199, 203, 211, 238
Turner, Kay, 38
Twagiyaresu, Michel, 246

U
Ulster Defence Association (UDA), 163
Ulster Volunteer Force (UVF), 163
University of São Paulo (USP) (São Paulo, Brazil), 128, 131
Unspoken, 2, 13, 18, 20, 48, 51, 76, 102, 208, 230

V
Valdina, 58, 92–96, 99, 100, 103
Vale (Brazilian mining company), 192
Valle, Marcos, 65
Van Boeschoten, Riki, 178
Vanguarda Paulista (Brazilian musical movement), 123
Vanguarda Popular Revolucionária (VPR) (Brazilian guerilla group), 200n2
Van 't Spijker, Gerard, 242
Varda, Agnès, 97–99, 101, 103, 104
Vaughan, Sarah, 65
Viana Filho, Oduvaldo, 64, 65
Vianna, Herbert, 60
Víctor Hugo, 149
Vieira, Leylianne Alves, 179, 211, 212
Vilanova, Mercedes, 253
Violence, 179, 194, 217, 231, 234, 239, 240, 242
  epistemic violence, 239
  military violence, 148, 152
  sexual violence, 19, 30, 32, 33, 35, 48, 230
  State-sponsored violence, 254
  symbolical violence, 252
Vogel, Lisa, 20, 38, 40–44, 49–51
Von Plato, Alexander, 5n4
Vulnerability, 24, 30, 36, 41, 43, 178

W
Wagner, Roy, 208, 209
Western literary tradition, 8
Whiteness, 74, 76, 102
Wikipedia, 94, 100

Williams, Raymond, 249, 250
Witness testimony, 110
Witter, José Sebastião, 128–133
Woodrow Wilson International Center for Scholars, Smithsonian Institute (Washington, D.C.), 5
Workers of Fiat Concord Union and Works of Materfer Union (SITRAC-SITRAM) (Argentina), 148, 150
Working class, 148, 257, 258
World War I, 29, 164, 173
World War II, 29, 51, 158, 162, 242, 246

X
Xakriabá, Domingos, 236
Xakriabá (Brazilian indigenous people), 217, 235–240, 251

Y
Yow, Valerie Raleigh, 216
Yuri, 224

Z
Zembrzycki, Stacey, 11

GPSR Compliance

The European Union's (EU) General Product Safety Regulation (GPSR) is a set of rules that requires consumer products to be safe and our obligations to ensure this.

If you have any concerns about our products, you can contact us on

ProductSafety@springernature.com

In case Publisher is established outside the EU, the EU authorized representative is:

Springer Nature Customer Service Center GmbH
Europaplatz 3
69115 Heidelberg, Germany

www.ingramcontent.com/pod-product-compliance
Lightning Source LLC
Chambersburg PA
CBHW071702100426
42873CB00017B/387